BUSINESS GUIDE
TO THE URUGUAY ROUND

**International Trade Centre
UNCTAD/WTO**

Commonwealth Secretariat

ABSTRACT FOR TRADE INFORMATION SERVICES

1995   07.03
                                                        BUS

INTERNATIONAL TRADE CENTRE UNCTAD/WTO (ITC)
COMMONWEALTH SECRETARIAT (CS)
Business Guide to the Uruguay Round
Geneva: ITC/CS, 1995. xviii, 392 p.

Guide explaining rules of the Uruguay Round **trade agreements** and their implementation — provides overview of achievements of the Uruguay Round and legal system established by it; explains role of World Trade Organization (WTO); presents rules applicable to trade and examines their implications for **trade liberalization**; reviews main features of General Agreement on Trade in Services (GATS); rules applicable to government procurement and State trading; describes provisions of the Agreement on Trade-Related Aspects of Intellectual Property Rights (TRIPS).

English, French, Spanish

ITC, Palais des Nations, 1211 Geneva 10, Switzerland
CS, Marlborough House, London, United Kingdom

ITC/226/1/95-XII   ISBN 0-85092-443-X
EIDD/E/GATT/5

Roberto Azevêdo
Embaixador

ACKNOWLEDGEMENTS

This Guide is published jointly by the International Trade Centre UNCTAD/WTO (ITC) and the Commonwealth Secretariat. It is based on the work of Mr Vinod Rege, a former Director at the General Agreement on Tariffs and Trade. It was reviewed and approved by the World Trade Organization and also benefited from comments received from officials of the United Nations Conference on Trade and Development and the World Intellectual Property Organization.

Roberto Azevêdo
Embaixador

CONTENTS

PART TWO: INTERNATIONAL RULES GOVERNING TRADE IN GOODS (GATT 1994 AND ITS ASSOCIATE AGREEMENTS) **59**

Section 1
OBJECTIVES AND BASIC RULES OF GATT 61

CHAPTER 2

FOUR MAIN RULES OF GATT 63

Section 2
RULES OF GENERAL APPLICATION   81

CHAPTER *3*

VALUATION OF GOODS FOR CUSTOMS PURPOSES   83

CHAPTER *4*

PRESHIPMENT INSPECTION   97

CHAPTER 10

CHAPTER 11

APPENDICES

INDEX

LIST OF BOXES

NOTE

The following abbreviations are used:

ACV	Agreement on Implementation of Article VII of GATT 1994 (Customs Valuation)
ADP	Agreement on Implementation of Article VI of GATT 1994 (Anti-dumping)
AMS	Aggregate Measurement of Support
AS	Agreement on Safeguards
ATC	Agreement on Textiles and Clothing
BOP	Balance of payments
DSB	Dispute Settlement Body
DSU	Understanding on Rules and Procedures Governing the Settlement of Disputes
Forex	Foreign exchange contracts
GATS	General Agreement on Trade in Services
GATT	General Agreement on Tariffs and Trade
ILP	(Agreement on) Import Licensing Procedures
IPR	Intellectual property right
ISO	International Organization for Standardization
ITC	International Trade Centre UNCTAD/WTO
LDC	Least developed country
MFA	Multi-Fibre Arrangement
MFN	Most favoured nation
PSI	(Agreement on) Preshipment Inspection
SCM	(Agreement on) Subsidies and Countervailing Measures
SME	Small and medium-sized enterprise
SPS	(Agreement on the Application of) Sanitary and Phytosanitary Measures
TBT	(Agreement on) Technical Barriers to Trade
TPRM	Trade Policy Review Mechanism
TRIMs	(Agreement on) Trade-Related Investment Measures

TRIPS	(Agreement on) Trade-Related Aspects of Intellectual Property Rights
UNCTAD	United Nations Conference on Trade and Development
VAT	Value-added tax
VERs	Voluntary export restraints
WIPO	World Intellectual Property Organization
WTO	World Trade Organization

INTRODUCTION

The Uruguay Round of Multilateral Trade Negotiations was the most comprehensive and ambitious among the rounds of negotiations to be held under the auspices of the General Agreement on Tariffs and Trade (GATT). It has resulted in:

- The improvement of the rules of GATT and its associate agreements. These apply to trade in goods.

- The adoption of the General Agreement on Trade in Services (GATS), bringing the growing trade in services under international discipline for the first time.

- The adoption of the Agreement on Trade-Related Aspects of Intellectual Property Rights (TRIPS). The Agreement lays down uniform standards for the protection of these rights.

The Round has also brought about the further liberalization of trade.

One of the other achievements of the Round is the establishment of the World Trade Organization (WTO) which entered into force on 1 January 1995. On that date, GATT ceased to be a separate institution and became part of WTO.

All WTO member countries are required to adopt national legislation and regulations to implement the rules prescribed by the three Agreements — GATT 1994 (as the GATT is now called), GATS and the Agreement on TRIPS — and other legal instruments. WTO is responsible for the surveillance of the implementation of these rules by its Members. Any Member that considers another Member to be flouting the discipline of the system or infringing any of its rules can bring a complaint to WTO and request a settlement of differences.

WTO is also responsible for arranging continuing negotiations for the liberalization of trade among its member countries.

The successful conclusion of the Uruguay Round, the coming into existence of WTO, and the commencement of the implementation of the Round's results are regarded as marking a new era in international trade and economic relations.

Objectives of the Guide

The improved and strengthened rule-based system developed by the Uruguay Round is expected to promote the smooth and orderly development of international trade. It is important to note that governments have negotiated the Round's legal instruments to ensure that their industries and business enterprises can trade with other countries on a fair and equitable basis and that their sales in foreign markets are not disrupted by the sudden imposition of restrictions. The detailed rules, in addition, give industries and business enterprises certain rights vis-à-vis their own governments. Exporting industries also have in certain cases the right to defend their interests in export markets against the imposition of measures affecting their trade.

Almost all developing countries are now pursuing policies promoting export-oriented growth, making their industries increasingly dependent on foreign trade. It would not be an exaggeration to say that in a number of developing countries, virtually all industries — whether large or small — today depend on foreign trade either as exporters or importers. They have therefore the same vital interest as their counterparts in developed countries in seeing that the uniform rules embodied in the Uruguay Round legal instruments are applied by all countries.

The ability of industries and business enterprises to benefit fully from this rule-based system, however, depends on their knowledge and understanding of the detailed rules. These rules are both voluminous and complex. The Final Act Embodying the Results of the Uruguay Round of Multilateral Trade Negotiations, which contains the texts of the legal instruments, runs over 400 pages. These are supplemented by national schedules which list in more than 22,000 pages the liberalization commitments assumed by member countries. In addition, it is difficult for business persons not trained in law to understand the system's legal language.

Against this background, the Commonwealth Secretariat and the International Trade Centre UNCTAD/WTO (ITC) have jointly prepared this Guide to explain in simple terms the rules of the Uruguay Round system. The Guide emphasizes aspects important to persons engaged in, or concerned with, foreign trade. In addition, each chapter has a section on the business implications of specific rules.

Target audience

The Guide is addressed primarily to:

• Industries;

• Business enterprises, particularly small and medium-sized enterprises (SMEs);

• Associations of industries and trade; and

• Research and other institutions directly or indirectly associated with foreign trade.

Organization of the Guide

The Guide begins with an overview. The primary purpose of the overview is to give the reader an overall picture of the achievements of the Uruguay Round and of the benefits that the business community can derive from improved knowledge and understanding of the legal system it has established.

The overview should be useful to those who wish to have a general impression of the system but whose needs do not call for a detailed knowledge of its rules. For those who, for professional and other reasons, require a deeper understanding, the overview should make it easier for them to follow the detailed explanations given later in the Guide.

The Guide is divided into five main parts.

- **Part I** explains the role of the WTO as a forum for negotiations and as an organization responsible for reducing trade friction among countries and for settling disputes between them.

- **Part II** presents in six sections the rules applicable to trade in goods as embodied in GATT 1994 and its associate agreements. It also describes the results of the negotiations in terms of the liberalization of trade in goods.

- **Part III** reviews the main features of the rules of GATS and of the commitments that countries have assumed to liberalize trade in services.

- **Part IV** explains the rules applicable to government procurement and State trading.

- **Part V** describes the provisions of the Agreements on TRIPS.

The Guide is user friendly. It assumes no prior knowledge on the part of the readers of the Uruguay Round legal system or of its rules. However, while the rules are explained in simple language, care has been taken to ensure that the Guide correctly reflects the legal situation. The text has been reviewed and approved by the WTO secretariat.

A summary of the main rules and points made is given at the beginning of each chapter. This is followed by a more detailed description of the rules applicable in the subject area. To facilitate reference to provisions of the WTO legal instruments, the relevant Articles are indicated in the margin. Each chapter ends with an analysis of the business implications of the issues covered.

The lack of information on national laws and regulations applicable to imported products is one of the problems faced by exporters in their markets. To alleviate this difficulty, some Agreements require countries to establish *enquiry, information* or *contact points* from which information on national laws and regulations in the areas covered by them and other specific matters can be obtained. Appendices I and II list the addresses of these national points. The Guide also explains how interested business enterprises can obtain information on WTO laws, the specific liberalization commitments undertaken by countries, and WTO's ongoing work.

With the establishment of WTO, the system of periodic multilateral negotiations came to an end. WTO now provides a continuous forum for negotiations. A number of Uruguay Round agreements provide timetables for further negotiations. Moreover, negotiations on rule-making do not end with the adoption of agreements. They continue during the implementation stage, when decisions are taken to interpret and improve the rules in the light of the practical difficulties encountered in their application. This Guide will be revised and updated from time to time to take into account developments in WTO discussions and negotiations. Future editions will also reflect the views of its users, thus making it more responsive to the needs and requirements of the business community.

Overview

This overview introduces the legal system of the Uruguay Round and briefly describes the progress achieved in trade liberalization. It is divided into three sections.

To enable readers to appreciate the results achieved by the Round in their correct perspective, section I gives an account of the background leading to the launching of the negotiations. This is followed in section II by a résumé of the main principles and rules embodied in the legal instruments that were either revised or newly negotiated in the Round. This section also gives a short description of the trade liberalization commitments undertaken by various countries. Section III explains the implications for business of these results. It stresses that governments negotiated the legal instruments and improvements in access to foreign markets primarily for the benefit of their industries, business enterprises and the trading community. The basic responsibility for taking advantage of the new trade opportunities that have been created as a result now falls on the business and trading communities. To assist them in converting these opportunities into business orders and in their overall efforts to develop trade, the legal system provides them with security of access and creates certain rights in their favour. Their ability, however, to derive full advantage from the system will greatly depend on their knowledge and understanding of its rules.

1. General

The Uruguay Round was the eighth of the rounds of negotiations to be held under the auspices of the General Agreement on Tariffs and Trade (GATT). The Round got its name from the Ministerial Conference launching the negotiations in September 1986, which was held in Punta del Este, Uruguay. The negotiations were to have been completed in four years, but because of the crises and deadlocks that developed from time to time, they dragged on for over seven years. They were formally concluded at the Ministerial Meeting held in April 1994 in Marrakesh, Morocco. The Final Act embodying its results came into force on 1 January 1995.

I. BACKGROUND TO THE LAUNCHING OF THE NEGOTIATIONS

2. Factors influencing the launching

Broadly speaking, three developments made some GATT member countries feel that there was a need to hold a new round of negotiations.

First, it had become evident that, although as a result of the adoption of associate agreements the rules of GATT in a number of areas had been strengthened, its rules were not being applied in two important trade sectors, viz. agriculture and textiles. In the agricultural sector, most developed countries had taken advantage of the loophole to establish policies that were not always consistent with GATT principles. In the textile sector, a number of these countries imposed restrictions on imports, particularly from developing countries. They did this under the so-called Multi-Fibre Arrangement (the Arrangement Regarding International Trade in Textiles or MFA), which provided a legal cover for derogation from GATT rules against the use of quantitative restrictions. Arrangements like the voluntary export restraints (VERs) proliferated, under which some developed countries restricted competitive imports of certain products. These measures had come to be called "grey area measures" as there were doubts about their consistency with GATT principles and rules.

Second, by about the same time, it had become evident that trade in services had grown into an important component of international trade. The rules of GATT applied to trade in goods and there were no international rules on measures taken by countries to protect their service industries. Opinion was growing therefore that, both for the efficient development of the service industries in different countries and to develop trade in services, it was necessary to bring this trade under international discipline.

Third, industries and trading organizations were complaining that because of differing national standards for the protection of intellectual property rights, such as patents and trademarks, and ineffective enforcement by governments of the national rules providing for such rights, trade in counterfeit goods was on the increase. The absence of adequate protection was also considered a deterrent to foreign investment in the production of patented goods and a reason for the reluctance of industries in developed countries to sell or license technology to industries in developing countries.

3. Positive factors influencing the negotiations

The Uruguay Round negotiations lasted, as noted earlier, over seven years. The reasons for the crises that occurred from time to time are now of historical interest. It would be sufficient to note for the purpose of this Guide that, in the Round's last phase and especially during its last two years, the deadlock among the major players (particularly the United States of America and the European Union) on certain crucial elements in the areas of agriculture and trade in services delayed the successful conclusion of the Round.

On the other hand, certain developments elsewhere had a positive impact on both the negotiating process and its final results. These were:

❑   A shift in the trade policies of developing countries from import substitution to policies encouraging export-oriented growth;

❑   The breakdown of communism and the end of the cold war; and

❑   The adoption of market-oriented reforms.

In many ways, the launching of the negotiations coincided with the decision of a number of developing countries to reorient their trade and economic policies away from import substitution to export-oriented growth. The measures they were taking to reduce tariffs, to liberalize their import control system and to open their doors to foreign investment were consistent with GATT principles, its philosophy and approach. Though these measures were unilateral and were not influenced by the launching of negotiations, they enabled developing countries, including those that were initially sceptical, to take a more constructive attitude to the issues being discussed and to agree to integrate themselves more fully into the legal system that was being formulated. This shift in trade policies and the adoption of market-oriented reforms also led a number of developing countries to seek GATT membership. Simultaneously, with the breakdown of communism, policies favouring privatization and market-oriented reform in the countries that are now called transitional economies prompted most of them to apply for GATT membership.

II. BRIEF DESCRIPTION OF THE RESULTS

4. General

As multilateral negotiations generally involve compromises, the results do not always meet the expectations of individual countries. It is often said that no country leaves the negotiating table as a winner or as a loser. On the whole, however, the negotiations have brought about positive outcomes. In particular they have resulted in:

❏   An improved framework of multilateral rules governing international trade; and

❏   Further improvements in access to foreign markets for both goods and services.

One of the other achievements of the Round is the establishment of the World Trade Organization (WTO). GATT has ceased to be a separate institution and has become part of WTO. The organization is responsible for overseeing the implementation of the multilateral rules. The improved mechanism that has been adopted for consultations among member countries when differences arise and for the settlement of disputes is expected to reduce trade friction. The organization also provides a continuing forum for negotiations among its member countries on further trade liberalization and for the elaboration of rules in other areas with an impact on international trade.

5. Improved framework of rules

The improved rules governing international trade are contained in three main legal instruments:

❏   General Agreement on Tariffs and Trade (GATT) and its associate agreements. These apply to trade in goods.

❑   General Agreement on Trade in Services (GATS) which applies to trade
     in services.

❑   Agreement on Trade-Related Aspects of Intellectual Property Rights
     (TRIPS).

   Box A lists the main legal instruments that now form the Uruguay Round
legal system.

Box A

**THE MAIN LEGAL INSTRUMENTS NEGOTIATED
IN THE URUGUAY ROUND**

A.   **Marrakesh Agreement Establishing the World Trade Organization**
B.   **Multilateral agreements**
  1.   Trade in goods
    • General Agreement on Tariffs and Trade 1994 (GATT 1994)

      Associate Agreements

      Agreement on Implementation of Article VII of GATT 1994
      (Customs Valuation)

      Agreement on Preshipment Inspection (PSI)

      Agreement on Technical Barriers to Trade (TBT)

      Agreement on the Application of Sanitary and Phytosanitary
      Measures (SPS)

      Agreement on Import Licensing Procedures

      Agreement on Safeguards

      Agreement on Subsidies and Countervailing Measures
      (SCM)

      Agreement on Implementation of Article VI of GATT 1994
      (Anti-dumping) (ADP)

      Agreement on Trade-Related Investment Measures (TRIMs)

      Agreement on Textiles and Clothing (ATC)

      Agreement on Agriculture

      Agreement on Rules of Origin
    • Understandings and Decisions

      Understanding on Balance-of-Payments Provisions of GATT
      1994

      Decision Regarding Cases where Customs Administrations
      Have Reasons to Doubt the Truth or Accuracy of the
      Declared Value (Decision on Shifting the Burden of Proof)

Understanding on the Interpretation of Article XVII of GATT 1994 (State trading enterprises)

Understanding on Rules and Procedures Governing the Settlement of Disputes

Understanding on the Interpretation of Article II:1(b) of GATT 1994 (Binding of tariff concessions)

Decision on Trade and Environment

Trade Policy Review Mechanism

2. Trade in services
    - General Agreement on Trade In Services (GATS)

3. Intellectual property rights (IPRs)
    - Agreement on Trade-Related Aspects of Intellectual Property Rights (TRIPS)

C. **Plurilateral trade agreements**
    - Agreement on Trade in Civil Aircraft
    - Agreement on Government Procurement
    - International Dairy Agreement
    - International Bovine Meat Agreement

5.1 Objective, principles and rules of GATT

The basic objective of GATT, which lays down multilateral rules for trade in goods, is to create a liberal and open trading system under which business enterprises from its member countries can trade with one another under conditions of fair and undistorted competition. Even though the detailed rules which GATT and its associate agreements (see box A) prescribe may appear complex and their legal terminology often bewildering, they are based on a few simple principles and rules. In effect, the entire framework of GATT is based on four basic rules.

5.1.1 Four basic rules

Protection to domestic industry through tariffs. Even though GATT stands for liberal trade, it recognizes that its member countries may have to protect domestic production against foreign competition. However, it requires countries to keep such protection at low levels and to provide it through tariffs. To ensure that this principle is followed in practice, the use of quantitative restrictions is prohibited, except in a limited number of situations.

Binding of tariffs. Countries are urged to reduce and, where possible, eliminate protection to domestic production by reducing tariffs and removing other barriers to trade in multilateral trade negotiations. The tariffs so reduced are bound against further increases by being listed in each country's national schedule. The schedules are an integral part of the GATT legal system.

Most -favoured-nation (MFN) treatment. This important rule of GATT lays down the principle of non-discrimination. The rule requires that tariffs and other regulations should be applied to imported or exported goods without discrimination among countries. Thus it is not open to a country to levy customs duties on imports from one country at a rate higher than it applies to imports from other countries. There are, however, some exceptions to the rule. Trade among members of regional trading arrangements, which is subject to preferential or duty-free rates, is one such exception. Another is provided by the Generalized System of Preferences. Under the system, developed countries apply preferential or duty free rates to imports from developing countries, but apply MFN rates to imports from other countries.

National treatment rule. While the MFN rule prohibits countries from discriminating among goods originating in different countries, the national treatment rule prohibits them from discriminating between imported products and equivalent domestically produced products, both in the matter of the levy of internal taxes and in the application of internal regulations.

Thus it is not open to a country, after a product has entered its market on payment of customs duties, to levy an internal tax [e.g. sales tax or value-added tax (VAT)] at rates higher than those payable on a product of national or domestic origin.

5.1.2 Rules of general application

The four basic rules described above are complemented by rules of general application governing goods entering the customs territory of an importing country. These include rules which countries must follow:

❑ In determining the dutiable value of imported goods where customs duties are collected on an *ad valorem* basis;

❑ In applying mandatory product standards, and sanitary and phytosanitary regulations to imported products;

❑ In issuing licences for imports.

The detailed rules applicable in these and other areas are contained in the relevant associate agreements. The main features of these rules are described in box B.

Box B

SUMMARY OF GATT RULES APPLICABLE AT THE BORDER

Determination of dutiable customs values. [See chapter 3.] The Agreement on Customs Valuation protects the interests of importers by stipulating that value for customs purposes should be determined on the basis of the *price paid or payable* by the importer in the transaction that is being cleared by Customs. However, Customs can reject the declared value when it has *reasonable doubts* about the truth or accuracy of the declared value. In all such cases, it has to give importers an opportunity to justify their declared value. Where Customs is not satisfied with the justification, the Agreement limits its discretion by requiring that the value is determined on the basis of one of five prescribed standards.

Application of mandatory standards. [See chapter 5.] Countries often require imported products to conform to the mandatory standards they have adopted to protect the health and safety of their people. The Agreement on Technical Barriers to Trade provides that such product standards should not be formulated and applied in a way as to cause *unnecessary barriers to trade.* Towards this end it calls on countries to use *international standards* where they exist and, where they do not, to base their mandatory standards on scientific information and evidence.

Application of sanitary and phytosanitary regulations. [See chapter 5.] Such regulations are applied by countries to protect their plant, animal and human life from the spread of pests or diseases that may be brought into the country by contaminated fruits, vegetables, meat and other food products. The Agreement on the Application of Sanitary and Phytosanitary Measures requires countries not to apply such regulations in a way that would cause unreasonable barriers to trade and urges them to base their regulations on international standards and guidelines wherever possible.

Import licensing procedures. [See chapter 6.] The Agreement on Import Licensing Procedures sets out guidelines for licensing authorities to follow in issuing import licences and the time limits within which they should be issued, where countries require such licences as a precondition for import.

5.1.3 Other rules

In addition to the rules of general application described above, the GATT multilateral system has rules governing:

☐ The grant of subsidies by governments;

☐ Measures which governments are ordinarily permitted to take if requested by industry; and

☐ Investment measures that could have adverse effects on trade.

5.1.3.1 Rules governing the use of subsidies

Governments grant subsidies for diverse policy objectives. Such subsidies could in practice distort conditions of competition in international trade. The basic aim of GATT rules, which have been further elaborated by the Agreement on Subsidies and Countervailing Measures (SCM), is to prohibit or restrict the use of subsidies that have trade-distorting effects.

The SCM Agreement divides subsidies granted by governments in the industrial sector into prohibited and permissible subsidies.

Prohibited subsidies include export subsidies and subsidies that aim at encouraging the use of domestic rather than imported goods. Prior to the Uruguay Round, the rule prohibiting the use of export subsidies was mandatory only for developed countries. It now applies also to developing countries. The latter have, however, a transitional period of eight years to modify their subsidy practices. Developing countries with a per capita gross national product (GNP) of less than $1,000 and least developed countries are exempted from the rule prohibiting export subsidies.

Permissible subsidies are further divided into two categories: actionable and non-actionable. When imports of products receiving actionable subsidies cause *adverse* trade effects, the affected importing countries can have recourse to remedial measures. Such remedial measures can take the form of countervailing duties when the subsidized imports cause injury to the domestic industry (see below). However, importing countries cannot levy countervailing duties on products that have benefited from the limited number of subsidies that are considered non-actionable.

5.1.3.2 Measures which governments of importing countries can take if requested by domestic industry

The rules further stipulate that certain types of measures, which could have restrictive effects on imports, can ordinarily be imposed by governments of importing countries only if the domestic industry which is affected by increased imports petitions that such actions should be taken. These measures include:

❑ Safeguard actions;

❑ Levy of anti-dumping and countervailing duties.

Safeguard actions. The Agreement on Safeguards permits importing countries to restrict imports of a product for a temporary period by either increasing tariffs or imposing quantitative restrictions. Such safeguard actions can be resorted to only when it has been established through properly conducted investigations that a sudden increase in imports (both absolute and relative to domestic production) has caused or threatens to cause *serious injury* to the domestic industry. Safeguard actions cannot be taken if only one or two companies producing a product similar to the imported product are affected. They are permitted solely when it is established that increased imports are causing *serious injury* to the producers accounting for a major proportion of the total domestic production of a product similar to the imported product.

The primary purpose of providing such temporary increased protection is to give the affected industry time to adjust to, and prepare itself for, the increased competition that it will have to face after the restrictions are removed. The Agreement ensures that such restrictions are applied only for temporary periods by stipulating a maximum period of eight years for the imposition of a safeguard measure on a particular product.

Even though the initiative for the commencement of investigations can be taken by governments themselves, in most countries the practice is to initiate such investigations only on the basis of a petition from the affected industry.

Anti-dumping and countervailing duties. It is also open to governments to levy compensatory duties on imported products where it is alleged that foreign suppliers are resorting to *unfair* trade practices. The rules deal with two types of unfair practices that can distort conditions of competition in international trade.

The first is dumping of goods in foreign markets. In common parlance, it is usual to categorize all low-cost imports as dumped imports. The Agreement on Anti-dumping Practices (ADP) lays down strict criteria for the determination of dumping. It stipulates that a product should be treated as being dumped where its *export price* is less than the price at which it is offered for sale in the *domestic market of the exporting country*.

The second is unfair competition, which could result when a foreign company is able to charge low export prices because it has been subsidized by the government.

The ADP Agreement authorizes countries to levy anti-dumping duties on products that are being dumped. Likewise, the Agreement on SCM permits countries to levy countervailing duties on imported products that have benefited from subsidies. The levy of such duties is, however, subject to two important conditions. First, the duties cannot be levied simply on the grounds that the product is being dumped or subsidized. It is essential for the importing country to establish, through investigations carried out at national level, that increased imports are causing *material injury* to the domestic industry. Second, as noted earlier, governments can initiate such investigations if a petition is submitted by or on behalf of the domestic industry, claiming that dumped or subsidized imports are causing material injury to producers accounting for at least 25% of total domestic production.

It should be noted that the standard for determining injury to industry in safeguard actions is much higher than that required for determining injury for the levy of countervailing duties. For safeguard actions, it must be established that the injury to the industry is *serious*, while for anti-dumping and countervailing measures, a lower standard of proof of *material injury* is adequate. The difference is due to the fact that in the case of the former, the problems of the domestic industry in the importing country are not caused by foreign competition, which is fair; in the case of the latter these problems do arise from the unfair trade practices of foreign suppliers. The two Agreements further lay down factors (such as fall in turnover or profits or decline in the labour force) which should be taken into account by the investigating authorities in determining whether industry is being injured by imports.

5.1.3.3 Trade-Related Investment Measures (TRIMs)

Countries often impose conditions on foreign investors to encourage the use of investment according to certain national priorities. Where they have adverse effects on trade, such conditions are known as *trade-related investment measures*.

The Agreement on TRIMs, which has been negotiated in the Uruguay Round, now prohibits countries from using five types of measures that are considered to be inconsistent with the GATT rule of national treatment and the rule which prohibits the application of quantitative restrictions to imported products.

5.2 General Agreement on Trade in Services (GATS)

The General Agreement on Trade in Services aims at extending the rules covering trade in goods to trade in services. The detailed rules have been adjusted to take into account the differences between goods and services and therefore the way in which trade in services takes place.

5.2.1 How trade in services takes place

Services cover a wide range of activities in the areas, for example, of banking, insurance, information, telecommunications, education and recreation. WTO has identified over 150 service sub-sectors.

Whereas goods are tangible and visible, services are intangible and invisible. This basic difference also influences the way in which international trade in services takes place. While goods cross the border of one country and enter the customs territory of another country, very few service transactions involve cross-border movements. In fact, the few services that move across the border are those embodied in goods such as consultants' reports on diskettes. For most service transactions, however, *proximity* between the service provider and the consumer is required. This makes it necessary for service providers to move to the importing country to provide the service. They may do this by establishing a *commercial presence* in the importing country (for instance, by setting up a branch or a subsidiary company). Alternatively, the service providers or experts (natural persons as distinct from legal persons) may go to the importing country for a temporary period to carry out the service activity. Thus, in addition to cross-border movements, trade in services takes place through the *establishment of commercial presence* and the *movement of natural persons*. It is generally believed that the trade in these two modes is significantly larger than that which takes place through cross-border movements.[1]

5.2.2   How protection is granted to service industries

Another major difference between goods and service relates to the way governments grant protection to domestic industries. Industries producing goods are generally protected through the imposition of tariffs and other border measures such as quantitative restrictions. Because of the intangible nature of services and as many services do not involve cross-border movements, protection to service industries cannot be granted through measures applicable at the border. The main means used to protect service industries are *domestic regulations* governing the establishment and operation of service industries. Such regulations may, for instance, prohibit foreign suppliers from establishing branches or impose conditions on foreign suppliers that are more onerous than those applicable to domestic service producers.

5.2.3   Objective and main provisions of GATS

The basic objective of GATS is to establish a framework for liberalizing trade in services. It tries to achieve this by requiring countries to undertake through negotiations *commitments* to modify their *domestic regulations*. Such modifications should result in the gradual removal and, where possible, the elimination of restrictions applied to service products entering the country as well as those applicable to foreign service suppliers carrying out business in the various modes described above.

As with trade in goods, countries are expected to treat foreign suppliers and service products according to the MFN and national treatment principles. The first obliges them to treat foreign suppliers and service products from different countries in the same way. Because of the special features of trade in services, particularly the way in which protection is granted to domestic industries, the obligation to extend national treatment is, however, not as

---

1   There is a fourth mode in which international trade in services takes place. This happens when it is necessary for consumers, rather than service suppliers, to move to the country of importation. An example of such a trade transaction is tourism.

binding as for trade in goods. Countries are merely urged to undertake *commitments* gradually to reduce the elements in their regulations that discriminate between foreign and domestic service suppliers or result in foreign service suppliers being treated less favourably than domestic suppliers.

These commitments are set out in the national schedules of member countries. GATS obliges its Members not to take measures that would in any way reduce the value of their commitments.

5.3. Agreement on TRIPS

5.3.1   The nature of intellectual property

The Agreement on Trade-Related Aspects of Intellectual Property Rights forms with GATT 1994 and GATS the tripod for the WTO legal system. The objects of intellectual property are the creation of the human mind, the human *intellect*. The rights of creators of innovative or artistic work are known as intellectual property rights. They include copyright (which protects the rights of authors of books and other artistic creations), patents (which protect the rights of inventors) and industrial designs (which protect rights to ornamental designs). They also cover trademarks and other signs that traders use to distinguish their products from those of others and thus build consumer loyalty and goodwill for their marks or brand names.

5.3.2   Background to the negotiations on TRIPS

The unauthorized use of intellectual property is an infringement of the right of the owner. The years before the Uruguay Round witnessed a considerable increase in the production of, and international trade in, counterfeit and pirated goods. This was largely due to the unsatisfactory enforcement of trademark and copyright laws in many countries. In addition, patented technology was being used by manufacturers without licensing from patent owners. The standards of protection as well as the periods for which rights were protected also varied widely from country to country.

5.3.3   Main provisions of the Agreement

The Agreement on TRIPS complements agreements on the protection of intellectual property rights developed by the World Intellectual Property Organization (WIPO). In particular, it prescribes uniform minimum standards and periods for which protection should be granted to different intellectual property rights. Countries are further required not to discriminate among foreign nationals and between foreign and their own nationals in the *acquisition, scope and maintenance* of IPRs (extension of MFN and national treatment). The Agreement also places considerable emphasis on the surveillance of enforcement at the national level of intellectual property legislation and regulations.

5.4 Single undertaking rule

The multilateral legal instruments resulting from the Uruguay Round are treated as a single undertaking. All WTO member countries are required to adopt national legislation and regulations to implement the rules prescribed by GATT 1994 and its associate agreements, GATS and the Agreement on TRIPS. The obligation to abide by the discipline of the plurilateral agreements, however, applies only to WTO member countries which choose to accede to these agreements.

This membership requirement in regard to the multilateral agreements is new. Prior to the Uruguay Round, individual members were free to decide whether to accede to associate agreements. The result was that very few developing countries joined associate agreements such as those on Customs Valuation, Import Licensing and Technical Barriers to Trade. The single undertaking rule has automatically made all WTO members, including developing countries and transitional economies, parties to the associate agreements and other multilateral agreements.

The multilateral agreements, however, recognize that developing, least developed and transitional economies may have difficulties in immediately accepting all or some of the obligations which they impose and provide for the extension of special and differential treatment to these countries. This treatment takes the form of:

❑ Longer transitional periods for the implementation of some of the obligations the agreements impose. For instance, developing countries have a transitional period of five years — up to 1 January 2000 — to implement the provisions of the Agreement on Customs Valuation and those of the Agreement on Trade-Related Aspects of Intellectual Property Rights.

❑   For LDCs, longer transitional periods and exemption from some obligations.

❑   Provision of technical assistance to developing and least developed countries.

6. Improvements in market access

In addition to improving the legal and institutional framework for international trade, the Uruguay Round has significantly widened access to export markets.

6.1 The industrial sector

6.1.1 Reductions in tariffs

As a result of reductions made in earlier GATT rounds, the average tariff levels on industrial products were already low in most developed countries. Under the Uruguay Round agreements, these are to be cut further by 40% in five equal annual instalments. However, the percentage of tariff reductions on some products of export interest to developing countries, such as textiles and clothing and leather and leather products, is much lower than the average, as they are considered import sensitive. A number of developing countries and economies in transition will be reducing their tariffs by nearly two thirds of the percentage achieved by developed countries. As a result, the weighted level of tariffs applicable to industrial products is expected to fall from:

❑   6.3% to 3.8% in developed countries;

❑   15.3% to 12.3% in developing countries;

❑   8.6% to 6% in the transitional economies.

6.1.2 Agreement on Textiles and Clothing

Another important achievement of the Uruguay Round is the decision to phase out restrictions on imports of textiles and clothing. These restrictions were imposed by developed countries mainly on imports from developing countries under bilateral agreements negotiated under MFA, which provided an exception to the GATT rules prohibiting the use of discriminatory quantitative restrictions. The Agreement on Textiles and Clothing (ATC), which now replaces MFA, provides for the removal of restrictions on textiles in four phases over a period of 10 years. This phasing-out programme will end on 1 January 2005. From then on, the trade in textiles will be completely integrated into GATT 1994 and will be governed by its rules.

6.2 Agreement on Agriculture

In the past, the rules of GATT were not always applied fully in the agricultural sector. Some developed countries in particular protected their costly and inefficient production of temperate zone agricultural products (e.g. wheat and other grains, meat and dairy products) by imposing, in addition to high tariffs, quantitative restrictions and/or variable levies on imports. This level of protection often resulted in increased domestic production which, because of high prices, could be disposed of in international markets only under subsidy. Such subsidized sales depressed international prices. They also took away from competitive producers their legitimate market shares.

The Agreement on Agriculture, negotiated in the Uruguay Round, aims at ensuring that basic GATT rules are also applied by all countries to trade in agricultural products. The negotiations undertaken in pursuance of these rules have resulted in some progress in the liberalization of trade in these products. The Agreement has also established a mechanism for future negotiations on the further liberalization of this trade.

Thus the developed countries have agreed to replace quantitative restrictions and other non-tariff measures on agricultural products with tariffs. The new tariffied rates (arrived at by adding the incidence of non-tariff measures to existing tariffs) as well as other tariffs are to be reduced by 30%. For their part, developing countries and economies in transition have agreed to cut their tariffs by nearly two thirds of this average. In addition, all countries have bound all tariffs applicable to agricultural products. In most cases, however, developing countries have given bindings at rates that are higher than their current applied or reduced rates. The countries using subsidies, mostly the developed ones, have agreed to reduce both production and export subsidies by an agreed percentage.

III. BENEFITS TO THE BUSINESS COMMUNITY

7. General

What is the relevance of the Uruguay Round to the decisions that industries and business enterprises make in their international trade activities? When considering this question, one must bear in mind that governments have negotiated improved market access to enable business enterprises to convert trade concessions into new trade opportunities. The objective behind the strengthened rules of the Round is to ensure that the markets remain open and that this access is not disrupted by sudden and arbitrary impositions of import restrictions.

Business communities are, however, not fully aware at present of the advantages which the multilateral trading system resulting from the Uruguay Round can generate for them. The main reason for this is the immense complexity of the system, which has so far prevented these communities from taking an interest in, and getting acquainted with, its rules. It is, for instance, not widely known that the legal system not only confers benefits on producing industries and business enterprises but also creates rights in their favour.

7.1 Benefits of the legal system to the business community

The benefits which the legal system confers on business enterprises and the advantages they can derive from it can be viewed from two different perspectives:

❑   From the perspective of enterprises as exporters of goods and services;

❑   From the viewpoint of enterprises as importers of the raw materials, and other inputs and services required for export production.

7.2 Benefits to exporters of goods and services

7.2.1   Security of access

In trade in goods, almost all tariffs of developed countries and a high proportion of those of the developing and transitional economies have been bound against further increases by the Uruguay Round. Binding ensures that the improved market access resulting from the tariff reductions agreed in the Round will not be disrupted by sudden increases in rates of duties or the imposition of other restrictions by importing countries. In trade in services, countries have made binding commitments not to restrict access to service products and foreign service suppliers beyond the conditions and limitations specified in their national schedules.

The secured access to markets which bindings provide enables exporting industries to make investment and production plans under greater conditions of certainty.

7.2.2 Stability of access

The system also provides stability of access to export markets by requiring all countries to apply at the border the uniform set of rules elaborated by the various agreements. Thus countries are obliged to ensure that their rules for determining dutiable value for customs purposes, for inspecting products to ascertain conformity to mandatory standards, or for the issue of import licences, conform to the provisions of the relevant agreements. The adoption of such uniform rules helps export enterprises by eliminating dissimilarities in the requirements of different markets.

7.3 Benefits to importers of raw materials and other inputs

Enterprises often have to import raw materials, intermediate products and services for export production purposes. The basic rule requiring imports to be allowed in without further restrictions upon payment of duties, and the obligation to ensure that the other national regulations applied at the border conform to the uniform rules laid down by the agreements facilitate importing. They give exporting industries some assurance that they can obtain their requirements without delay and at competitive costs. Furthermore, the general increase in tariff bindings under the agreements indicates to importers that their importing costs will not be inflated by the imposition of higher customs duties.

8. Rights which the legal system confers on the business community

In addition to these benefits, the legal system has created certain rights in favour of business enterprises. These rights can be divided into two categories. In the first category are the rights domestic producers and importers obtain vis-à-vis their own governments. In the second are the rights of exporting enterprises to defend their interests when authorities in importing countries contemplate taking action to curtail their exports.

8.1 Rights of domestic producers and importers

A number of agreements require the legislation of member countries to provide certain rights to domestic producers and importers. Governments are obliged to enforce some of these rights under their legal system. In regard to other rights, governments are merely asked to use their *best endeavours* to ensure that the parties concerned can benefit fully from them.

Enforceable rights include those provided for by the Agreement on Customs Valuation which obliges governments to legislate that importers have a right:

❑   To justify declared value, where Customs expresses *doubts* about the truth or accuracy of that value; and

❑   To require Customs to give them in writing its reasons for rejecting the declared value, so that they can appeal to higher authorities against the decision.

Rights requiring governments merely to use their best endeavours include those covered by provisions in the Agreement on Import Licensing which call for import licences to be issued within *specified periods* after receipt of application. In this example, unless the national legislation provides otherwise, the importer only has a *right to expect* that the licence will be issued within the stipulated time.

The claim to such rights is often subject to conditions that the domestic industry or enterprise must fulfil. For instance, as noted earlier, an industry has a right to request its government to take safeguard actions or to levy anti-dumping or countervailing duties only if it is possible for the petitioning producing units to satisfy the investigating authorities that its request is supported by *producers who account for a substantial proportion of total production*. The investigating authorities are further required to ascertain whether the petitioner has such *standing* before commencing investigations.

8.2 Rights of exporting enterprises

An example of the rights which the agreements create in favour of exporting enterprises is the *right to give evidence* during investigations in importing countries for the levy of anti-dumping or countervailing duties.

When the authorities in the importing countries fail to honour their rights, the exporting enterprises cannot approach them directly for redress. They must take the matter up with their own governments and leave it to the latter to pursue it on a bilateral basis with the government of the importing country and, if necessary, to raise it under WTO procedures for the settlement of differences and disputes.

8.3 Illustrative list of rights

Box C presents an illustrative list of the benefits and rights which the various legal instruments confer on industry and the trading community. They are taken up in detail in the various chapters of this Guide.

8.4 Effective utilization of WTO dispute settlement procedures

Knowledge of the system will also enable the business and trading communities to help their governments to take full advantage of the WTO mechanism for the surveillance of the implementation of the legal instruments and for the settlement of differences and disputes. Governments will be able to take up such measures for discussion and solution in the appropriate committees only if the exporting enterprises bring marketing problems resulting from violation of the rules to their notice. Furthermore, governments can raise a complaint under the WTO dispute settlement procedures only if the affected industry first raises the complaint and provides the required information.

8.5 Influencing the future course of negotiations

The responsibility of producing and exporting enterprises, however, should not end with bringing to the notice of their governments the practical problems they are encountering. Either they or their national associations must exercise continuous vigilance and closely follow the ongoing work of WTO. It is important to note that negotiations do not end with the adoption of agreements. Further negotiations with important implications for trade are often held during the implementation stage. Unlike the previous GATT system, WTO provides a forum for continuous negotiations. A number of agreements call for

Box C

ILLUSTRATIVE LIST OF BENEFITS ARISING FROM THE URUGUAY ROUND

A. Binding of concessions and commitments

Business implication

Security of access to foreign markets

Rights of exporters

Trade in goods. Right to expect that the exported product will not be subject to customs duties that are higher than the bound rates or that the value of the binding will be reduced by the imposition of quantitative and other restrictions.

Trade in services. Right to expect that access of service products and of foreign service suppliers to a foreign market will not be made more restrictive than indicated by the terms and conditions given in the country's schedule of commitments.

Rights of importers

Trade in goods. Right to expect that imported raw materials and other inputs will not be subject to customs duties at rates higher than the bound rates.

Trade in services. Right to expect that the domestic service industries will be permitted to enter into joint ventures or other collaboration arrangements, if the conditions provided in the schedule of commitments are complied with.

B. Valuation of goods for customs purposes (Agreement on Customs Valuation)

Business implication

Assurance that the value declared by the importer will, as a rule, be accepted as a basis for determining the value of imported goods for customs purposes.

Rights of importers

Importers have a right:

- To expect that they will be consulted at all stages of the determination of values;

- To justify the declared value, where Customs expresses doubts about the truth or accuracy of the declared value or about the documents submitted;

- To require Customs to give in writing the reasons for rejecting the declared value, so that they can appeal to the higher authorities against the decision.

C. Use of preshipment inspection services (Agreement on Preshipment Inspection)

Business implications

By assisting governments in controlling such malpractices as the over-valuation and under-valuation of imported goods, PSI services help improve the trading environment. Experience has shown that these services speed up clearance of goods through Customs and reduce customs-related corruption.

Rights of exporters

Exporters to developing countries using mandatory PSI services have a right:

- To be informed of the procedures that PSI companies follow for physical inspection and price verification;

- To expect that any complaint they may have regarding the prices determined by the inspectors is considered sympathetically by designated higher officials in the PSI company; and

- To appeal to the Independent Review Entity when they are not satisfied with the decisions of the above-mentioned senior officials.

Benefits to importers

Importers benefit as:

- The utilization of PSI services speeds up customs clearance and in some cases reduces customs-related corruption;

- The physical inspection carried out by PSI companies prior to price verification provides an assurance that imported products will conform to the quality and other terms of the contract.

D. Import licensing procedures (Agreement on Import Licensing Procedures)

Business implication

Assures importers and foreign suppliers that for products for which import licences are required these licences will be issued expeditiously.

Rights of importers

Importers and foreign suppliers have a right to expect:

- That the procedures adopted for the issue of licences at the national level conform to the guidelines prescribed by the Agreement;

- That they will not be penalized unduly for clerical and other minor errors in the application;

- That the licences will be issued within the time periods prescribed by the Agreement.

E. Rules applicable to exports

Reimbursement of indirect taxes borne by exported products

Rights of exporters

Exporters have a right to expect that they will be:

- Either exempted from payment of, or reimbursed for, customs duties on inputs used in the manufacture of exported products;

- Reimbursed for all indirect taxes borne by the exported products.

Export duties

In addition, exporters have a right to expect that where governments levy export duties for revenue or other considerations, these will be applied at the same rates to exports to all destinations.

F.   Anti-dumpling and countervailing actions

Rights of exporters

- Right to expect that exporters alleged to be dumping or exporting subsidized products will be notified immediately after the investigations begin.

- Right to give evidence to defend their interests in such investigations.

- Right to expect that procedures will be terminated when preliminary investigations establish that the dumping margin/subsidy element is *de minimis* and imports are negligible.

Rights of domestic producers

- Right to petition for the levy of anti-dumping or countervailing duties where dumped or subsidized imports are causing material injury to the domestic industry, provided the petition is supported by producers accounting for at least 25% of the industry's production.

---

negotiations to review some or all of their provisions after the expiry of specific periods. In addition, proposals for developing international rules in such areas as *foreign direct investment* and *trade and environment* are being made and decisions to begin negotiations in these and other areas may be taken at the Ministerial Conference scheduled for the end of 1996. Only by following the discussions and making known to their governments their views and concerns will business communities in individual countries be able to ensure that the decisions taken during the implementation of the WTO agreements, as well as the policy approaches adopted by their governments in the negotiations on new subjects, are responsive to their needs and fully reflect the realities of business.

9.   Trade and income gains from liberalization

The responsibility falls on business enterprises to convert the tariff reductions and other liberalization commitments which governments have obtained into opportunities for trade by adopting appropriate export promotion and development strategies.

9.1 Estimates of income and trade gains

Various estimates have been made at the macroeconomic level of the gains in income and of the benefits to international trade that will flow from the implementation of the results of the Uruguay Round. These estimates, however, are confined to trade in goods. Detailed trade statistics on services are not yet available. The estimates also exclude the beneficial effects which strengthened international rules and the ensuing increased security and stability of access can have on the growth of international trade.

Estimates of gains vary according to the assumptions made and the methodologies used. WTO has, for instance, estimated, by using three different versions of its analytical model, that the annual gain in world income will range from $110 billion to $510 billion in 2005. The distribution of gains could vary from region to region. The income gain of developing countries is expected to be equivalent to about one third of the total. While the dynamic economies of East and South-East Asia will be the main beneficiaries, the African countries and the least developed countries in other regions will benefit only marginally, if at all.

As regards trade, the same estimates indicate that merchandise trade will increase by 9% to 24% in the year 2005, depending on the version used. This growth will be higher than the current average rate of 4% by which world trade in goods is growing. The product groups in which higher growth rates are expected are in the sector of industrial goods, including textiles and clothing, transport equipment, fishery products and other manufactures. In the agricultural sector, products in which higher growth is expected include forestry products and selected agricultural products. In general, developing countries are expected to increase their trade in labour-intensive goods and developed countries in products that require high capital inputs.

9.2 Need for caution in interpreting macroeconomic studies

While macroeconomic studies provide guidelines that may be useful to the business community, their findings have to be interpreted with caution, particularly in planning for the future and in day-to-day decision-making. There are three reasons, among others, for such caution. First, the estimates are susceptible both to the assumptions made and the methodologies used. Even the three versions of the WTO model mentioned above give widely different results. Second, the realization of the estimated gains may be delayed, and even frustrated, if commitments are implemented in form rather than in substance. There are growing apprehensions that this may happen in relation to at least some of the commitments undertaken in the Uruguay Round. In the case of textiles, for instance, the major trade gains are expected to result from removal over a period of 10 years of the discriminatory import restrictions applied in developed country markets under MFA. There are, however, new definite indications that very few restrictions will be lifted in the first half of the 10-year period and that the bulk of the restrictions could be eliminated only in the last stage of that period.

The impact of liberalization may also differ for enterprises in different countries. Take the case of textiles, on which restrictions are applied on a discriminatory basis by importing countries. Enterprises in country A whose exports had been restricted may find that they can benefit from the removal of restrictions on their main markets and therefore adopt production and export strategies to take advantage of the improved opportunities for trade. By contrast, enterprises in country B whose exports had not been so restricted will have to prepare themselves to cope with the increased competition that will follow the removal of restrictions on imports from country A.

Likewise, enterprises from countries benefiting from preferential tariff access in their major developed markets may find this access cut back by the MFN reductions resulting from commitments made in the Uruguay Round. The macroeconomic studies indicate that the reductions in preferential margins may not have any overall negative effects on the trade of preference-receiving countries. However, individual exporting enterprises may find that the loss of these margins could, in fact, have adverse trade effects. This could happen if the preferential margins were meaningful in actual trade, taking into account such factors as the prices charged by other suppliers in the importing market.

It is therefore important for business enterprises to supplement macro-economic studies with microeconomic reviews assessing the impact on their products of tariff reductions and the removal of barriers in their target markets. As the lack of financial and technical resources may prevent enterprises, particularly SMEs, from carrying out such studies themselves, national research institutions will have to take the initiative in this regard. International organizations like the Commonwealth Secretariat and ITC could also assist by preparing such studies for products in which a number of developing and least developed countries have an export interest.

9.3 Trade in services

In trade in services, the adoption of GATS has mainly created a framework for future trade liberalization. At present, most of the commitments given reaffirm or bind existing practices, and do not involve any significant removal of barriers. These commitments in effect amount to a halt in the introduction of new restrictive measures. Only a few of the commitments made genuinely provide for the liberalization of trade.

10. Summing up

The primary responsibility for taking advantage of the liberalization measures negotiated by governments now falls on business enterprises. Trade does not expand automatically in the wake of tariff reductions and the removal of trade barriers. This will happen only if business enterprises adopt appropriate export development strategies to take into account the impact of the liberalization measures on the products they export.

The implementation of the Uruguay Round results will create both opportunities and challenges for the business community. The challenge will come from the increased competition in both domestic and foreign markets that will follow the removal of tariffs and other barriers. The establishment of the WTO and the improved legal system that has emerged from the Round is expected to ensure that such increased competition remains fair and equitable. The legal system has also created in favour of the business community a number of rights. As has been said repeatedly, its ability to benefit from the system and these rights will depend on its knowledge and understanding of the system's detailed rules.

The chapters that follow elaborate on the points made in this overview and explain in detail both the rules and the trade and income gains that could result from the implementation of the Round's liberalization package.

PART ONE

WORLD TRADE ORGANIZATION: ITS ROLE AND FUNCTIONS

CHAPTER 1

World Trade Organization: forum for negotiations, dispute settlement and trade policy reviews

Summary of the main rules

One of the major achievements of the Uruguay Round is the strengthening of the institutional mechanism for enforcing the rules and the commitments assumed by countries through the establishment of the World Trade Organization (WTO).

WTO is an umbrella organization responsible for the surveillance of the implementation of:

- *GATT and its associate agreements,*

- *GATS,*

- *The Agreement on TRIPS, and*

- *WTO's other legal instruments.*

The organization provides a forum for continuous negotiations among its member countries for the further liberalization of trade in goods and services and for negotiations on other trade-related issues that may be selected for the development of rules and disciplines.

In addition, it carries out periodic reviews of the trade policies of individual member countries. The organization is also responsible for settling trade disputes among its member countries on the basis of the rules of its legal instruments.

By 25 October 1995, WTO had 110 members.

I. WORLD TRADE ORGANIZATION: ITS OBJECTIVES, FUNCTIONS AND STRUCTURE

1.   Objectives and mandate of WTO

The WTO is the umbrella organization responsible for overseeing the implementation of all the multilateral and plurilateral agreements that have been negotiated in the Uruguay Round and those that will be negotiated in the future. Its basic objectives are similar to those of GATT, which has ceased to exist as a separate institution and has become part of WTO. These objectives have been expanded to give WTO a mandate to deal with trade in services. Furthermore, they clarify that, in promoting economic development through the expansion of trade, adequate attention has to be given to protecting and preserving the environment.

Marrakesh Agreement Establishing the World Trade Organization (WTO Agreement), Preamble

---

Box 1

OBJECTIVES OF THE WTO

In its preamble, the Agreement Establishing the World Trade Organization reiterates the objectives of GATT. These are: raising standards of living and incomes, ensuring full employment, expanding production and trade, and optimal use of the world's resources. The preamble extends these objectives to services and makes them more precise:

• It introduces the idea of "sustainable development" in relation to the optimal use of the world's resources, and the need to protect and preserve the environment in a manner consistent with various levels of national economic development.

• It recognizes that there is a need for positive efforts to ensure that developing countries, and especially the least developed among them, secure a better share of the growth in international trade.

2.   Functions of WTO

The Agreement establishing WTO provides that it should perform the following four functions:

WTO Agreement, Article III, 1   ❏   First, it shall facilitate the implementation, administration and operation of the Uruguay Round legal instruments and of any new agreements that may be negotiated in the future.

WTO Agreement, Article III, 2   ❏   Second, it shall provide a forum for further negotiations among member countries on matters covered by the agreements as well as on new issues falling within its mandate.

WTO Agreement, Article III, 3   ❏   Third, it shall be responsible for the settlement of differences and disputes among its member countries.

WTO Agreement, Article III, 4   ❏   Fourth, it shall be responsible for carrying out periodic reviews of the trade policies of its member countries.

3.   Structure of WTO

WTO Agreement, Article IV, 1   The apex WTO body responsible for decision-making is the Ministerial Conference. It is expected to meet every two years. The first WTO Ministerial Conference is scheduled to be held in Singapore before the end of 1996.

WTO Agreement, Article IV, 2   During the two years between meetings, the functions of the Conference are performed by the General Council.

WTO Agreement, Article IV, 3   The General Council meets as a Dispute Settlement Body when it considers complaints and takes necessary steps to settle disputes between member countries. It is also responsible for carrying out

WTO Agreement, Article IV, 5   reviews of the trade policies of individual countries on the basis of the reports prepared by the WTO secretariat.

The General Council is assisted in its work by the:

WTO Agreement, Article IV, 5   ❑   Council for Trade in Goods, which oversees the implementation and operation of GATT 1994 and its associate agreements;

❑   Council for Trade in Services, which oversees the implementation and operation of GATS; and

❑   Council for TRIPS which oversees the operation of the Agreement on TRIPS.

Annex I to this chapter presents a chart on the organizational structure of WTO. It also indicates the various committees established by the WTO Agreement itself and the other committees that have been established for detailed work at the operational level under the various associate agreements.

3.1 Decision-making process

WTO Agreement, Article IX, 1   The Agreement stipulates that WTO shall continue the GATT practice of decision-making by *consensus*. Consensus is deemed to have been reached when, at the time a decision is being taken, not a single member country voices opposition to its adoption. When a consensus is not possible, the WTO Agreement provides for decision by majority vote, with each country having one vote.[2] The special voting requirements for the interpretation and amendment of provisions are listed in box 2.

---

2 Unlike IMF and other organizations, WTO does not have a *weighted voting* system, under which some countries have right to more votes than others.

Box 2

SPECIAL VOTING REQUIREMENTS

The Agreement lays down different voting requirements for decisions in the following cases:

- The interpretation of the provisions of any of the agreements requires a three-fourths majority. [WTO Agreement, Article IX, 2]

- Amendments generally require a two-thirds majority. However, amendments to: [WTO Agreement, Article X:1, 2]

  - The provisions in the WTO Agreement on amendments and decision-making;

  - MFN provisions in GATT 1994, GATS and the TRIPS agreement

  will take effect only upon acceptance by all members.

- Requests for a temporary *waiver* by any member country from its WTO obligations require a three-fourths majority. [WTO Agreement, Article IX, 2]

Despite these provisions, decisions on all important policy matters (like launching negotiations in areas not so far covered by the WTO legal instruments) are expected to continue to be taken by consensus. The rule of consensus prevents "tyranny of the majority" particularly where a sizeable section of opinion strongly opposes the decision being taken.

3.2   The Secretariat

WTO Agreement, Article VI, 1   WTO is located at Geneva in Switzerland. It is headed by a Director-General. The current Director-General, Mr Renato Ruggiero, who took office on 1 May 1995, has been elected for a period of four years. There are four Deputy Directors-General,

WTO Agreement, Article VI, 3   who assist him in the operational work. They are appointed by him, in consultation with member countries.

WTO Agreement, Article VI, 4

The WTO secretariat has a staff of 450 of varying nationalities.[3] In performing their duties, the Director-General and his staff are expected not to "seek or accept any instructions from any government or any other authority external to the WTO" and thus maintain the international character of the secretariat.

3.3 Membership

WTO Agreement, Article XI

WTO Agreement, Article XIV

By 25 October 1995, 110 countries had joined WTO. GATT member countries that have not so far acceded to WTO can do so during the transitional period of two years from 1 January 1995.

Final Act, para. 5
WTO Agreement, Article XII
Decision on the Acceptance of
and Accession to the Agreement Establishing the WTO

Countries that are at present not GATT members can become members of WTO by negotiating for accession. In such negotiations, they have to agree to take steps to bring their national legislation in conformity with the rules of the multilateral agreements. In addition they have to make commitments to reduce tariffs and modify their regulations so as to provide improved access for foreign goods and services. These commitments are often referred to as the price of the "entry ticket" entitling the acceding country to benefit on an MFN basis from all tariff reductions and other commitments undertaken by member countries in the past.

Annex II to this chapter lists the Members of WTO as of 25 October 1995.

---

3   On its establishment on 1 January 1995, WTO absorbed all the staff of GATT.

II. WTO AS A FORUM FOR NEGOTIATIONS

4. Continuous negotiation

WTO Agreement, Article III, 2

WTO is expected to bring to an end the GATT practice of holding negotiations in periodic rounds and to provide a forum for negotiations on a continuous basis. The Final Act itself contains an agenda for such negotiations (see annex III to this chapter).

This agenda first requires WTO members to complete the unfinished business of the Uruguay Round. For example, negotiations are to continue up to 30 June 1996 on certain service sectors. GATS further provides that negotiations should be held early for the elaboration of rules on emergency safeguards and the use of subsidies in the area of trade in services.

GATS, Article X

GATS, Article XV

Second, a number of WTO agreements themselves require regular review of specific provisions and/or of the entire agreement itself.

Third, several WTO agreements contain commitments to launch new negotiations after a period, to build on the results achieved in the Uruguay Round. Thus, further negotiations must be initiated by 1 January 2000 in two critical areas: agriculture, to continue the reform process begun in the Uruguay Round, and services, to promote additional liberalization of trade.

Agreement on Agriculture,
Article 20; Article 1(f)

GATS, Article XIX

Fourth, the WTO agenda will continue to expand to include new problems and issues that are encountered in trade relations among countries. Al-

Decision on Trade and Environment

ready at the Marrakesh meeting, the Ministers, while adopting the Uruguay Round results, decided to establish a Committee on Trade and Environment. The preparatory work which the Committee is doing at present may provide a basis for a decision at the 1996 Ministerial Conference to launch negotiations in this area.

Finally, new subjects are being proposed for inclusion in the agenda for negotiations in WTO. The United States and some other developed countries, for instance, had proposed at the Marrakesh meeting that the link between trade and labour standards should be included in the work programme. This was not done because of the opposition of developing countries, which feared that developed countries could use alleged abuses of workers' rights as a rationale for protectionist measures. In the coming months, particularly before the 1996 Ministerial Conference, fresh efforts will be made to secure the inclusion of this item in the agenda for negotiations. Among the other items being proposed for coverage are foreign direct investment and the related question of competition policy.

III. WTO SYSTEM FOR THE SETTLE-MENT OF DISPUTES

5.   General

For a multilateral trading system to function properly and without friction, it is not enough to have an agreed set of rules. The rules have to be supplemented by other rules giving countries the right of redress when infringements occur and for settling their differences and disputes. Developing a strong multilateral dispute settlement mechanism, which would remove some of the weaknesses of the earlier GATT system, was thus one of the most critical objectives of the Uruguay Round talks.

6.   Dispute Settlement Body (DSB)

WTO Agreement, Article III, 3
WTO Agreement, Article IV, 3

Understanding on Rules and Procedures Governing the Settlement of Disputes (DSU)

The WTO Agreement provides for a common system of rules and procedures applicable to disputes arising under any of its legal instruments. The main responsibility for administering these rules and procedures lies with the General Council, which as noted in earlier, acts as the Dispute Settlement Body (DSB).

7.   Importance of consultations and conciliation

DSU, Article 4

One of the important principles which these procedures lay down is that a dispute should be brought to DSB by the government of a member country for settlement only after efforts to settle it through consultations on a bilateral basis have failed. The procedures also provide that, in order to reach mutually acceptable solutions, the two parties may request the Director-General or any other person to use his or her good offices to conciliate and mediate between them.

DSU, Article 5

Only when consultations or efforts at conciliation have not produced the desired results within 60 days may the complaining party request DSB formally to commence the dispute settlement mechanism by establishing a *panel* to examine the com-

DSU, Article 5.4

DSU, Article 6

plaint.[4] In order to expedite the settlement of disputes and to ensure that the establishment of a panel is not delayed by the country against whom a complaint is made, the procedures require DSB to establish the panel, when requested by the complaining country, unless there is a consensus against the establishment of such a panel.

DSU, Article 8

DSU, Article 8.5

DSU, Article 8.4

DSU, Article 12.8

DSU, Article 11

8.   Panels

A panel normally consists of three persons, unless parties to the dispute agree that it should have five persons. The names of the persons to be appointed to the panel are proposed by the WTO secretariat from the list maintained by it of governmental and non-governmental experts. The persons in the list are well-qualified senior officials of member countries, members of their delegations to WTO, senior officials who have worked in the secretariat, and persons who have taught international trade law or policy. The panels are required to submit to DSB within a period of six to nine months reports containing their recommendations after making *an objective assessment* of the facts of the case and of the conformity of the measures complained about with the relevant provisions of the legal instruments.

9.   Appellate body

The establishment of an appellate body — a kind of court of appeal — is a new addition to the dispute settlement system. The body consists of seven persons of recognized authority, with expertise

---

4 The procedures recognize that the parties may in certain cases by mutual consent agree to refer the dispute to arbitration. However, they provide that, in such cases, the award shall be binding on the parties and that it should be reported to DSB.

DSU, Article 17.2

DSU, Article 17.5

in law, international trade and the subjects covered by the various agreements. They should be unaffiliated to any government. Of the seven, only three persons will be called to serve in any one case. The appeal can be made by any one of the parties to the dispute. The report of the appellate board, which will be confined to issues of law in the panel report and the legal interpretations developed by it, has to be submitted to DSB within a period of 60 to 90 days.

10.   Consideration of the reports by DSB

DSU, Article 20

The report of the panel or of the appellate body, where one of the parties has appealed against the panel's report, is submitted to DSB for appropriate recommendations, decisions and rulings. In order to ensure prompt settlement of disputes, it is provided that the period "from the date of the establishment of the panel by the DSB" and the date "when it considers the panel or appellate report" should not exceed nine months when the panel report is not appealed and 12 months when it is appealed.

DSU, Article 21

11.   Implementation of the reports

The procedures visualize that the reports of the panels may be implemented by the parties in the three ways described below.

DSU, Article 21.1

11.1   Compliance

DSU, Article 21.3

First, the procedures emphasize that the party which is in breach of obligations must promptly comply with the recommendations of the panel or appellate body. If it is not possible for the party to implement the recommendations immediately, DSB may on request grant it a reasonable period for implementation.

DSU, Article 22

11.2 Provision of compensation

Second, where the party which is in breach does not comply within a reasonable period, the party that has invoked the dispute settlement procedure may request for compensation. Alternatively, the party in breach of the obligations may itself offer to pay compensation.

11.3 Authorization of retaliatory action

DSU, Article 22.2 ff.

Third, where the party in breach fails to comply and refuses to provide compensation, the aggrieved party may request DSB to authorize it to take retaliatory action *by suspending concessions or other obligations* under the agreements that would hurt the trade of the former country. In simple language this means that, where the party is for instance in breach of its obligations under GATT or under one of its associate agreements, the aggrieved party may be authorized by DSB to raise tariffs on products which it imports from the party in breach; the trade in such products should be approximately equal to that affected by the measures complained about.

DSU, Article 22.3

The rules provide that such retaliatory actions shall be authorized by DSB as far as possible in the same sectors of GATT, GATS or the Agreement on TRIPS in which the panel or appellate body has found violation. However, where it considers that this is not possible, it can authorize retaliation under other sectors of the same agreement. Only in rare cases and as a last resort can DSB authorize retaliation across agreements, i.e. imposition of higher tariffs on goods for breach of an obligation under GATS or the Agreement on TRIPS.

The provision of compensation and authorization by DSB of retaliatory measures are, however,

DSU, Article 2

temporary measures. The ultimate solution is for the country which is in breach of the obligation to implement the recommendations. The rules require DSB to keep such cases under review to secure their full implementation.

IV. TRADE POLICY REVIEW MECHANISM (TPRM)

12. General

WTO Agreement, Article III

Trade Policy Review Mechanism (TPRM), A

In addition to providing a mechanism for settling disputes, WTO acts as a forum for the periodic review of the trade policies of member countries. The objectives of these reviews are twofold. First, they aim at finding out how far the countries are following the disciplines of, and commitments made, under the multilateral agreements (and, where applicable, under the plurilateral agreements). By carrying out such reviews periodically, WTO acts as a watchdog to ensure that its rules are carried out and thus contributes to the prevention of trade friction. The provisions establishing the review mechanism, however, clarify that it is not intended to serve as a basis for enforcement of obligations; nor should such reviews be used for the settlement of disputes. The second equally important objective of these reviews is to provide greater transparency and understanding of the trade policies and practices of member countries.

TPRM, B

TPRM, C.ii

13. Periodicity of reviews

The frequency with which such reviews are carried out depends on the share of the individual member countries in world trade. The top four are to be examined every two years: at the moment these are the European Union (counted as one), the United States, Japan and Canada. The next 16 are to be reviewed every four years, and the rest every six, except that longer intervals may be fixed for least developed countries.

TPRM, C.v

The basis for the review is provided by:

❑   A full report prepared by the Member whose trade policy is being reviewed; and

❑   The report prepared by the secretariat on its own responsibility, taking into account the information provided by the Member and other information, including that obtained during visits to the country.

TPRM, C.i

The reviews are carried out by the General Council, which for the purpose of such reviews acts as Trade Policy Review Body. The country report and the reports prepared by the secretariat, together with the minutes on the discussions, are published promptly after the review.

TPRM, C.vi

V. IMPLICATIONS

Business persons are often sceptical of the benefits they can derive from the strengthened multilateral rules and the institutional framework for their enforcement resulting from the establishment of WTO. After all, they argue, it is the governments and not they which participate in WTO negotiations and discussions. Furthermore, WTO meetings are closed to the general public and the business community becomes aware of what is happening in these discussions only through press reports.

The main reason for this scepticism is, however, the lack of knowledge of the general public and the business community of how the system works in practice. It is true that only governmental representatives participate in trade negotiations. It is also true that meetings of the various committees, established to ensure national enforcement of the rules agreed by countries at the international level, are attended only by governmental representatives. Again, when an exporting enterprise encounters a problem in selling to a foreign market, it cannot bring the complaint direct to the WTO Dispute Settlement Body; this is the prerogative of governments.

14. WTO-related consultations

14.1 Mechanism for consultations between governments and the private sector

Governments, however, do not act in isolation. In most developed countries and a large number of developing countries, formal institutional mechanisms have been established for consultations with industries and their associations, chambers of commerce and other trade associations on issues discussed in WTO. In these consultations, governments seek to obtain the views of the business community on:

❑   The policy approaches they should adopt on the specific issues under negotiation;

❑   The stand they should take on proposals made for the inclusion of new subjects in the agenda for negotiations (e.g. development of disciplines similar to that of GATT and GATS on foreign direct investment).

The mechanism also provides an opportunity for industries and businesses to raise any problems they may be confronting in their target export markets because of the measures taken by governments of importing countries. In fact, most of the complaints brought by governments to WTO emanate from specific problems and issues raised by affected industries in their consultations with these governments. Box 3 illustrates how in practice it is only when the exporting industry brings to the notice of the government the problems and difficulties it is facing in foreign markets that the government is able to take up the matter for discussion in WTO.

In developing countries where such a mechanism for consultations does not exist, it will be necessary to develop it. In countries where it does, it may be necessary to improve it to ensure that different business interests are adequately represented and able to bring to the notice of their governments the problems they encounter abroad.

14.2 Influence of associations of industries and chambers of commerce

In addition to participating in consultations arranged by governments, industries and trade enterprises in developed countries make known their concerns and views on subjects under negotiation in WTO by holding discussions under the auspices of chambers of commerce or federations of industries. Furthermore, pressure groups try to ensure that their sectoral interests are adequately taken into account by their governments when specific issues are discussed at the international level. The reports on these

---

Box 3

THE ROLE OF INDUSTRIES AND THEIR ASSOCIATIONS IN THE SETTLEMENT OF DISPUTES

Recently an ambassador from a country which had a case before the Dispute Settlement Body made the following statement in reply to a question from a journalist as to how it was decided to bring the matter to WTO:

"The petrochemical industry brought the problem to our notice and furnished us with the information on the restrictive licensing procedure which the importing country had introduced. We requested our commercial representative to check the facts and obtain more detailed information on regulations. When we were satisfied on the basis of the information provided by the affected industry and the report received from our commercial representative that there was a violation of the rules by the importing country, we decided to invoke the dispute settlement procedures by requesting the importing country for bilateral consultations. When we found that these bilateral consultations were not resulting in solutions, we decided to request the Dispute Settlement Body for the appointment of a panel."

Almost all, if not all, disputes brought to GATT in the past were the result of information provided by industries or their associations to their governments on breach of rules by the country with which they were trading. This will continue to be so for disputes brought before WTO. The ability of industries and their associations to raise such problems with their governments will depend to a large extent on their knowledge of the rules of the system. This further emphasizes the need for the business community to keep well informed of existing rules and of the rules that are being developed in new areas.

It is important to note that only a few of the problems raised by governments under dispute settlement procedures, at the instance of their industries, result in the establishment of panels. A significant number of them are settled through bilateral consultations.

---

discussions are widely publicized to influence public opinion in favour of the groups' views. The reports are also used to lobby members of national legislatures to ensure that governments ultimately adopt policy approaches to negotiations in WTO which adequately reflect their views and concerns.

For instance, the basic groundwork on a number of subjects in the agenda for the Uruguay Round negotiations was carried out by associations of industries and trade. The detailed studies prepared by national and international federations of industries on the implications of the trade in counterfeit goods were to influence the governments of developed countries in pressing for inclusion of this item in the agenda, ultimately leading to the Agreement on TRIPS. Again, the genesis of the Agreement on TRIMs can be traced to the studies prepared by organizations of industries and other research institutes on the adverse implications for trade of the local content and export performance requirements imposed on foreign investors. Many of the proposals for improved rules in the Agreement on Anti-dumping Practices originated from the problems and concerns expressed by industries to their governments.

The interest taken by associations of industries does not end with suggesting subjects for inclusion in negotiations. In most cases they closely follow developments in these negotiations, and make their views known to their governments when they consider that the proposed new rules would not be to their benefit. In the Uruguay Round, for instance, the final outcome of the negotiations on textiles was greatly influenced by the pressures exerted by textile lobbies on the governments of the importing developed countries. It is well known that the Uruguay Round negotiations were held in abeyance for over two years because of the pressures brought to bear on the governments of some countries by agricultural lobbies, which considered that they would be adversely affected by the liberalization proposals under discussion.

Trade and industry associations must continue to follow WTO's ongoing work on the implementation of the rules of the various agreements and the sectoral negotiations that are under way in the service sector.

In most developing countries, however, chambers of commerce and trade associations have not so far shown an active interest in the subjects discussed in international organizations like WTO. This in the past was partly due to the fact that, until a few years ago, a number of these countries were pursuing import substitution policies. Consequently they focused mainly on domestic policy issues. With the shift to policies promoting export-oriented growth, these associations are becoming increasingly conscious of their members' need to become familiar with the WTO legal system and of their own need to pay more active attention to WTO's ongoing work. Many of them require assistance in improving their understanding of the system's substantive and procedural rules. International organizations could assist such associations by holding for the benefit of their members:

❑ General seminars on the WTO legal system; and

❑ Workshops on rules applicable to specific areas, such as mandatory standards and sanitary and phytosanitary regulations, customs valuation, subsidies, countervailing and antidumping measures, and intellectual property rights.

14.3 Effective utilization of the trade information available in WTO

One of the other less publicized advantages to the business person of the WTO system arises from the increasing availability at the WTO secretariat of information on national legislation and rules in the foreign trade sector. Almost all WTO agreements require member countries to notify the WTO secretariat of national legislation, rules and regulations in the subject areas covered by them. The secretariat is expected to bring out in the coming years compendiums of, for instance, the rules of different countries in such areas as customs valuation or the levy of anti-dumping and countervailing duties.

In addition, valuable information on products is available in the country reports prepared for consultations with individual countries under the trade policy review mechanism. This information should be useful to enterprises exporting or considering the export of specific products. By studying the report on consultations with a particular country, it may be possible for an exporter to obtain information on the tariffs, mandatory standards and other regulations that are applicable to specific products or product groups in his or her target market. Although these reports are published, they are rarely mentioned in the national business journals of developing countries.

14.4 Summing up

To sum up, the ability of business persons to benefit from the improved institutional framework that has resulted from the Uruguay Round will depend greatly on:

❑   Their knowledge of the trade rules and of the rights which these give as well as the obligations they impose.

❑   Their knowledge of the new opportunities for trade that have been created by the liberalization commitments undertaken by countries during the negotiations.

❑   The initiative they show in bringing to the notice of their governments their problems in selling to international markets so that their governments can raise the issues in appropriate WTO forums and, if necessary, invoke WTO's dispute settlement procedures.

Parts Two to Five of this Guide explain the rules of the system, the new opportunities that have been created as well as the challenges which business enterprises may encounter in both domestic and foreign markets as a result of the liberalization of trade.

How the WTO works

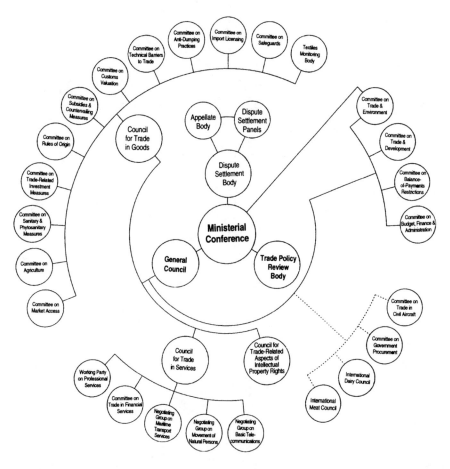

Source: WTO secretariat.

ANNEX II

WTO membership
(As of 25 October 1995)

The following 110 Governments have accepted the Marrakesh Agreement Establishing the World Trade Organization and their membership in the World Trade Organization is effective as of the dates indicated:

Government	Entry into force/ Membership	Government	Entry into force/ Membership
Antigua and Barbuda	1 January 1995	Denmark	1 January 1995
Argentina	1 January 1995	Djibouti	31 May 1995
Australia	1 January 1995	Dominica	1 January 1995
Austria	1 January 1995	Dominican Republic	9 March 1995
Bahrain	1 January 1995	Egypt	30 June 1995
Bangladesh	1 January 1995	El Salvador	7 May 1995
Barbados	1 January 1995	European Community	1 January 1995
Belgium	1 January 1995	Finland	1 January 1995
Belize	1 January 1995	France	1 January 1995
Bolivia	13 September 1995	Gabon	1 January 1995
Botswana	31 May 1995	Germany	1 January 1995
Brazil	1 January 1995	Ghana	1 January 1995
Brunei Darussalam	1 January 1995	Greece	1 January 1995
Burkina Faso	3 June 1995	Guatemala	21 July 1995
Burundi	23 July 1995	Guinea Bissau	31 May 1995
Canada	1 January 1995	Guinea, Rep. of	25 October 1995
Central African Republic	31 May 1995	Guyana	1 January 1995
Chile	1 January 1995	Honduras	1 January 1995
Colombia	30 April 1995	Hong Kong	1 January 1995
Costa Rica	1 January 1995	Hungary	1 January 1995
Côte d'Ivoire	1 January 1995	Iceland	1 January 1995
Cuba	20 April 1995	India	1 January 1995
Cyprus	30 July 1995	Indonesia	1 January 1995
Czech Republic	1 January 1995	Ireland	1 January 1995

Government	Entry into force/ Membership	Government	Entry into force/ Membership
Israel	21 April 1995	Poland	1 July 1995
Italy	1 January 1995	Portugal	1 January 1995
Jamaica	9 March 1995	Romania	1 January 1995
Japan	1 January 1995	Saint Lucia	1 January 1995
Kenya	1 January 1995	Saint Vincent & the	
Korea	1 January 1995	Grenadines	I January 1995
Kuwait	1 January 1995	Senegal	1 January 1995
Lesotho	31 May 1995	Sierra Leone	23 July 1995
Liechtenstein	1 September 1995	Singapore	1 January 1995
Luxembourg	1 January 1995	Slovak Republic	1 January 1995
Macau	1 January 1995	Slovenia	30 July 1995
Malawi	31 May 1995	South Africa	1 January 1995
Malaysia	1 January 1995	Spain	1 January 1995
Maldives	31 May 1995	Sri Lanka	1 January 1995
Mali	31 May 1995	Suriname	1 January 1995
Malta	1 January 1995	Swaziland	1 January 1995
Mauritania	31 May 1995	Sweden	1 January 1995
Mauritius	1 January 1995	Switzerland	1 July 1995
Mexico	1 January 1995	Tanzania	1 January 1995
Morocco	1 January 1995	Thailand	1 January 1995
Mozambique	26 August 1995	Togo	31 May 1995
Myanmar	1 January 1995	Trinidad and Tobago	1 March 1995
Namibia	1 January 1995	Tunisia	29 March 1995
New Zealand	1 January 1995	Turkey	26 March 1995
Nicaragua	3 September 1995	Uganda	1 January 1995
Nigeria	1 January 1995	United Kingdom	1 January 1995
Norway	1 January 1995	United States	1 January 1995
Pakistan	1 January 1995	Uruguay	1 January 1995
Paraguay	1 January 1995	Venezuela	1 January 1995
Peru	1 January 1995	Zambia	1 January 1995
Philippines	1 January 1995	Zimbabwe	3 March 1995

ANNEX III

Timetable for further WTO negotiations

DATE		ITEM
1995	1 January	WTO enters into force
	30 June	Deadline for negotiations on financial services and on movement of natural persons
1996	1 January	Agreement on Government Procurement enters into force
	30 April	Deadline for negotiations on basic telecommunications services
	30 June	Review of operation of provisions on R & D subsidies
	30 June	Deadline for negotiations on maritime services
1997	1 January	Start of negotiations on government procurement of services
	1 January	First review of provisions on preshipment inspection (reviews every three years thereafter)
	1 January	First review of TRIPS section on geographical indications
	31 December	Deadline for negotiations on emergency safeguards for services
1988	1 January	Examine standard of review for anti-dumping disputes, and consider its application to countervailing cases
	1 January	First review of operation and implementation of provisions on technical barriers (reviews are to be held every three years thereafter)
	1 January	Deadline for report with recommendation from the Working Party on Trade in Services and the Environment on modifications of GATS Article XIV (general exceptions)

	1 January	Review of operation and implementation of sanitary and phytosanitary provisions (further reviews to be held as need arises)
1999	1 January	Start negotiations on further improvement of the Agreement on Government Procurement (extension of coverage)
	1 January	Deadline for review of provision on patent or *sui generis* protection of plant varieties
	1 January	Deadline for review of dispute settlement rules and procedures
	30 June	Start review of provisions on serious prejudice and non-actionable subsidies
2000	1 January	Start first round of negotiations on progressive liberalization of services (new negotiations to increase the general level of specific commitments)
	1 January	Review of Article II (MFN) exemptions
	1 January	Launch new negotiations to continue reform process in agriculture
2000	1 January	First review of TRIPS agreement, reviews to be held every two years thereafter
	1 January	Deadline for review of TRIMs agreement and consideration of whether to complement it with provisions on investment and competition policy
	1 January	Review of interpretation of the rules on modification and withdrawal of concessions
	1 January	Deadline for appraisal of Trade Policy Review Mechanism
	Unspecified	Negotiations on increased protection for geographical indications for wines and spirits
	Unspecified	Subsidies in services

PART TWO

INTERNATIONAL RULES GOVERNING TRADE IN GOODS (GATT 1994 AND ITS ASSOCIATE AGREEMENTS)

Section 1

OBJECTIVES AND BASIC RULES OF GATT

CHAPTER 2

Four main rules of GATT

Summary

The entire edifice of GATT's open and liberal multilateral trading system is built on four basic and simple rules.

The first rule, while recognizing that it is important for member countries to follow open and liberal trade policies, permits them to protect domestic production from foreign competition, provided that such protection is extended only through tariffs and is kept at low levels. To this end, it prohibits countries from using quantitative restrictions, except in specified cases. The rule against the use of quantitative restrictions has been strengthened in the Uruguay Round.

The second rule provides for the reduction and elimination of tariffs and other barriers to trade through multilateral negotiations. The tariffs so reduced are listed on a tariff-line basis in each country's schedule of concessions. The rates given in these schedules are known as **bound** rates. Countries are under an obligation not to increase tariffs above the bound rates shown in their schedules.

The third rule requires countries to conduct their trade without discriminating among countries from which goods are imported or to which goods are exported. This rule is embodied in the most-favoured-nation (MFN) principle. An important exception to this rule is permitted in the case of regional preferential arrangements.

The fourth rule is known as the national treatment rule. It requires countries not to impose on an imported product, after it has entered their domestic markets on paying customs duties at the border, internal taxes such as sales or value-added tax at rates higher than those levied on a similar domestic product.

1.   General

GATT 1994, Preamble

The objective of the multilateral system for trade in goods created by GATT is to provide industries and business enterprises from different countries a stable and predictable environment in which they can trade with one another under conditions of fair and equitable competition. This open and liberal trading system is expected to promote through increased trade, greater investment, production and employment and thus facilitate the economic development of all counries.

2.   First rule: protecting the domestic industry by tariffs only

The legal system which GATT has created to attain the above objective is complex, but it is based on a few basic and simple rules.

GATT 1994, Article XI

GATT 1994, Article XII

GATT 1994, Article XVIII

While GATT stands for liberal trade, it recognizes that countries may wish to protect their industries from foreign competition. It urges them to keep such protection at reasonably low levels and to provide it through tariffs. The principle of protection by tariffs is reinforced by provisions prohibiting member countries from using quantitative restrictions on imports. The rule, however, is subject to specified exceptions. An important exception permits countries that are in balance-of-payments (BOP) difficulties to restrict imports in order to safeguard their external financial position. This exception provides greater flexibility to developing countries than is available to developed countries to use quantitative restrictions on imports if they are necessary to forestall a serious decline in their monetary reserves.

2.1 Non-observation of the rule against quantitative restrictions

2.1.1 Agricultural sector

In the past, a number of countries did not abide by the GATT rule on protection by tariffs alone. In the agricultural sector for instance, a number of developed countries maintained quantitative restrictions which went far beyond those warranted by the exceptions provided in GATT. In addition to these restrictions, some of these countries, particularly those belonging to the European Union, applied variable levies instead of fixed tariffs to imports of temperate zone agricultural products such as wheat and other grains, meat and dairy products. The primary purpose of those levies was to ensure a reasonable income to farmers and to maintain a certain parity between the income earned by them and that earned by industrial workers. The levies payable were determined periodically and were generally equal to the difference between the landed import price and the guaranteed reference domestic price. The variable levies thus resulted in domestic production being fully insulated from foreign competition, as the levies completely offset the competitive price advantages of foreign suppliers.

2.1.2 Trade in textiles and clothing

In the industrial sector, most developed countries did not apply the rule against the use of quantitative restrictions to trade in textiles, a sector of particular interest to developing countries. There was one significant difference between the restrictions applied in the agricultural sector and those applied to textiles. With some notable exceptions, the restrictions maintained in the agricultural sector were outside the scope of GATT rules. In the case of textiles, the restrictions were authorized under the provisions of MFA, an arrangement negotiated under GATT auspices. MFA permitted countries to derogate from their basic obligation and to impose restrictions on imports of textiles and textile products, provided the conditions it laid down were met.

2.1.3 Developing countries

A number of developing countries applied, in addition to high tariffs, quantitative restrictions on imports in both the agricultural and industrial sectors. Such use of restrictions was, however, in most cases justifiable from the legal point of view, under the exceptions to the GATT rules which permit countries in balance-of-payments difficulties to impose quantitative restrictions on imports.[5]

GATT 1994, Article XII;
Article XVIII:B

2.2 Reinforcement of the discipline against the use of quantitative restrictions

2.2.1 Tariffication in the agricultural sector

The WTO legal system has brought about a considerable change in the use of quantitative restrictions and other non-tariff measures affecting imports. In the agricultural sector for instance, in accordance with the provisions of the Agreement on Agriculture, WTO member countries have abolished quantitative restrictions and their systems of variable levies, replacing these with tariffs. The new tariff rates have been determined by *tariffication,* i.e. calculating the incidence of quantitative restrictions and

---

5   Countries are considered to be in balance-of-payments difficulties when their external earnings from trade in goods and services and the flow of investment and loans are far from adequate for their external payments liabilities, and when monetary reserves for meeting immediate liabilities are declining. GATT rules provide developing countries in balance-of-payments difficulties a greater flexibility to use quantitative restrictions on imports.

other measures on the price of the imported products and adding it to the then-prevailing tariffs. As a result of this tariffication, countries may henceforth protect their domestic agricultural protection only by means of tariffs.

2.2.2 Phased removal of restrictions on textiles and clothing

In the area of textiles and clothing, the new Agreement on Textiles and Clothing (ATC) requires member countries maintaining restrictions to phase them out gradually in four stages, so as to abolish them completely by 1 January 2005.

2.2.3 Developing countries in balance-of-payments difficulties are urged to use price-based measures

Understanding on BOP Provisions of GATT 1994, 2, 3

In addition, the Understanding on Balance-of-Payments Provisions of GATT 1994 strongly urges member countries not to use quantitative restrictions to safeguard their BOP situations. It requires countries, whether developed or developing, to prefer in such situations *price-based measures* (such as import surcharges and import deposit requirements) to quantitative restrictions as their impact on the price of imported products is transparent and measurable. Quantitative restrictions can be resorted to only when, because of a critical BOP situation, it is perceived that price-based measures cannot arrest a further sharp deterioration in the external payments position.

The WTO legal system has thus, by strengthening the rules against the use of quantitative restrictions, further reinforced the basic GATT rule that protection to domestic production should be given primarily through tariffs.

3.   Second rule: tariffs should be reduced and bound against further increases

3.1   Reductions in tariffs

GATT 1994, Preamble; Article XXVIII bis

The second important rule of GATT is that tariffs and other measures that countries maintain to protect their domestic production should be reduced and, where possible, eliminated through negotiations among member countries and that the tariffs so reduced should be bound against further increases.

3.2   Binding against further increases

GATT 1994, Article II:1(b); Understanding on the Interpretation of Article II:1(b)

The concept of binding needs some explanation. The rates of tariffs agreed in the negotiations as well as the other commitments assumed by countries are listed in *schedules of concessions*. Each WTO member country has a separate schedule and is under an obligation not to impose tariffs or other duties or charges which "are in excess of those set forth" in its schedule. It is also obliged not to take measures — such as the imposition of quantitative restrictions — which would reduce the value of the tariff concessions. The rates of tariffs listed in the schedule are known as *bound* rates of tariffs (see box 4).[6]

3.3   Principle governing the exchange of concessions in negotiations

What is the principle by which countries agree in trade negotiations to reduce tariffs, to bind

---

6   It is possible for a country which has bound its tariffs to secure release from the binding and to raise the tariff above the bound rate. It does this by entering into *renegotiations* with the countries with which it had initially negotiated the concession as well as with the principal supplying countries of the product concerned and which therefore benefit from the concession. In such negotiations, the country requesting release is expected to make compensatory tariff concessions on other products in which the countries with which it is negotiating have trade interest.

them against further increases and to remove other barriers to trade? The basic principle governing the exchange of such concessions is the principle of *reciprocity and mutual advantage*. A country requesting improved access to the market of other countries, through tariff reductions or the removal of

---

Box 4

BINDING OF TARIFFS

It is not open to a country to increase the rates of tariffs above the *bound rate* indicated in its *schedule of concessions*. The schedule, *inter alia,* lists on a product-by-product basis the *pre-negotiation* tariff rate on a product and the rate of tariff at which the country has agreed "in the negotiations to bind the tariff rate". In trade negotiations, a country could agree:

- To bind its existing positive rate (e.g. 10 %) or zero rate; or

- To reduce the rate, for example from 10 % to 5 %, and to bind the reduced rate.

It is also possible for a country to bind its tariffs at a *ceiling rate* which is higher than the rate resulting from the tariff reductions agreed in the negotiations. Thus a country which has agreed to reduce a tariff from 10 % to 5 % may indicate that, while it will apply the reduced rate to imports, the bound rate of the tariff will be 8 %. In that case, the country is free to raise its tariffs to 8 % at any time without infringing any of its GATT obligations.

The Uruguay Round has brought about substantial progress in the binding of tariffs of all countries. All countries — developed, developing and transitional economies — have bound their tariffs in the agricultural sector. In the industrial sector over 98 % of imports into developed and transitional economy countries will be entering under bound rates of tariffs.

In the case of imports into developing countries, the proportion of imports entering under bound rates is around 73 %. A number of developing countries have, however, given ceiling bindings in certain instances. Such ceiling bindings take the form of a commitment not to raise the tariff:

- Over the ceiling rates shown for each product;

- Over the ceiling rate applicable to a particular sector;

- Over the ceiling rate applicable across the board to all products.

other barriers such as quantitative restrictions, must be ready to make concessions in tariffs and other areas that the other countries consider to be advantageous and of reciprocal or equivalent value to the concessions they are making.

GATT 1994, Part IV (Trade and Development), Article XXXVI:8; Tokyo Round Decision on Differential and More Favourable Treatment, Reciprocity and Fuller Participation of Developing Countries, para. 5, 6 and 7

The rule of full reciprocity does not, however, apply to negotiations between developed and developing countries. Developing countries are required to make concessions in the form of tariff reductions on the basis of *relative reciprocity*, which takes into account the fact that, because of their lower level of economic development and their *trade and financial needs*, they may not be able to make concessions on the same basis as developed countries. The rule, however, recognizes that developing countries are not all at the same level of development; some of them, particularly the newly industrializing countries (NICs), have reached higher stages of growth. These countries are required to make larger contributions and concessions in the form of tariff reductions and bindings than those at lower rungs of economic growth. This concept is also known as *graduation*, since it visualizes that as a developing country develops, it will graduate to a higher status and ultimately may be able to make tariff concessions and accept disciplines in other areas on the same basis as developed countries.

3.4 Greater contributions from developing countries in the Uruguay Round

Because of the rule of relative reciprocity only a few developing countries made tariff concessions in the Tokyo Round and earlier rounds of negotiations. Furthermore, those that made concessions did so on only a few products. This situation changed considerably in the Uruguay Round, and almost all developing countries have agreed to make concessions by reducing tariffs on a percentage basis. However, in accordance with the principle of relative reciprocity, these concessions have been made at a lower percentage than that applicable to developed countries.

During the Uruguay Round, two factors were responsible for the greater willingness of developing countries to make concessions and to accept through negotiations higher obligations. First, a significant number of these countries have expanded economically in recent years. The second factor, which is closely related to the first, is the dramatic shift which has taken place in the trade policies of almost all developing countries. In the past, when they followed import substitution policies, built high tariff walls and insulated domestic production from foreign competition, it was difficult for them to offer concessions in the form of tariff reductions.

These countries are now following policies promoting export growth and are reducing tariffs and eliminating the plethora of licensing and other systems they maintained to restrict imports. These open and liberal trade policies enabled them in the Uruguay Round not only to take credit for their unilateral tariff reductions by binding them but also to improve their bargaining position in negotiations with their developed country partners.

4.   Third rule: trade according to the most-favoured-nation clause

GATT 1994, Article I

The third basic GATT rule, which provides that trade must not be discriminatory, is embodied in the famous most-favoured-nation clause. In simple terms, the principle means that if a member country grants to another country any tariff or other benefit to any product, it must immediately and unconditionally extend it to the *like product* of other countries. Thus if country A agrees, in trade negotiations with country B, to reduce custom duties on imports of tea from 10% to 5%, the reduced rate must be extended to all WTO member countries. The obligation to extend such MFN treatment applies not only to imports but also to exports. Thus, if a country levies duties on exports of a product to one destination, it must apply it at the same rate to exports to all destinations.

GATT 1994, Article I.1

Moreover, the obligation to provide MFN treatment is not confined to tariffs. It also applies to:

❑ Charges of any kind imposed in connection with importation and exportation;

❑ The method of levying tariffs and such charges;

❑ Rules and formalities in connection with importation and exportation; and

❑ Internal taxes and charges on imported goods, and laws, regulations and requirements affecting their sales;

GATT 1994, Article XIII ❑ The administration of quantitative restrictions (e.g. by allocating quotas among supplying countries on a non-discriminatory basis) where such restrictions are permitted under the exceptions provisions.

The principle thus implies that, by agreeing to give MFN treatment, member countries undertake not to *discriminate* among countries and not to treat a country *less favourably* than another in all matters connected with foreign trade in goods.

4.1   Exceptions to the MFN rule

GATT 1994, Article XXIV   The GATT rules, however, recognize that tariffs and other barriers to trade can be reduced on a preferential basis by countries under regional arrangements. The lower or duty-free rates applicable to trade among members of regional arrangements need not be extended to other countries. Regional preferential arrangements thus constitute an important exception to the MFN rule. In order to protect the trade interests of non-member countries, GATT lays down strict conditions for forming such arrangements. These conditions, *inter alia,* provide that:

GATT 1994, Article XXIV:5   ❏   Member countries of regional arrangements must remove tariffs and other barriers to trade affecting *substantially all trade* among themselves; and

❏   The arrangement should not result in the imposition of new barriers to trade with other countries.

Such arrangements may take the form of customs unions or free-trade areas. In both instances, trade among member States takes place on a duty-free basis while trade with other countries continues

GATT 1994, Article XXIV:8   to be subject to MFN tariff rates. In the case of customs unions, tariffs of member countries are harmonized and applied to imports from outside countries on a uniform basis. In free-trade areas, member countries continue to use, without harmonization, the tariffs set out in their individual national schedules.

The annex to this chapter lists selected regional arrangements. As a result of such regional arrangements, a high proportion of world trade takes place today on a preferential basis.

In addition to these arrangements, developed countries have introduced one-way free-trade arrangements under which imports from either all or a limited number of developing countries enter their markets duty free. These arrangements are non-reciprocal as the developing countries benefiting from preferential access do not extend any preferential treatment to imports from developed countries. Examples of such one-way preferential arrangements are:

GATT 1994; Tokyo Round Decision on Differential and More Favourable Treatment, Reciprocity and Fuller Participation of Developing Countries, para. 2(a)

❏ The Generalized System of Preferences (GSP) under which developed countries allow imports from all developing countries of industrial products and selected agricultural products on a preferential and duty-free basis;

❏ The Lomé Convention under which member States of the European Union allow imports from a number of countries in Africa and the Caribbean and LDCs in Asia and the Pacific (ACP countries) to enter on a duty-free basis;

❏ The Caribbean Basin Arrangement, under which the United States allows imports from countries belonging to the Caribbean region on a duty-free basis.

5. Fourth rule: national treatment

The MFN principle, as has been noted, requires members not to discriminate among countries. The national treatment principle, which complements the MFN principle, requires that an imported

GATT 1994, Article III

product which has crossed the border after payment of customs duties and other charges should not receive treatment that is *less favourable* than that extended to the *like product produced domestically*. In other words, the principle requires member countries to treat imported products on the same footing as similar domestically produced products. Thus it is not open to a country to levy on an imported product, after it has entered the country on payment of customs duties at the border, internal taxes (such as a sales tax) at rates that are higher than those applied to comparable domestic products. Likewise, regulations affecting the sale and purchase of products in the domestic market cannot be applied more rigorously to imported products.

6.   Business implications

The new framework of rules covering agricultural products and textiles which the Uruguay Round has developed will help ensure that GATT's basic rules against the use of quantitative restrictions and requiring that protection to domestic production is given only through tariffs are followed in practice by all countries. Exporting enterprises prefer tariffs to quantitative restrictions for many reasons. Tariffs are transparent and their incidence on price is predictable. The use of quantitative restrictions imposes a certain uncertainty on trade, as administering authorities have the power to adjust the sizes of quotas from time to time. Finally, as the operation of quota restrictions requires licensing, enterprises can export only if their foreign buyers are able to obtain a licence.

The Uruguay Round has also resulted in significant progress in tariff binding by all countries (see box 4). The assurance that, because of the binding, the lower rates agreed in the negotiations will not be raised by countries to which exports are being made encourages enterprises to invest in manufacturing plants, equipment and distribution networks and to take other measures to develop trade. Furthermore, the bindings give enterprises a guarantee that the tariffs that are payable on the raw materials and inputs which they have to import for use in export production will not be increased by their own governments.

Lastly, the national treatment rule assures exporting enterprises that once their products have entered the importing market after payment of customs duties and other charges payable at the border, they will not be required to pay internal taxes at rates that are higher than those payable on products of domestic origin. The national treatment rule applies not only to internal taxes, but also to the rules governing mandatory standards for products and those applicable to the sale and distribution of goods. As governments are increasingly imposing taxes and adopting product regulations for the protection of the environment and for the health and safety of consumers, the rule that such taxes and regulations should be applied to domestic and imported products on a non-discriminatory basis is of vital importance to exporting enterprises.

ANNEX

Selected regional and intraregional preferential arrangements

Arrangement	No. of members	Current members
European Union (EU)	15	United Kingdom, France, Germany, Belgium, Netherlands, Luxembourg, Italy, Spain, Portugal, Austria, Sweden, Denmark, Finland, Ireland, Iceland
EU - East Europe Free Trade Arrangements	EU 15 plus 6	EU plus Poland, Czech Republic, Slovak Republic, Hungary, Romania, Bulgaria
Australia, New Zealand Closer Relations Trade Agreement (CER)	2	Australia, New Zealand
North American Free Trade Agreement (NAFTA)	3	United States, Canada, Mexico
ASEAN Free Trade Area	6	Malaysia, Thailand, Singapore, Philippines, Indonesia, Brunei Darussalam
Mercado Commun del Sur (Mercosur)	4	Brazil, Argentina, Uruguay, Paraguay
Andean Pact	5	Peru, Venezuela, Bolivia, Colombia, Ecuador
Common Market for Eastern and Southern Africa (COMESA)	23	Angola, Burundi, Comoros, Djibouti, Eritrea, Ethiopia, Kenya, Lesotho, Madagascar, Malawi, Mauritius, Mozambique, Namibia, Rwanda, Seychelles, Somalia, Sudan, Swaziland, United Republic of Tanzania, Uganda, Zaire, Zambia, Zimbabwe

Section 2

RULES OF GENERAL APPLICATION

CHAPTER 3

Valuation of goods for customs purposes

Summary

When customs duties are levied on an **ad valorem** basis (e.g. 10 % of the value of imported goods), the actual incidence of duty depends on how Customs determines dutiable value. The Agreement on Customs Valuation requires Customs to determine the value on the basis of the **price paid or payable** by the importer in the transaction that is being valued. As a result of a Decision adopted in the Uruguay Round, Customs can reject transaction values when it has reasons to doubt the **truth or accuracy** of the value declared by importers or of the documents submitted by them. In order to protect the interests of importers in such situations, Customs is required to provide them with an opportunity to justify their price. Where Customs is not satisfied with the justifications given, it is obliged to give to these importers in writing its reasons for not accepting the transaction value declared by them.

The Agreement limits the discretion available to Customs in determining dutiable value when the transaction value is not accepted by laying down five specific methods for establishing value. In determin-

ing value on the basis of these methods, Customs is required to consult the importers and take their views into account.

A number of developing countries currently use valuation systems based on the Brussels Definition of Value, developed by the World Customs Organisation (WCO). These countries will have to modify their systems to bring them in conformity with the rules of the Agreement on Customs Valuation within the transitional period of five years (i.e. up to 1 January 2000) that has been accorded to developing countries for changing over to the system established by the Agreement.

1.   Types of customs duties

Customs duties are levied on an *ad valorem* basis (e.g. 20% of the value of the imported product) or as specific duties (e.g. $2 per kilogram or per litre). Combined or mixed duties containing both *ad valorem* and specific rates are also levied (10% of the value + $2 per kilogram) on some products.

With a few exceptions, most countries levy *ad valorem* duties. Governments prefer to levy such duties for three broad reasons. First, it is easier for the authorities to estimate collectable revenue from *ad valorem* duties, which are assessed on the basis of value, than revenue from specific duties, which are levied on the basis of volume or weight. Second, *ad valorem* duties are more equitable than specific duties as their incidence is lower on cheaper products and higher on more expensive goods. For instance, a specific duty of $2 per litre would have an incidence of 50% on a bottle of wine costing $2, and 10% on a higher-priced wine costing $2 a bottle. An *ad valorem* duty of 10% would have an incidence of $0.20 on the cheaper bottle and $2 on the more expensive bottle. Third, in international negotiations for reductions in tariffs it is far easier to compare the level of tariffs and negotiate reductions if the duties are *ad valorem*.

However, the incidence of *ad valorem* duties depends to a large extent on the methods used to determine dutiable value. Thus, if Customs determines the dutiable value at $1,000, an *ad valorem* duty of 10% will result in a duty of $100. If, on the other hand, it determines value at $1,200, the importer will have to pay an import duty of $120 for the same goods. The benefits to the trade arising from tariff bindings could fall considerably if Customs uses prices other than invoice prices for determining values for customs purposes. The rules that are applied for the valuation of goods are therefore of crucial importance in ensuring that the incidence of duties as perceived by the importer is not higher than that indicated by the nominal rates shown in the importing country's tariff schedules.

2. Rules of the Agreement on Customs Valuation

The detailed GATT rules on the valuation of goods for customs purposes are contained in the Agreement on Customs Valuation (full title: Agreement on Implementation of Article VII of GATT 1994). The Agreement's valuation system is based on simple and equitable criteria that take commercial practices into account. By requiring all member countries to harmonize their national legislation on the basis of the Agreement's rules, it seeks to ensure uniformity in the application of the rules so that importers can assess with certainty in advance of imports the amounts of duties payable.

ACV, Preamble

2.1 The main standard: transaction value

The basic rule of the Agreement is that the value for customs purposes should be based on the *price actually paid or payable* when sold for export to the country of importation (e.g. the invoice price), adjusted, where appropriate, to include certain payments made by buyers such as the costs of packing and containers, assists, royalties and license fees (see box 5). The rules exclude buying commissions and special discounts obtained by sole agents and sole concessionaires from being taken into account in arriving at dutiable value.

ACV, Article 1:1

ACV, Article 8:1

Box 5

DETERMINING CUSTOMS VALUE: PERMITTED ADJUSTMENTS TO THE PRICE PAID FOR GOODS

(ACV, Article 8)

In order to arrive at the transaction value, Article 8 of the Agreement on Customs Valuation provides that payments made for the following elements can be added to the price actually paid or payable (i.e. the invoice price) by the importer for the imported goods:

- Commissions and brokerage, except buying commissions;

- Costs of, and charges for, packing and containers;

- Assists, i.e. goods (materials, components, tools, dies, etc.) or services (designs, plans, etc.) supplied free or at reduced cost by the buyer for use in the production of the imported goods;

- Royalties and license fees;

- Subsequent proceeds of any sale accruing to the seller as a result of the resale or use of imported goods;

- The cost of transport, insurance and related charges to the place of importation, if the country bases its valuation on CIF prices.

The Article further clarifies that no additions other than for the elements mentioned above shall be made to the price paid or payable in order to arrive at the transaction value. The Article, in addition, enumerates charges or costs that should not be added to customs value, if they can be distinguished from the price actually paid or payable. These are:

- Freight after importation into the customs territory of the importing country;

- Cost of construction, erection, assembly, maintenance or technical assistance occurring after importation;

- Duties and taxes of the importing country.

The Tokyo Round Agreement strictly limited the discretion available to Customs to reject *transaction value* to the small number of cases listed in box 6. This was a matter of concern to numerous developing countries. They considered that the rule unduly inhibited the ability of their Customs administrations to deal with the traders' practice of under-

---

Box 6

INSTANCES WHEN CUSTOMS CAN REJECT
THE TRANSACTION VALUE DECLARED BY THE IMPORTER

1. When there is no sale.

2. When there are restrictions on the disposition or use of the goods by the buyer. The transaction value need not be accepted if the sale contract imposes some restrictions on the use or disposition of goods except where:

   — The restriction is imposed by law (e.g. packaging requirements);

   — The restrictions limit the geographical area in which the goods may be sold (e.g. distribution contract which limits sales to European countries);

   — The restrictions do not affect the value of goods (e.g., the new model imported should not be sold before a particular date).

4. When the sale or price is subject to some conditions for which the value cannot be determined (e.g., the seller establishes the price of the imported goods on condition that the buyer also buys other goods in specified quantities).

5. When part of the proceeds of any subsequent resale by the buyer accrues to the seller.

6. Where the buyer and seller are related and if the price is influenced by the relationship.

---

valuing imported goods in order to reduce the incidence of customs duties. This was one reason for the reluctance of a large number of developing countries to accede to the Agreement in the pre-WTO period.

The Decision Regarding Cases where Customs Administrations Have Reasons to Doubt the Truth or Accuracy of the Declared Value (also known as the Decision on Shifting the Burden of Proof), adopted as a result of the initiative taken by developing countries during the Uruguay Round, corrects this lacuna. The Tokyo Round Agreement placed the burden of proof on Customs if it rejected the transaction value declared by the importer. The Uruguay Round decision shifts the burden of proof on to the importers when Customs, on the basis of the information on prices and other data available to it, "has reason to doubt the truth or accuracy of the particulars or of documents produced in support" of declarations made by the importers.

Decision on Shifting the Burden of Proof, para. 1

In order to ensure that the transaction value is rejected by Customs in such cases on an objective basis, the new Agreement stipulates that national legislation should provide certain rights to importers. First, where Customs expresses doubts as to the truth or accuracy of a declared value, importers should have a right to provide an explanation, including documents or other evidence to prove that the value declared by them reflects the correct value of the imported goods. Second, where Customs is not satisfied with the explanations given, importers should have a right to ask Customs to communicate to them in writing its reasons for doubting the truth or accuracy of the declared value. This provision is intended to safeguard the interests of importers, by giving them the right to appeal against the decision to higher authorities and, if necessary, to a tribunal or other independent body, within the Customs administration.

ACV, Article 2(a)

The rule that transaction values declared by importers should be used for valuation of goods applies not only to *arms-length transactions* but also to *transactions between related parties*. In the latter transactions, which generally take place among transnational corporations and their subsidiaries or affiliates, prices are charged on the basis of *transfer pricing* which may not always reflect the correct or true value of the imported goods. Even in such cases, the Agreement requires Customs to enter into consultations with the importer, in order to ascertain the type of relationship, the circumstances surrounding the transaction and whether the relationship has influenced the price. If Customs after such examination finds that the relationship has not influenced the declared prices, the transaction value is to be determined on the basis of those prices. Further, in order to ensure that in practice the transaction value is not rejected simply on the grounds that the parties are related, the Agreement gives importers the right to demand that the value should be accepted when they demonstrate that the value *approximates* the *test values* arrived at on the basis of:

ACV, Article 2(b)

❑   Customs value determined in past import transactions occurring at about the same time between unrelated buyers and sellers of identical or similar goods; or

❑   Deductive or computed values calculated for identical or similar goods (see below).

2.2   Five other standards

How should Customs determine dutiable value when it decides to reject the transaction value declared by the importer? In order to protect the interests of importers and to ensure that the value in such cases is determined on a *fair and neutral* basis, the Agreement limits the discretion available to Customs to using the five standards it lays down. The Agreement further insists that these standards should be used in the sequential order in which they appear in the text, and only if Customs finds that the first standard cannot be used should the value be determined on the basis of the following standards.

ACV, Annex I, General Note

The standards to be used in sequential order are discussed below.

ACV, Article 2

2.2.1 The transaction value of identical goods

Where value cannot be determined on the basis of the transaction value, it should be established by using an already determined transaction value for identical goods.

ACV, Article 3

2.2.2 The transaction value of similar goods

Where it is not possible to determine value on the basis of the above method, it should be determined on the basis of the transaction value of similar goods.

Under both these methods, the transactions selected must relate to imported goods that were sold for export to the country of importation and at about the same time as goods being exported.

Box 7 describes the rules to be followed in determining whether the goods that are used for determining dutiable value are identical or similar to imported goods.

2.2.3 Deductive value

The next two methods are the deductive method and the computed value method.

ACV, Article 5

Deductive value is determined on the basis of the unit sales price in the domestic market of the imported goods being valued or of identical or similar goods after making deductions for such elements as profits, customs duties and taxes, transport and insurance, and other expenses incurred in the country of importation.

Box 7
RULES FOR DETERMINING WHETHER GOODS
ARE IDENTICAL OR SIMILAR
(ACV, Article 15:2)

Whether the goods are identical or similar to those in the transaction to be valued
is determined by taking into account the characteristics described below.

Goods are identical if they:

Are the same in all respects including physical characteristics,
and quality and reputation.

Goods are similar if they:

Closely resemble the goods being valued in terms of components, materials
and characteristics;

Are capable of performing the same
functions and are commercially inter-
changeable with the goods being valued.

In addition, in order to be treated as identical or similar, the goods must have
been produced:

— in the same country
— and by the same producer

as the goods being valued.

Where, however, import transactions involving identical or similar goods *produced by the same person in the country of production of the goods being valued*
do not exist, goods produced by a different person in the same country must be
taken into account.

ACV, Article 6

2.2.4 *Computed value*

The computed value is determined by adding
to the cost of producing the goods being valued, "an
amount for profit and general expenses equal to that
usually reflected in sales of goods of the same class
or kind as the goods being valued which are made by
producers in the country of exportation for export to
the country of importation."

ACV, Article 7

2.2.5 *Fall-back method*

Where customs value cannot be determined
by any of the four methods described above, it can

be determined by using any of the previous methods in a flexible manner, provided that the criteria employed are consistent with Article VII of the General Agreement. The value so fixed should not, however, be based on the following factors, among others:

❑ The price of goods for export to a third country market,

❑ Minimum customs values,

❑ Arbitrary or fictitious values.

ACV, Article 6, General Note   As a general rule, the Agreement visualizes that where a transaction value is not accepted, the value should be determined by using the above standards *on the basis of the information available within the country of importation.* However, it recognizes that in order to determine a computed value, it may be necessary *to examine the costs of producing the goods being valued* and other information which has to be obtained from outside the country of importation. The Agreement therefore suggests, in order to ensure that the importer is not subjected to unnecessary burdens, that the computed value standard should be used only when *buyer and seller are related* and the producer is prepared to provide to the Customs authorities in the importing country the necessary cost data and facilities for their subsequent verification.

3.   Developing countries and the Agreement

Before 1 January 1995, only 11 of the developing country members of GATT had acceded to the Agreement on Customs Valuation. The coming into existence of WTO on that date changed the situation. As noted earlier, the Agreement establishing WTO requires its member countries to accept all multilateral agreements negotiated in the Uruguay Round. As the Agreement on Customs Valuation is a multilateral agreement, developing country members of WTO join it automatically.

ACV, Article 20:1

Developing countries have been given a delay period of five years to implement the provisions of the Agreement.[7] Those among the WTO's original members who invoke this provision will therefore need to apply the Agreement only from 1 January 2000.

This delay period is intended to provide them with sufficient time to take gradual steps to change over from their current systems to the Agreement's valuation system.[8] In order to facilitate such change-over, the Agreement calls on developed countries and international organizations like WCO to provide technical assistance in the preparation of implementation measures and for personnel training.

ACV, Article 20:3

4.   Business implications

The basic aim of the Agreement is to protect the interests of honest traders by requiring that Customs should accept for determining dutiable value the price actually paid by the importer in the particular transaction. This applies to both arms-length and related-party transactions. The Agreement recognizes that the prices obtained by different importers for the same products may vary. The mere fact that the price obtained by a particular importer is lower

---

7   The delay period of five years may be extended by the Committee on Customs Valuation, which has been established under the Agreement, if a developing country so requests and shows good cause.

8   A number of developing countries use a system based on the Brussels Definitions of Value (BDV), a system of valuation developed by the World Customs Organisation (WCO).

than that at which other importers have imported the product cannot be used as a ground for rejecting the transaction value. Customs can reject the transaction value in such situations only if it has reasons to doubt the truth or accuracy of the declared price of the imported goods. Even in such cases, it has to give importers an opportunity to justify their price and if this justification is not accepted, to give them in writing the reasons for rejecting the transaction value and for determining the dutiable value by using other methods. Furthermore, by providing importers the right to be consulted throughout all stages of the determination of value, the Agreement ensures that the discretion available to Customs for scrutinizing declared value is used objectively.

In addition to the rights of importers to be consulted at all stages of the determination of dutiable value, the Agreement requires national legislation on the valuation of goods to provide the following rights to importers:

❑ Right to withdraw imported goods from Customs, when there is likely to be a delay in the determination of customs value, by providing sufficient quantities, in the form of surety or a deposit, covering the payment of customs duties for which goods may be liable.

❑ Right to expect that any information of a confidential nature that is made available to Customs shall be treated as confidential.

❑ Right to appeal, without fear of penalty, to an independent body within the Customs administration and to judicial authority against decisions taken by Customs.

CHAPTER 4

Preshipment inspection

Summary

The Agreement on Preshipment Inspection (PSI), negotiated in the Uruguay Round, provides developing countries with a means for dealing with the problem of under- or over-valuation of imported goods. Over 30 developing countries currently use the services of PSI companies for mandatory and independent verification in the exporting country of the prices of goods to be imported. The Agreement recognizes that the use of such services by developing countries may be necessary to prevent **over- and under-invoicing and fraud**. It states that these countries may use the services of such companies "for as long as and in so far as it is necessary to verify the quality, quantity or price of imported goods".

In order to ensure that PSI companies do not arbitrarily reject the price agreed voluntarily between importers and exporters, the Agreement lays down the principles and rules which these companies must follow in verifying prices in exporting countries. In particular, it states that in verifying export prices, PSI companies should use for comparison purposes the prices of identical or similar goods offered for exportation:

- *To the country of importation, or*

- *To other markets.*

Where prices charged for goods exported to countries other than the country of importation are used, the economic and other factors that influence the different export prices charged to different markets should be taken into account.

The Agreement also establishes a mechanism for reviewing exporters' complaints when they consider that decisions to revise prices have been taken by PSI companies arbitrarily and without following its rules.

In countries using PSI services, Customs administrations cannot automatically determine the transaction value on the basis of the price recommended by PSI companies in their reports of findings. The Agreement on Customs Valuation clarifies that Customs in using PSI-recommended prices must take into account its obligations under that Agreement. This implies that Customs will have to treat PSI-recommended prices as advisory opinions. When, on scrutinizing the prices declared by the importer and that recommended by the PSI company, Customs finds that the latter price does reflect the true value of the goods, it can determine the transaction value on the basis of that price if the importer does not contest it. Where, however, the importer challenges the PSI-recommended price, Customs will have to determine value by using the methods prescribed in the Agreement on Customs Valuation.

1.   General

Since about the second half of the last century importers have used the services of independent inspection companies to certify the quality and quantity of products they want to import. These inspections, which are conducted in most cases prior to shipment and in the country of exportation, assure the importer that the goods conform to the technical specifications and the quality standards laid down in the contract and that the quantities exported are correct. The services of such inspection companies are utilized not only by private business firms, but also by State-owned enterprises and government departments. In fact, the regulations in many countries require goods procured by government departments to be inspected and certified for quality and quantity by independent and competent inspection companies.

Since the mid-1960s, the governments of some developing countries have also been using the services of PSI companies to inspect goods to be imported and to verify their prices, prior to shipment and in the exporting countries. Their basic purpose in doing so is to bring under control the under- or over-invoicing of imported goods and other unfair or improper practices. Today, over 30 countries in Asia, Africa and Latin America use the services of PSI companies:

❑   For the physical inspection of the goods to be imported in order to ensure that they conform to the terms of the contract;

❑   To verify their prices; and

❏   To ensure that they are classified by the exporter under the correct tariff classification of the importing country.

The physical inspection of goods is an integral part of the procedures adopted by PSI companies to ensure that the prices indicated by the exporter in the invoice reflect the true value of the goods and that there is no under- or over-invoicing. Such inspections also help importers as they are assured that the goods they have ordered meet contractual specifications and quality standards, thereby reducing possibilities for dispute after the goods arrive at destination. These inspections also prevent the import of products that are considered harmful to health and therefore cannot be sold (e.g. banned chemicals and pharmaceutical products, substandard food products) in the exporting countries.

PSI companies carry out a physical inspection and price verification of almost all goods imported by the countries using their services. Most contracts, however, exempt goods with values below the specified threshold for preshipment inspections.

There are currently five PSI companies providing preshipment inspection services on a worldwide or a regional basis.[9] They are all members of the Preshipment Inspection Committee of the International Federation of Inspection Agencies (IFIA). The main objective of the Federation is to establish a basis for common rules governing their operations.

---

9 The largest among them is the Société générale de surveillance (SGS) of Geneva. It has over 130 affiliated companies, with a presence in more than 140 countries and a staff of over 30,000. The other four companies are BIVAC International of Paris, COTECNA of Geneva, Inchape Testing Services International (ITSI) of London, and Inspectorate of the United States. There are indications that a number of other companies may enter the market in the future.

2. Objectives for using PSI services

Contracts for mandatory preshipment inspections can be grouped into two broad categories according to the purpose for which the services of PSI companies are employed. In the terminology used by PSI companies, these are *foreign exchange contracts (Forex)* and *customs contracts.* The first is usually employed to designate contracts whose basic objective (and that of the government requiring them) is to prevent the flight of capital through over-invoicing. The second is used for contracts undertaken when the governments' main aim is to prevent slippage of customs revenue as a result of undervaluation or deliberate misclassification by traders of goods to be imported under low-duty headings.

Until about a few years ago, the predominant government objective was to prevent the overvaluation of imports. Traders tend to overvalue imports when the import trade and foreign exchange transactions are subject to restrictions. As most developing countries are now liberalizing their trade regimes and are removing restrictions on foreign exchange, they are relying increasingly on PSI services to detect the undervaluation of imported goods and thus to prevent slippage of customs revenue. The result has been that, as box 8 shows, a large majority of the countries using PSI services rely on them to prevent both the loss of revenue from under-invoicing and the loss of foreign exchange from over-invoicing.

While PSI services are mainly used for the preshipment inspection of imports, a few governments also utilize them to control the flight of capital through the undervaluation of exports.

Box 8

COUNTRIES/AREAS USING PSI SERVICES

Country/area	Nature of contract
Angola	Forex
Benin	Customs/Forex
Bolivia	Customs
Burkina Faso	Customs/Forex
Burundi	Forex
Cameroon	Customs/Forex
Central African Rep.	Customs/Forex
Chad	Customs
Congo	Customs
Côte d'Ivoire	Customs
Ecuador	Customs
Ethiopia	Forex
Ghana	Customs/Forex
Guinea	Customs/Forex
Haiti	Customs/Forex
Indonesia	Customs
Kenya	Customs
Mali	Customs
Madagascar	Customs/Forex
Malawi	Customs/Forex
Mauritania	Customs/Forex
Mexico	Forex
Mozambique	Customs/Forex
Nigeria	Customs/Forex
Pakistan	Customs
Peru	Customs
Philippines	Customs
Rwanda	Customs/Forex
Senegal	Customs/Forex
Sierra Leone	Customs/Forex
Tanzania, United Rep. of	Customs/Forex
Togo	Customs
Uganda	Customs
Zaire	Forex
Zambia	Customs/Forex
Zanzibar	Forex

3. Background to the negotiations

3.1 Concerns of exporters from developed countries

This expansion of PSI services to the mandatory verification of the prices agreed between importer and exporter was viewed with concern by business and industry, especially in some developed countries. They were particularly worried by the fact that they were asked to revise their prices downward when the PSI companies found contractual prices to be overvalued. They argued that the criteria used by PSI companies for price comparison was not always known to the exporters. The lack of transparency not only created uncertainty about the acceptability of prices negotiated with buyers but also put exporters in a disadvantageous position, as there were no procedures for appealing to independent bodies against the decisions of PSI companies. The delays in carrying out physical inspections and price verifications also delayed shipment, adding to the exporters' costs.

3.2 Response of countries using PSI services

In the initial phase of the discussions in the Uruguay Round the developed countries therefore argued that the use of PSI services for mandatory physical inspection and verification of prices constituted a non-tariff barrier. This view was challenged by developing countries. They maintained that far from constituting non-tariff measures, the prices re commended by PSI companies in their reports of findings facilitated clearance of goods at the importing end. In their view, it was not appropriate to look at the impact the use of these services had on trade without taking into account the broader policy objectives for which they were being utilized. Their experience had shown that the PSI service was the most effective means of preventing capital flight through over-invoicing and the loss of customs revenue through under-invoicing by traders.

4.   Main provisions of the Agreement on Preshipment Inspection

4.1   Objectives and scope

The Agreement on Preshipment Inspection, negotiated in the Uruguay Round, attempts to strike a balance between the concerns expressed by exporting enterprises in developed countries and the need to safeguard the essential interests of developing countries that consider PSI services useful. It clari-

Agreement on Preshipment Inspection (PSI), Article 1

fies that its provisions apply only to preshipment activities carried out in exporting countries that are "contracted or mandated by the government". The term "preshipment inspection" is defined as "all activities relating to the verification of the quality, the quantity, the price, including currency exchange rate and financial terms and/or the customs classification of goods to be exported".

PSI, Preamble

The Agreement further recognizes that a number of developing countries use PSI services, and allows their use "for as long as and in so far as" they are "necessary to verify the quality, quantity or price of imported goods." The basic aim of the Agreement is to lay down a set of principles and rules for countries using PSI services and for exporting countries to ensure that their activities do not cause barriers to trade. Its substantive provisions ensure that the practical problems encountered by exporters as a result of delays in carrying out physical inspections and price verifications by PSI companies, the lack of transparency in the procedures they follow, and the treatment of confidential information are reduced or eliminated. Box 9 summarizes these and other provisions.

4.2 Price verification provisions

PSI, Article 2.20

The Agreement further lays down guidelines and rules which PSI companies must follow when verifying prices in exporting countries of the products to be imported. In particular it states that, in order to determine whether the export price reflects the correct value of the goods, it should be compared with the prices of identical or similar goods offered for export from the same country of exportation to the country of importation, or to other markets.

However, where for price comparison purposes the prices charged for export to countries other than the country of importation are used, the economic and other factors that influence the prices charged to different countries should be taken into account. In other words, the rules recognize that firms often charge varying prices in different markets, taking into account demand and growth potential as well as such factors as per capita income and standards of living in these markets. An exporting firm may thus charge higher prices for its exports of, say, shirts to Europe than it does for exports to Africa. The Agreement stipulates that when third-country prices are used for price-comparison purposes, the factors responsible for variations in the prices charged to importers in different countries should be taken into account and PSI companies should not "arbitrarily impose the lowest price upon the shipment". In addition, it states that PSI companies should make appropriate allowances for certain "applicable adjusting factors" in regard to the export

Box 9

COUNTRIES USING PSI SERVICES AND EXPORTING COUNTRIES: MAIN OBLIGATIONS

Obligations of importing countries using PSI services

Non-discrimination. Procedures and criteria should be applied on an equal basis to all exporters. There should be uniform performance of inspection by all inspectors. [PSI, Article 2.1]

National treatment. Countries using PSI services should not apply national regulations in a manner that will result in less favourable treatment of the goods being inspected in comparison to the like domestic product. [PSI, Article 2.2]

Site of inspections. Physical inspection should be carried out in the exporting country and, only if this is not feasible, in the country of manufacture. [PSI, Article 2.3]

Standards. Quality and quantity inspections should be conducted according to the standards agreed between buyer and seller or, in their absence, international standards. [PSI, Article 2.4]

Transparency. Transparency should be ensured by providing exporters with information, *inter alia,* on the laws and regulations of user countries on PSI activities, and the procedures and criteria used for inspection. [PSI, Article 2.5 to 2.8]

Protection of confidential information. Confidential information should not be divulged to third parties. [PSI, Article 2.5 to 2.13]

Delays. Unreasonable delays should be avoided. [PSI, Article 2.15 to 19]

Price verification. See box 10.

Appeals procedures. See box 11.

Obligations of exporting countries in relation to PSI activities

Non-discrimination. Laws and regulations should be applied on a non-discriminatory basis. [PSI, Article 3.1]

Transparency. All laws and regulations should be published. [PSI, Article 3.2]

Technical assistance. Technical assistance should be provided to user countries with a view to gradually reducing their reliance on PSI services for the verification of prices. [PSI, Article 3.3] price of the goods being inspected and the prices of identical or similar goods being used for price comparison. (See box 10.)

Since one of the main aims of governments in using PSI services is to prevent the loss of customs revenue from undervaluation of goods, the question arises of how Customs should use the prices recommended by PSI companies in determining value for customs purposes. The Agreement on Customs Valuation clarifies the role of Customs in such situations by stating that the obligations of user member countries "with respect to the services of preshipment inspection entities (in connection with customs valuation) shall be the obligations which they have accepted" under the Agreement (on Customs Valuation). The aim of the complex legal language is to ensure that Customs administrations in countries using PSI services do not automatically determine dutiable value on the basis of prices recommended by the PSI company in its report of findings. Customs have to examine each case. If on the basis of the examination and a comparison of price declared by the importer and that recommended by the PSI company, it finds that the latter reflects the correct price and the importer does not contest it, the value can be determined on the basis of that price. In all cases, it will be necessary to ensure that, in arriving at the recommended price, the PSI company has followed the rules relating to adjustments for various elements (e.g. buying commissions and sole agency commissions) laid down by the Agreement on Customs Valuation.

There will always be a few importers who will contest the PSI-recommended prices that are acceptable to Customs, and maintain that the prices declared by them reflect the true value of goods. In

Box 10

AGREEMENT ON PRESHIPMENT INSPECTION: PROVISIONS ON PRICE VERIFICATION
(the text of Article 2.20)

User Members shall ensure that, in order to prevent over- and under-invoicing and fraud, preshipment inspection entities conduct price verification according to the following guidelines:

(a) preshipment inspection entities shall only reject a contract price agreed between an exporter and an importer if they can demonstrate that their findings of an unsatisfactory price are based on a verification process which is in conformity with the criteria set out in subparagraphs (b) through (e) below;

(b) The preshipment inspection entity shall base its price comparison for the verification of the export price on the price(s) of identical or similar goods offered for export from the same country of exportation at or about the same time, under competitive and comparable conditions of sale, in conformity with customary commercial practices and net of any applicable standard discounts. Such comparison shall be based on the following:

   (i)   only prices providing a valid basis of comparison shall be used, taking into account the relevant economic factors pertaining to the country of importation and a country or countries used for price comparison;

   (ii) the preshipment inspection entity shall not rely upon the price of goods offered for export to different countries of importation to arbitrarily impose the lowest price upon the shipment;

(c) When conducting price verification, preshipment inspection entities shall make appropriate allowances for the terms of the sales contract and generally applicable adjusting factors pertaining to the transaction; these factors shall include but not be limited to the commercial level and quantity of the sale, delivery periods and conditions, price escalation clauses, quality specifications, special design features, special shipping or packing specifications, order size, spot sales, seasonal influences, licence or other intellectual property fees, and services rendered as part of the contract if these are not customarily invoiced separately; they shall also include certain elements relating to the exporter's price, such as the contractual relationship between the exporter and importer;

(d) The verification of transportation charges shall relate only to the agreed price of the mode of transport in the country of exportation as indicated in the sales contract;

Box 10 (cont'd)

(e) The following shall not be used for price verification purposes:

(i)   the selling price in the country of importation of goods produced in such country;

(ii)   the price of goods for export from a country other than the country of exportation;

(iii) the cost of production;

(iv)   arbitrary or fictitious prices or values.

---

such cases, importers have a right to expect Customs to give them the opportunity to produce documentary and other evidence to justify their declared price. If, after examining the evidence, Customs still maintains that the price declared by the importer involves either under- or over-valuation, it cannot under the provisions of the Agreement on Customs Valuation determine value on the basis of the PSI-recommended price.[10] It will have to determine it by using the methods laid down in the Agreement for the determination of value when the transaction value declared by the importer is not acceptable.

PSI, Article 2:21, Article 4

4.3 Appeal, revision and dispute settlement provisions

One of the other major criticisms made by exporters of PSI activities was the absence of an institutional mechanism for considering complaints. When they regarded a decision to revise prices as arbitrary or wrong, and the PSI company concerned refused to review its decision, the exporters found it

---

10 This applies even when the PSI company has arrived at the price by adhering to the rules of the Agreement on Customs Valuation.

PSI, Article 2:21

PSI, Article 4

PSI, Article 8

difficult to obtain a hearing for their grievances. To facilitate consideration of such complaints, the Agreement establishes a three-tier mechanism (see box 11). First, it calls on PSI entities to designate officials to whom exporters can appeal against the decisions of PSI inspectors. Second, it establishes an Independent Review Entity (IRE) to which both exporters and PSI entities can submit grievances. Complaints made to the IRE are to be examined by a panel consisting of three experts — one member to be nominated by the International Chamber of Commerce (ICC), the second by the International Federation of Inspection Agencies (IFIA), and the third, who should be a trade expert and who will act as chairman, to be nominated by the IRE itself. Third, it recognizes that governments of countries using PSI services and exporting countries could bring disputes on any matter related to the operation of the Agreement to WTO for settlement.

5.   Business implications

By laying down rules on PSI activities, the PSI Agreement seeks to reduce, if not completely eliminate, the difficulties exporting enterprises experience in regard to transactions with countries using PSI services. In addition, the Agreement has created a mechanism for the consideration of complaints. This will enable exporters who believe that their prices have been revised arbitrarily by the verifying inspector to complain to a designated senior official of the inspecting company, and, if they are not satisfied, to bring the matter up for consideration by the Independent Review Entity, which has been established under the Agreement.

Governments of PSI-using countries benefit from the increased customs revenue resulting from

---

Box 11

AGREEMENT ON PRESHIPMENT INSPECTION: PROVISIONS ON APPEALS, REVIEWS AND DISPUTE SETTLEMENT
(PSI, Article 4)

Appeals procedures

The Agreement imposes an obligation on user member countries to require PSI entities whose services they employ to designate one or more officials "who shall be available during normal business hours in each city or port in which they maintain preshipment inspection administrative office, to receive, consider and render decisions on exporter's appeals or grievances". The designated officials are expected to take decisions on such complaints promptly.

Independent review mechanism

Where a dispute cannot be settled through mutual consultations between exporters and PSI entities, either party can, within two days after its submission under the appeals procedures, refer it to the Independent Review Entity established under the Agreement and administered jointly by IFIA and the ICC. This entity is required to establish a list of experts who can serve as members of panels considering the complaints brought to it.

A panel shall consist of three experts. One member is to be nominated by the exporter; the second by the PSI entity. The experts so nominated should not, however, be affiliated to these two nominating parties. The third expert, who is to be nominated by the Independent Review Entity, shall be a trade expert and is to act as chairman.

The decisions of the panel shall be taken by majority vote and in eight working days of the request for independent review. The panel decisions are binding on the parties to the dispute.

Settlement of disputes between governments

However, where either the user or the exporting country considers that its right under the PSI Agreement or under the General Agreement is infringed, it may request consultations. If the consultations do not succeed in reaching a mutually satisfactory solution, it may invoke the GATT dispute settlement procedures.

---

the detection of undervaluation and from the decline in the flight of capital through overvaluation. The employment of PSI services also brings indirect benefits to business enterprises. First, by speeding up the clearance of goods, it greatly reduces the inventories which manufacturers have to maintain and thus enables them to cut costs. Second, the use of PSI services lowers the level of customs-related corruption, thereby reducing demands for under-the-table payments for imported goods to be cleared. As has been said, one of the objectives of governments using PSI services is to bring customs-related corruption under control. Third, when verifying prices, PSI companies carry out physical inspections of all goods to be imported in order to ensure that they conform to the conditions stipulated in contracts between importers and exporters in regard to quality and quantity. Except therefore in cases of low-value imports, which are not inspected, importers obtain an assurance that the goods they will receive will be in conformity with the terms of their contracts. However, as PSI companies enter into contracts with governments, importers have no right of recourse to these companies if they (the importers) ultimately find that the imported goods do not, in fact, meet the terms of their contracts.

CHAPTER 5

Mandatory and voluntary product standards and sanitary and phytosanitary regulations

Summary of the main rules

Countries often require imported products to conform to the mandatory standards they have adopted for the protection of the health and safety of their people or for the preservation of their environment.

The Agreement on Technical Barriers to Trade (TBT) provides that such mandatory product standards should not be so applied by countries as to cause **unnecessary obstacles to international trade.** *Furthermore, they should be based on scientific information and evidence.*

The Agreement visualizes that mandatory product standards do not create unnecessary barriers to trade if they are based on **internationally agreed standards.** *Where for geographical, climatic and other reasons, it is not possible for member countries to base their mandatory regulations on international regulations, they are obliged to publish these regulations in draft form to give producers in other countries an opportunity to comment on them. The Agree-*

ment also obliges member countries to take such comments into consideration when the standards are finalized, thus ensuring that the characteristics of products produced in, and exported by, other countries are taken into adequate account.

Voluntary standards, with which compliance is not mandatory, may also pose problems in international trade if they differ widely from country to country. The Code of Good Practice for the Preparation, Adoption and Application of Standards, an integral part of the Agreement on TBT, therefore urges countries to use their best endeavours to require national standardizing bodies to use the same principles and rules in preparing and applying voluntary standards as are laid down for mandatory standards.

Countries also require the compliance of imported agricultural products with their national sanitary and phytosanitary regulations. The primary aim of these regulations is to protect human, animal or plant life or health from pests and diseases that may be brought in by imported agricultural products. The rules which the Agreement on the Application of Sanitary and Phytosanitary Measures (SPS) lay down are similar to those applicable to mandatory product standards. There are, however, some important differences.

The Agreement on TBT requires mandatory product standards to be applied on a non-discriminatory basis to imported products. The Agreement on SPS permits countries to apply measures on a discriminatory basis, taking into account such factors as the differences in the level of prevalence of specific diseases or pests. The SPS Agreement further permits countries to take measures to restrict imports on a *provisional basis, as a precautionary step, in cases where there is imminent risk of the spread of diseases, but the "scientific evidence is insufficient". There is no such provision in the TBT Agreement.*

1.   Role of standards

Product standards play an important role in cutting costs by reducing the variety of inputs and machine tools used in production. This leads to savings in the costs of design, production, handling, storing. Standards are indispensable in international business transactions because they ensure a uniform level of quality in merchandise. Standards also reduce disputes over specifications and the quality of goods and services exported or imported.

Many standards used in business transactions are voluntary. In practice, exporting enterprises may find that some of these have the effect of mandatory standards. This happens when large industries refuse to buy goods that do not conform to the standards they impose.

Governments often lay down health and safety standards for various products. These laws have been passed to protect consumers who have no means of assessing the risks involved in using these goods. Standards are also established to protect the environment and natural resources. In recent years, increasing environmental awareness has led to the promulgation of new health and safety regulations.

When product standards adopted at national level vary from country to country, manufacturers have to adjust their production processes to meet the differing technical specifications of their target markets. This increases tooling costs and prevents companies from taking advantage of economies of scale. This is why efforts are being made in international organizations to harmonize standards on a world-wide basis.

2.   Agreement on Technical Barriers to Trade (TBT)

2.1   Product standards

TBT, Annex I

International rules applicable to product standards are contained in the Agreement on Technical Barriers to Trade. The Agreement uses the term "technical regulations" to cover standards with which compliance is mandatory. The term "standard" is used for voluntary standards.

Both terms cover:

❑   Product characteristics;

❑   Process and production methods (PPM) that have an effect on product characteristics;

❑   Terminology and symbols; and

❑   Packaging and labelling requirements as they apply to the product.

The rules of the Agreement apply to process and production methods only if these methods have an effect on the quality or other characteristics of the product. Other processes and production methods are not covered by the provisions of the Agreement. (See box 12.)

2.2   Technical regulations

2.2.1   Main conditions

TBT, Preamble

The Agreement recognizes that countries have the right to adopt technical regulations which prescribe mandatory product standards (including packaging and labelling requirements). These regulations are enacted to ensure the quality of exports, to protect human health or safety, animal or plant life

---

Box 12

DISTINCTION BETWEEN PRODUCT STANDARDS
AND PPM STANDARDS

Product standards define product characteristics, or the product's quality, design or performance. They need to be distinguished from standards for process and production methods (PPMs, as they are commonly called) which specify norms relating to how goods should be produced. PPM standards apply before and during the production stage, i.e. before the product is placed on the market.

The provisions of the Agreement on TBT apply primarily to product standards. They do not cover PPM standards, except when the production process or method used has an effect on product quality.

Assume that country A prohibits imports of pharmaceuticals from country B. Its grounds are that country B has failed to meet its requirements for proper manufacturing practices and plant cleanliness, thereby affecting product quality. In this case the PPM standard is covered by the TBT Agreement and country A can justify its action if it can establish that its production and processing requirements have an impact on product quality.

Now assume that country A prohibits imports of steel on the grounds that pollution standards at the steel plant in country B are much lower than those enforced by country A. In this case, no environmental damage is done to the importing country; country A's process standard would therefore not be covered by the Agreement and its prohibition on imports would not be justifiable.

---

or the environment, among other objectives. The Agreement requires member countries to ensure that their technical regulations meet certain conditions:

TBT, Article 2.1   ❑   They should be applied on an MFN basis to imports from all sources;

TBT, Article 2.1   ❑   They should not extend to imported products treatment that is less favourable than that extended to domestically produced products (national treatment principle);

TBT, Article 2.2

❑ They should not be formulated and applied in a manner as to cause an "unnecessary obstacle to trade"; and

❑ They should be based on scientific information and evidence.

TBT, Article 2.2

The Agreement also specifies criteria which regulatory authorities have to bear in mind in formulating technical regulations, in order to ensure that they do not create unnecessary obstacles to trade.

2.2.2 Requirement to base technical regulations on international standards

TBT, Article 2.4

One way of ensuring that technical regulations do not create barriers to trade is to base them on international standards. The Agreement therefore imposes an obligation on countries to use international standards as a basis for their technical regulations. An exception is made when the regulatory authorities believe that the international standards would be ineffective or inappropriate in view of climatic, geographical, or technological factors. Further, in order to harmonize technical regulations on an international basis, the Agreement calls on WTO member countries to participate actively in the work of International Organization for Standardization (ISO) and other international standardization organizations.

2.2.3 Opportunity to comment on draft standards

The Agreement also prescribes certain procedural rules to be followed when countries are adopting mandatory technical regulations that are not based on existing international standards. Member countries are required to publish a notice and to

TBT, Article 2.9

notify the WTO secretariat when they adopt technical regulations not based on existing international standards. In addition, they must provide sufficient notice in advance of the adoption of the regulation. These provisions are intended to provide interested exporting countries with an opportunity to comment on the draft standards with a view to ensuring that, when the final regulations are adopted, the characteristics of products produced in their countries are taken into account. The Agreement imposes an obligation on countries proposing the adoption of a technical regulation to take the comments of the exporters into account when finalizing the regulation.

2.2.4 *Rules governing certification of conformity with standards*

For some of the products to which mandatory standards apply, the regulatory authorities may require that imports can be sold only if the manufacturer or exporter is able to obtain a certificate of *positive assurance* from a recognized institution or laboratory in the importing country that the product is in conformity with the standard. In order to ensure that foreign suppliers are not put in a disadvantageous situation when obtaining certificates of positive assurance of conformity, the Agreement stipulates that:

TBT, Article 5

❑   Conformity assessment procedures should not accord to foreign suppliers treatment which is less favourable than that accorded to domestic suppliers;

❑   Any fees charged to foreign suppliers should be equitable in relation to those chargeable for products of domestic origin; and

❑   The selection of samples for testing should not be made as to cause inconvenience to foreign suppliers.

2.2.5 Mutual recognition of certificates of conformity assurance

TBT, Article 6

For products for which regulatory authorities require assurance of conformity to standards, the Agreement encourages countries to accept the results of the inspections and tests carried out by competent certifying bodies in the exporting countries if they are satisfied that product standards and the procedures for assessment of conformity are *equivalent* to their own. However, it emphasizes that entering into arrangements for the mutual recognition of conformity assessment certificates will be possible only if the importing country has confidence in the technical competence of the conformity assessment body of the exporting country.

2.2.6 Obligations of local government bodies

In a number of countries, technical regulations imposing mandatory standards as well as systems for assessing conformity with such standards are formulated and applied not only by central government bodies but also by local and non-governmental bodies. The Agreement imposes a binding obligation on member countries to require their central government bodies to abide by its discipline in formulating and applying mandatory standards. However, as the central governments which are signatories to the Agreement are not allowed by the constitutions of some countries to assume binding obligations on behalf of local bodies, it calls on these

TBT, Article 7

governments to "take such reasonable measures as may be available to them" to ensure that these local bodies abide by the Agreement's discipline.

2.3 Voluntary standards

As noted earlier, many of the standards used by industries and exporters are voluntary standards.

TBT, Article 4; TBT, Annex 3

These are often formulated by national standardizing bodies in the various member countries. Voluntary standards can create problems in international trade if they vary widely from country to country. The Agreement has therefore developed a *Code of Good Practice* with which national standardizing bodies are expected to abide in preparing, adopting and applying standards. The code requires national standardizing bodies to follow principles and rules that are similar to those specified for mandatory standards. Thus the code urges them:

❑   To use international standards as a basis for its national standards;

❑   To participate fully, within the limits of their resources, in the preparation of international standards for products for which it proposes to adopt national standards.

Furthermore, in order to acquaint foreign producers with the work on standardization that is being undertaken by national bodies in different countries, it requires these bodies to publish their work programme "at least once every six months", giving information on the standards that they are preparing and the standards they have adopted in the preceding period. At the time of publication, the national bodies are also required to notify the ISO/IEC[11] Information Centre of the name of the publication and how and where it can be obtained.

The code also requires standardizing bodies to allow a period of at least 60 days for the submission of comments by interested parties in outside countries. The comments are usually forwarded

---

11 ISO/International Electrotechnical Commission.

through their national standardizing bodies. The code calls on the standardizing body formulating the standard to take these comments into account when finalizing the standard.

3. Sanitary and phytosanitary measures (SPS)

A number of imported agricultural products — particularly plants, fresh fruits and vegetables, meat, meat products and other food products — may be required to satisfy sanitary and phytosanitary regulations as well as product standards. In addition, many countries restrict the export of these products if they do not meet the quality requirements specified by regulations. Box 13 illustrates how these regulations can affect international trade.

The Agreement on the Application of Sanitary and Phytosanitary Measures, which was negotiated in the Uruguay Round, specifies the principles

---

Box 13

WHY KNOWLEDGE OF HEALTH AND SANITARY REGULATIONS IS IMPORTANT IN PLANNING FOR EXPORT: AN EXAMPLE FOR FRESH FRUITS AND VEGETABLES

A number of major importers of fresh fruits and vegetables have strict regulations on plant protection. These countries require fresh commodities from countries with specific pests, especially the fruit fly of the *Tephridiate* family, to be treated to prevent the establishment of the pests in their territories. In the past, ethylene dibromide (EDB) was widely used for the fumigation of such produce prior to importation. The prohibition of EDB by the United States, Japan, and other countries jeopardized trade in fresh fruits and vegetables originating from tropical and semi-tropical countries. Alternative treatments to EDB fumigation such as vapour and dry heat treatment, hot water dips, refrigeration at near 0°C for a specific duration, and treatment with other chemicals such as methyl bromide, phosphine and cyanide, are now used with varying degrees of success.

and rules which member countries must use in regulating imported products. The Agreement defines sanitary and phytosanitary measures as measures taken to protect human, animal or plant life or health:

SPS, Annex A

❑ "From risks arising from the entry, establishment or spread of pests, diseases, disease-carrying organisms or disease-causing organisms;

❑ ...from risks arising from additives, contaminants, toxins or disease-causing organisms in food, beverages or feedstuffs;

❑ ...from diseases carried by animals, plants or products thereof".

Like the Agreement on TBT, the SPS Agreement requires countries:

SPS, Preamble

❑ To base their SPS regulations on international standards, guidelines or recommendations;

SPS, Preamble

❑ To play a full part in the activities of international organizations, particularly the Codex Alimentarius Commission, International Office Epizootics and International Plant Protection Convention, in order to promote the harmonization of SPS regulations on an international basis;

SPS, Annex B:5

❑ To provide an opportunity to interested parties in other countries to comment on draft standards when they are not based on international standards or the international standards are not considered appropriate; and

SPS, Article 4

❑ To accept the SPS measures of exporting countries as equivalent if they achieve the same level of SPS protection.

The SPS Agreement, however, differs from the TBT Agreement in three important respects:

SPS, Article 2:3

❑ First, the TBT Agreement requires that product standards should be applied on an MFN basis. The SPS Agreement permits standards to be applied on a discriminatory basis provided that they "do not arbitrarily or unjustifiably discriminate between Members where identical or similar conditions prevail". The rationale for this rule is that, owing to differences in climate, the incidence of pests or diseases, and food safety conditions, it is not always appropriate to impose the same sanitary and phytosanitary standards on animal and plant products originating from different countries.

❑ Second, the SPS Agreement provides greater flexibility for countries to deviate from international standards than is permitted under the TBT Agreement. As noted earlier, the TBT Agreement allows a country to deviate from international standards if this is necessitated by "fundamental climatic or geographical factors or fundamental technological problems". Its provisions thus make it clear that the adoption of a standard which is different (either lower or higher) will have to be justified on scientific or technical grounds.

SPS, Article 3:3

The SPS Agreement, on the other hand, states that a country may introduce or maintain an SPS measure resulting in a higher level of SPS protection than that achieved by an international standard if there is scientific justification or when the country determines that a higher level of protection would be appropri-

SPS, Article 5.2

ate. In the latter case, the Agreement offers certain guidelines. It states that the appropriate level of protection should be based on an assessment of risk appropriate to the circumstances, available scientific evidence, relevant process and production methods, and the prevalence of specific diseases or pests.

SPS, Article 5.3

❏   Third, in assessing the risk to animal or plant life or health, economic factors such as the establishment or spread of pests or disease; the costs of control or eradication in the importing member country; and the relative cost-effectiveness of alternative approaches to limiting risks should be taken into consideration.

SPS, Article 5.4

❏   Fourth, in determining the appropriate level of SPS protection, the objective of minimizing negative trade effects should be borne in mind.

SPS, Article 5.7

❏   Fifth, the SPS Agreement permits countries to adopt SPS measures on a provisional basis, as a precautionary step, in cases where there is imminent risk of the spread of diseases, but the "scientific evidence" is insufficient.

4.   Business implications

The number of technical regulations laying down mandatory standards is steadily increasing in most countries. The trend is the response of governmental regulatory authorities to growing public demand that products marketed should meet minimum quality and safety standards, and not have any adverse impact on the health of the consuming public and on the environment. The same considerations often impel regulatory authorities to set and apply stricter health and sanitary regulations. Box 14 presents an illustrative list of products for which countries adopt mandatory safety or health standards. Box 15 lists agricultural products to which health and sanitary regulations are applicable in most countries.

One of the main problems enterprises face in developing export trade is the lack of adequate information about the standards and health and sanitary regulations applicable to their products in target mar-

---

Box 14

ILLUSTRATIVE LIST OF IMPORT PRODUCTS SUBJECT TO MANDATORY STANDARDS

Machinery and equipment

Boilers
Electrically driven construction and assembly tools
Metal and wood-working equipment
Medical equipment
Food processing equipment

Consumer articles

Pharmaceuticals
Cosmetics
Synthetic detergents
Household electric appliances
Video and TV sets
Cinematographic and photographic equipment
Automobiles
Toys
Certain food products

Raw materials and agricultural inputs

Fertilizers
Insecticides
Hazardous chemicals

Box 15

**LIST OF AGRICULTURAL PRODUCTS GENERALLY SUBJECT
TO HEALTH AND SANITARY REGULATIONS**

Fresh fruits and vegetables
Fruit juices and other food preparations
Meat and meat products
Dairy products
Processed food products

TBT, Article 10:3
SPS, Annex B:3

kets. To help enterprises obtain such information, the two Agreements require each member country to establish *enquiry points* from which information can be obtained by interested business enterprises on:

❑   Technical regulations and voluntary standards adopted or proposed to be adopted;

❑   Conformity assessment procedures, adopted or proposed to be adopted;

❑   Sanitary and phytosanitary regulations adopted or proposed to be adopted;

❑   Control and inspection procedures, production and quarantine treatment, pesticide tolerance treatment and food additive approval procedures;

❑   Risk assessment procedures.

Appendices I and II list the enquiry points that have been established by different member countries under the provisions of TBT and SPS Agreements.

As has been noted, the two Agreements aim at protecting the interests of foreign suppliers. They do this by requiring that standards — both mandatory and voluntary — as well as health and sanitary standards should not be formulated and applied in such a way as to cause *unreasonable barriers to trade*. It is therefore in the interest of exporting enterprises to examine whether the product standards, health or sanitary regulations or the testing and inspection requirements of their export markets conform with the criteria and rules laid down by the Agreements whenever they encounter difficulties in complying with them. If such examination shows non-conformity, they should bring the matter to the notice of the appropriate authorities in their national governments. This will enable their governments to raise the matter either bilaterally with the government of the importing country or in WTO forums with a view to securing modifications in the offending standards or regulations.

In effect, the ability of governments to derive full advantage from these Agreements will depend on how far the practical problems encountered by enterprises in their foreign markets are brought to their notice. Enterprises in turn can do this only if they have full knowledge and understanding of the provisions and rules of the Agreements.

The Agreements further visualize that, in certain areas, their implementation will be possible only if appropriate arrangements are established for consultations and cooperation between national standardizing bodies and authorities responsible for overseeing the operation of the Agreements on the one hand and exporting industries and/or their associations on the other hand. Thus, the Agreements require that in order to ensure that the adoption of standards does not create an unnecessary obstacle to trade, countries should participate actively in the work of international organizations developing international standards for the product for which they propose to adopt standards or regulations. This participation, however, calls for cooperation among national standardizing bodies, producing enterprises, and government departments. In most cases, responsibility for the research and the preparation of technical studies required for international discussions devolves on producing enterprises.

The Agreements further require that where the standards on which technical or health and sanitary regulations are based do not conform to international standards, the draft regulations should be published and an opportunity provided to member countries to comment on it. The basic purpose of this rule is to ensure that regulations adopted take into adequate account the production and other standards prevailing in other countries. The main responsibility for providing such comments falls on the producing and exporting industries.

CHAPTER 6

Import licensing procedures

Summary

National import licensing procedures can adversely affect the flow of imports, particularly if these procedures are not transparent or if they unnecessarily delay the issue of licences. The Agreement on Import Licensing Procedures divides licences into two categories: automatic and non-automatic. Automatic licences should be issued within a maximum period of 10 days after the receipt of applications. Non-automatic licences, which are generally used to administer quantitative restrictions, must be granted within a maximum period of 30 days from receipt of application where licences are issued on a **first-come first-served basis** and 60 days **if all applications are considered simultaneously**.

The Agreement further lays down certain principles and rules to ensure that the flow of international trade is not impeded by the **inappropriate use of import licensing procedures** and that procedures are administered fairly and equitably.

1. General

GATT's basic approach is that, in order to facilitate trade, formalities for, and documentation on, importation and exportation should be kept to the minimum. However, GATT recognizes that countries often, for various reasons, require importers to obtain import licences. Such licensing systems may be adopted to administer quantitative restrictions in the limited number of situations permitting member countries to use such restrictions. Alternatively, they may be used for the surveillance of trade statistics or the prices of certain goods.

Agreement on Import Licensing Procedures (ILP), Preamble

The Agreement on Import Licensing Procedures lays down rules for adopting and implementing national procedures for issuing import licences. It defines "import licensing" as "administrative procedures ... requiring the submission of an application ... to the relevant administrative body as a prior condition for importation ... of goods." It divides licensing systems into two categories: automatic and non-automatic. Under automatic systems, the authorities issue licences automatically without using any discretionary powers. Non-automatic licensing systems administer quota restrictions and other measures, and the authorities use their discretion in granting licences. The Agreement lays down general rules applicable to both systems and specific rules for each system. National licensing authorities must comply with these rules, the basic objective of which is to protect the interests of importers and foreign suppliers. The rules require national licensing authorities to ensure that licensing procedures:

ILP, Article 1.1

ILP, Articles 2 and 3

❑   Are not more burdensome than absolutely necessary to administer the licensing system, taking into account the purpose for which they are adopted;

❑ Are transparent and predictable; and

❑ Protect the interests of importers and foreign suppliers from unnecessary delays and arbitrary actions.

2. Common rules

ILP, Article 1.4(a)

The Agreement obliges member countries to publish all information on import licensing procedures, so that importers, exporters and their governments are fully aware of:

❑ The eligibility of persons, firms and institutions to make applications;

❑ The administrative body responsible for the issue of licences; and

❑ The products subject to licensing.

ILP, Article 1.5 - 11

To protect the interests of importers and to facilitate speedy and prompt issue of licences, the Agreement further stipulates that:

❑ Application forms and procedures, including procedures for the renewal of licences, should be as simple as possible;

❑ Applications should not be refused for minor documentation errors which do not alter the basic data contained therein;

❑ Penalties imposed for such errors, except where fraudulent intent or gross negligence is involved, should not be more severe than required to serve as a warning;

❑ Licensed imports should not be refused for minor variations in value, quantity or weight from those designated in a licence, where such differences are consistent with commercial practice or are due to losses in weight and quantities occurring in shipping or bulk loading.

ILP, Article 2

3.   Automatic import licensing

In systems where administrative authorities do not exercise any discretion and "licences are granted in all cases", the Agreement requires approval or licence to be granted immediately, on receipt of the application, and in any case "within a maximum period of 10 working days".

ILP, Article 3

4.   Non-automatic import licensing

Non-automatic licensing systems are used, as noted earlier, where the government's primary purpose is to restrict imports. Governments may do this by publicly announcing predetermined quota or quantitative limits applicable to restricted goods. Licensing systems may also be administered without a public announcement of the quantities allowed to be imported.

Where import licensing is utilized for the administration of quotas, the Agreement requires the publication of the overall amount of the quota (quantity and/or value), its opening and closing dates, so that all interested parties — importers, exporters and foreign producers and their governments — are fully aware of them. Further, where a quota is allocated among supplying countries, the country granting the quota is not only required to publish information on the shares allotted to each country, but must also specifically inform the governments of all interested supplying countries of the distribution of shares.

The Agreement requires import licences to be issued within 30 days of the receipt of the application where the procedures provide that licences should be issued "on a first-come first-served basis". They must be issued within 60 days of the date of closing for the receipt of applications where these applications "are considered simultaneously".

The rules further aim at ensuring that, in the distribution of licences, consideration is given to the practical difficulties that importers might have encountered in utilizing the licences issued to them. As a principle, licences should be issued to those importers who have made the best possible use of past licences. At the same time, care should be taken to ensure that importers who have not been able to use their licences for legitimate reasons are not "unduly penalized" by denial of a licence or by unduly reducing the value or quantity authorized under the licence. Licensing authorities are further required to give special consideration in distributing licences to new importers, particularly to those who import from developing and least developed countries.

5. Business implications

By obliging national licensing authorities to follow its principles and rules, the Agreement seeks to protect the interests both of foreign suppliers wanting to export products subject to licensing and of producing industries interested in importing such products. It further requires countries to adopt licensing procedures which, *inter alia,* would give importers the right to expect that:

❑ Licences will be issued promptly within the prescribed periods; and

❑ They will not be penalized for minor documentation errors.

CHAPTER 7

Rules applicable to exports

Summary of the main rules

*GATT rules permit an export product to be relieved of all **indirect taxes** borne by it in the exporting country. The rules further allow countries to levy **duties** on exports if these are necessary to control exports or to achieve any other policy objective. As with imports, the rules prohibit export restrictions except in a few specified situations.*

1.   General

The Guide has so far described the GATT rules applicable predominantly to imported products. This chapter briefly discusses the rules on exports.

2.   Export incentives providing for the reimbursement of indirect taxes

GATT rules permit countries to relieve a product to be exported of:

GATT 1994, Annex I, Ad
Article XVI
SCM, Footnote to Article 1 and
Annexes I to III

❏   Customs duties and other indirect taxes levied on inputs used and consumed in its manufacture;

❏   Indirect taxes on the exported product; and

❏   Indirect taxes on the production and distribution of the exported product.

SCM, Annex I, footnote 58

The term "indirect taxes" covers such taxes as "sales, excise, turnover, value added, franchise, stamp, transfer, inventory and equipment taxes". The Agreement on Subsidies and Countervailing Measures (SCM), which provides that foregoing by governments of the taxes that are due and payable constitutes an export subsidy, clarifies that:

> Exemption of an exported product from duties or indirect taxes borne by the like product when destined for domestic consumption, or the remission of such duties or taxes in amounts not in excess of those which have accrued, shall not be deemed to be a subsidy.

It is important to note the reasons for these rules. Under GATT's national treatment rule, a country may levy on an imported product, in addition to customs duties, all indirect taxes that it imposes on like products produced domestically, provided the duties are not levied at rates higher than those applied to domestic products. Unless therefore the exported product is either relieved or exempted from the indirect taxes payable in the exporting country, it becomes subject to double taxation — in both the exporting and importing country.

The rules, however, allow an exported product to be relieved of indirect taxes only. It may not be relieved of the direct taxes (such as income tax and taxes on profits) payable by producing enterprises. The SCM agreement clarifies that "exemption, remission or deferral specifically related to exports, of direct taxes or social welfare charges paid or payable" by the producing enterprise constitute a prohibited export subsidy. The economic rationale for this rule arises from the assumption that the burden of indirect taxes is generally shifted to the product and is reflected in its price, while direct taxes are not so shifted, but are absorbed by the tax payer producer.

Almost all countries today have *incentive schemes*. These schemes make it possible for exporting enterprises to claim exemption from, or drawback of, customs duties paid on inputs used in the manufacture of export products and the reimbursement of indirect taxes borne by such products. Further, in order to ensure that exporting enterprises are not disadvantaged in selling in outside markets, countries rarely impose taxes on exports.

3. Rule governing export control measures

GATT rules, however, recognize that in certain situations countries may have to take measures to control exports. As with imports, countries are required in such situations to give preference to price-based measures. The rules thus permit countries to use export taxes but prohibit restrictions on exports unless they can be justified under one of the exceptions.

3.1   Export taxes

Revenue considerations have led some developing countries to levy export duties. Today, these countries are reducing their dependence on these duties because of their adverse effects on the export trade.

However, apart from revenue considerations, export duties may also be levied to attain certain other policy objectives. They may, for example, be temporarily imposed immediately after a devaluation if the lower export prices in foreign currency terms do not bring about the expected rise in exports while providing undue benefit to exporters.

Duties are levied by countries exporting primary commodities to improve their terms of trade. They may also be used to control exports in order to increase the availability of resources to the domestic processing industry or to control for environmental or ecological reasons further exploitation of the country's natural resources.

One of the major advantages of export duties over export restrictions is that they provide governments with additional revenue. Governments often use such revenue to assist the producers of the taxed commodities and products.

GATT 1994, Article 1:1   The basic GATT rule requiring countries to extend MFN treatment applies to duties on both imports and exports. The MFN principle also applies to:

❏   The method of levying such duties; and

❏   All rules and formalities connected with exportation.

3.2   Export restrictions

The GATT provisions prohibiting restrictions on imports also apply to exports. There are, however, a few exceptions to this rule. Thus it is open to a country to restrict or prohibit exports, if this is necessary:

GATT 1994, Article XI:2(b)   ❏   To implement standards or regulations on the classification, grading or marketing of commodities in international trade; and

GATT 1994, Article XI:2(a)   ❏   To prevent or relieve critical shortages of foodstuffs or other essential products.

In addition, the rules prevent countries from imposing restrictions:

❏   On raw materials in order to protect or promote a domestic fabricating industry;

❏   To avoid competition among exporters.

4.   Business implications

It is important for the business person to note that GATT rules permit the reimbursement of customs duties paid on production inputs as well as the refund of the indirect taxes borne by exported products. As regards customs duties, the practice in most countries is either to exempt inputs imported for use in export production from payment of duties, or to permit exporters to claim a duty drawback after export. Most countries also have incentive schemes allowing exporters to claim the reimbursement of indirect taxes borne by the exported product. As relief from such taxes on products exported is granted by almost all countries, enterprises in countries that do not provide such a relief may find themselves at a disadvantage on foreign markets. It is necessary to ensure that the amount reimbursed does not exceed the actual incidence of the customs duties on inputs and of the indirect taxes on the exported product. Any payment in excess of the actual incidence would amount to an export subsidy.

As has been noted, countries are prohibited from granting export subsidies. Developing countries have a transitional period of eight years to phase out their existing export subsidy schemes. The rules do not permit these countries to grant during the transitional period subsidies on products that have not benefited from them earlier. Furthermore, the rules permit the refund only of indirect taxes borne by the exported product. Any exemption or payments to exporters to compensate for direct taxes payable on export earnings are not allowed.

GATT's basic approach that exported products should be relieved of all indirect taxes also implies that, where in special situations countries levy export duties, the need for maintaining them should be kept under continuous review. It is important for the business person to know that such duties, like import duties, can be applied by governments only on an MFN basis. It is not open to a country to levy a higher export duty on exports to one destination and lower or no duty on exports to other destinations.

Section 3

SUBSIDIES

CHAPTER 8

Rules governing subsidies on industrial products

Summary of the main rules

The GATT rules on subsidies stipulated in Article VI have been clarified and elaborated by the Agreement on Subsidies and Countervailing Measures (SCM) and the Agreement on Agriculture. Broadly speaking, the provisions of the Agreement on SCM apply to industrial products; those of the Agreement on Agriculture cover agricultural products.

The SCM Agreement recognizes that governments utilize subsidies to attain various policy objectives. However, it restrains the right of governments to grant subsidies that have significant trade-distorting effects. Its rules are complex.

The Agreement divides subsidies into prohibited and permissible subsidies. Prohibited subsidies include export subsidies. In the past, the rule against the use of export subsidies on industrial products applied only to developed countries; the Agreement extends this rule to developing countries. The latter countries have a transitional period of eight years within which to bring their subsidy practices into *conformity with the rule. During this period, they cannot increase the level of their export subsidies. The rule against the use of export subsidies does not apply to least developed countries and to developing countries with per capita GNPs of less than $1,000.*

All subsidies that are not prohibited are permissible. The permissible subsidies are divided into two categories: subsidies that are actionable and those that are not actionable.

The Agreement provides two types of remedies where the subsidies granted by governments cause "adverse effects" to the trade interests of other countries.

Where such adverse effects take the form of material injury to a domestic industry in the importing country, the Agreement authorizes that country to levy countervailing duties to offset the subsidy. Such duties can be levied only if, after duly conducted investigations, the investigating authorities are satisfied that there is a causal link between subsidized or dumped imports and material injury to the industry concerned. Furthermore, such investigations can normally be initiated only on the basis of a petition from the affected industry alleging that such imports are causing it damage.

Alternatively, both in the case of serious prejudice to a domestic industry and in the case of other adverse effects, the importing country can bring the matter before the Dispute Settlement Body (DSB) to secure withdrawal or modification by the subsidizing country of the subsidies that are causing adverse effects.

1. General

Governments grant subsidies to attain various policy objectives. Thus, subsidies may be made available to promote the development of new industries; to encourage investment and the establishment of industries in a country's backward regions; to assist industries in export development; to improve the infrastructure for agricultural production and to ensure a reasonable income level for farmers.

The GATT rules governing the use of subsidies are complex, and they differ for industrial and for agricultural products. The main GATT provisions on subsidies are elaborated in the Agreement on Subsidies and Countervailing Measures (SCM), and in the Agreement on Agriculture. The provisions of the Agreement on SCM apply, with a few exceptions, to industrial products; those of the Agreement on Agriculture relate to agricultural products. The rules of the SCM Agreement are described in this chapter, those applicable to agriculture are discussed in chapter 13.

2. Definition of subsidies; aim of the SCM Agreement

Under the SCM Agreement, an industry is deemed to have received a subsidy where a *benefit* is conferred on the industry as a result of:

Agreement on Subsidies and Countervailing Measures (SCM), Article 1

❏ Direct transfer from the government of funds (e.g. grants, loans or equity infusion) or government guarantees of payment of loans;

❏ The government foregoing the revenue that should otherwise have been collected;

❏ The government providing goods or services, or purchasing goods.

The concept of *benefit* is essential to determining whether a measure represents a subsidy. Although the Agreement provides only limited guidance on this point, as a general rule it may be said that a government action that is not consistent with commercial considerations confers a benefit. Thus, a government infusion of equity on terms a private investor would not accept, a loan on terms more favourable than those offered by commercial banks, or the provision by a government of goods or services for less than the prevailing market price, is likely to confer a benefit and may therefore be a subsidy.

The aim of the Agreement is not to restrain unduly the right of governments to grant subsidies but to prohibit or discourage them from using subsidies that have adverse effects on the trade of other countries. Towards this end, it categorizes subsidies into those that are prohibited and those that are permissible.

2.1   Prohibited subsidies (red light subsidies)

The following subsidies are prohibited:

SCM, Article 3   ❏   Export subsidies, i.e. subsidies that are contingent on export performance (see box 16 for illustrative list);

❏   Subsidies that are contingent on the use of domestic over imported goods.

In the past the rule prohibiting the use of export subsidies on industrial products applied only to developed countries. The Agreement extends the application of the rule to developing countries. These countries (with some exceptions) may, however, gradually abolish the use of such subsidies over a transitional period of eight years. They also have a

---

Box 16

ILLUSTRATIVE LIST OF PROHIBITED EXPORT SUBSIDIES

The Agreement's illustrative list of prohibited export subsidies includes the following:

- Direct subsidies based on export performance;

- Currency retention schemes involving a bonus on exports;

- Provision of subsidized inputs for use in the production of exported goods;

- Exemption from direct taxes (e.g. tax on profits related to exports);

- Exemption from, or remission of, indirect taxes (e.g. VAT) on exported products in excess of those borne by these products when sold for domestic consumption;

- Remission or drawback of import charges (e.g. tariffs and other duties) in excess of those levied on inputs consumed in the production of exported goods;

- Export guarantee programmes at premium rates inadequate to cover the long-term costs of the programme;

- Export credits at rates below the government's cost of borrowing, where they are used to secure a material advantage in export credit terms.

---

transitional period of five years to eliminate subsidies that are contingent on the use of domestic over imported products. Box 17 describes the provisions of the Agreement that extend special and differential treatment to developing countries in regard to the use of prohibited and permissible subsidies.

2.2 Permissible subsidies

Under the Agreement's rules, governments are in principle permitted to grant subsidies other than those described above, which are prohibited. However, the Agreement groups permissible subsidies into two categories: those that are actionable and

Box 17

FLEXIBILITY AVAILABLE TO DEVELOPING COUNTRIES IN THE USE OF SUBSIDIES
(SCM, Article 27)

The Agreement recognizes that "subsidies may play an important role in economic development programmes of developing country Members." Because of this, it further acknowledges that these countries may not be able to abide immediately by the full discipline of the rules which it lays down. To allow for flexibility in the application of the rules, the Agreement provides for special and differential treatment to developing countries.

Export subsidies

As noted earlier, the rule prohibiting export subsidies will apply to developing countries only after a transitional period of eight years, i.e. by 1 January 2003. These countries are, however, urged to phase out such subsidies progressively within the eight-year period and are not allowed to increase the level of their export subsidization. The transitional period may, if requested by a developing country, be extended by another two years.

These countries are further required to phase out within a period of two years export subsidies for any product in which they have become *export competitive*. A country is considered to have reached export competitiveness in a product if it has attained a share in the world market of 3.25% for two consecutive years. A product for this purpose is defined as a section heading of the Harmonized System Nomenclature, developed by the World Customs Organization for the classification of tariffs and trade statistics.

The least developed and low-income developing countries, with per capita GNPs of less than $1,000, are totally exempt from the rule prohibiting export subsidies.* If, however, they are found to have developed *export competitiveness* in any product, they are under an obligation to phase out the export subsidies granted to that product within eight years, rather than the two-year period provided for other developing countries.

Export subsidies by developing country Members remain actionable, however, both multilaterally and through countervailing duties.

Subsidies to promote the use of domestic goods

The rule prohibiting subsidies to promote the use of domestic over imported goods will be applicable to developing countries after a transitional period of five years (by 1 January 2000) and to least developed countries after eight years (by 1 January 2003).

Box 17 (cont'd)

Subsidies to encourage privatization

To encourage privatization, the Agreement provides that "direct forgiveness of debts, subsidies to cover social costs, in whatever form, including relinquishment of government revenue..." by the government of a developing country shall be treated as non-actionable multilaterally, provided such subsidies are granted for a limited period and are in accordance with a privatization programme. They remain subject to countervailing measures, however.

* The low-income countries whose per capita GNPs are currently less than $1,000 per annum are: Bolivia, Cameroon, Côte d'Ivoire, the Dominican Republic, Egypt, Ghana, Guatemala, Guyana, India, Indonesia, Kenya, Morocco, Nicaragua, Nigeria, Pakistan, the Philippines, Senegal, Sri Lanka and Zimbabwe. These countries will, however, be required to accept the obligation to prohibit the use of export subsidies when their per capita GNPs reach $1,000.

---

those that are non-actionable. It has become common practice to compare the Agreement's categorization of subsidies to the traffic light. Prohibited subsidies are called red light subsidies; those that are actionable, amber; and those that are non-actionable, green.

2.2.1 *Permissible subsidies that are actionable (amber subsidies)*

Broadly speaking the Agreement uses the concept of *specificity* to categorize subsidies that are actionable and those that are non-actionable. A subsidy is specific if it is limited to:

SCM, Articles 2, 5

❑   An enterprise or group of enterprises;

❑   An industrial sector or group of industries; or

❑   A designated geographic region within the jurisdiction of the granting authority.

All specific subsidies (other than those identified in the section that follows) are actionable if they cause what the Agreement calls "adverse effects to the interests of other Members". Such adverse effects take the form of:

❑   Serious prejudice to the domestic industry;

❑   Injury to the domestic industry in the importing country;

❑   Nullification and impairment of the benefits of bound tariff rates.

One basis for actionability is the existence of *serious prejudice* to the interests of other countries. This course of action is likely to be invoked when the subsidized product is displacing the complainant's exports from the market of the subsidizing country or of a third country. Box 18 describes the criteria which the Agreement lays down for determining whether a subsidy granted by a country is causing serious prejudice to the interests of other Members.

Material injury is another basis for actionability. In particular it is the basis under which an importing country can levy countervailing duties on subsidized imports that are causing injury to its domestic industry.

Subsidies that cause *nullification and impairment* of the benefits which the GATT system provides are also actionable. Such nullification and impairment of benefits could be deemed to have occurred when an exporting country finds that the value of the concession in the form of tariff binding it has obtained in trade negotiations by making a reciprocal concession has been greatly reduced because a domestic industry has lost market share to an industry in the importing country benefiting from subsidy.

Box 18

CRITERIA FOR DETERMINING *SERIOUS PREJUDICE* TO THE INTEREST OF ANOTHER COUNTRY

(SCM, Article 6)

The Agreement clarifies that *serious prejudice* to the interest of another country shall be presumed to have occurred, *inter alia*, where:

• Total *ad valorem* subsidization of a product exceeds 5%;

• Subsidies cover operating losses sustained by an industry;

• Subsidies other than one-time measures cover operating losses sustained by an enterprise; or

• There is direct forgiveness of debt by the government.

In all other cases, in order to establish that *serious prejudice* has actually occurred, the complainant must demonstrate that the effect of the subsidy is:

• To displace or impede imports from another member country into the subsidizing country;

• To displace exports to a third country market;

• Significantly to undercut or suppress prices in the subsidizing market;

• An increase in the world market share of the subsidizing country over its average share in the previous three years for the product or commodity benefiting from subsidy.

2.2.2 Permissible subsidies that are non-actionable (green subsidies)

SCM, Articles 2, 8

All permissible subsidies that are not "specific" are actionable. In particular, subsidy programmes under which subsidies are granted on the basis of objective criteria that are economic in nature and horizontal in application and "do not favour certain enterprises over others" are not specific. They are therefore non-actionable. Thus the subsidies given by governments to small and medium-sized enterprises, identified on the basis of their size or number of employees, would ordinarily be non-actionable.

In addition, certain subsidies that are specific are non-actionable, provided the specific conditions governing their grant comply with the rules of the Agreement. These include subsidies:

❑   For research activities conducted by firms, provided certain conditions are met.

❑   To adapt existing production facilities to new environmental requirements, provided that the subsidy is a one-time non-recurring measure and is limited to 20% of the cost of adaptation; and

❑   To assist in the development of industries in disadvantaged regions, provided that such assistance is not directed to specific enterprises or industries within the region.

Importing countries cannot levy countervailing duties on products benefiting from non-actionable subsidies.

3.   Remedies available to affected industries and to their governments

What are the remedies available to industries and to governments of Members which consider that their interests are being damaged by subsidized imports?

The Agreement provides for two types of remedies. First, a country which considers that either a prohibited subsidy is being used or that it is being adversely affected by the grant of a permissible subsidy, may raise the matter before the WTO Dispute Settlement Body (DSB) for redress. Where the adverse effects take the form of "material injury" to its domestic industry, the importing country may, instead of invoking dispute settlement procedures, levy countervailing duties on the imported subsidized products (see box 19). Such duties can however be levied only when investigations carried out at the national level and on the basis of a petition from the affected industry have established that the subsidized imports are causing injury to the domestic industry. Countervailing duties cannot be levied on products benefiting from non-actionable subsidies.

The Agreement on SCM lays down detailed rules and procedures for investigating authorities to follow in carrying out investigations and calculating the amount of countervailing duties that can be levied. Since the rules applicable to the levy of countervailing duties and to the use of anti-dumping measures are similar, and since in most countries the investigations for the levy of both these duties are carried out by the same investigating authorities, these rules are explained together in chapter 11.

4. Business implications

The rule against the use of export subsidies for industrial products, which in the past applied only to developed countries, is now also valid for developing countries. (The exceptions are least developed and developing countries with per capita GNPs of less than $1,000.) These countries have a transitional period of eight years within which to withdraw their existing subsidy systems. During this period, they may not increase the level of their subsidies or grant

---

Box 19

REMEDIES AVAILABLE TO IMPORTING COUNTRIES
UNDER THE AGREEMENT ON SCM
(SCM, Articles 4, 7 and 9)

Two types of remedies are available to an importing country which considers that the use of subsidies by other member countries is affecting its interests adversely. It may levy countervailing duties if, after investigations carried out in pursuance of a petition made by the affected industry, it is established that subsidized imports are causing the industry material injury. It may also bring the matter for redress before the Dispute Settlement Body (DSB).

Prohibited subsidies. Any country which considers that another country is using a prohibited subsidy may, if bilateral consultations with that subsidizing country do not lead to its withdrawal, bring the matter before DSB.

Actionable subsidies. A country which finds that an actionable subsidy granted by another country has adversely affected its interests may refer the matter to the DSB for settlement, if bilateral consultations fail to bring about a mutually agreed solution.

Non-actionable subsidies. Countervailing duties cannot be levied on products that have benefited from non-actionable subsidies. However, where a country "has reasons to believe" that the subsidy programmes have had "serious adverse effects" on its domestic industry as to cause damage which would be difficult to repair, it may request the country granting subsidies for consultations. If the consultations fail, it may request the Committee on Subsidies and Countervailing Measures (SC), which has been established under the Agreement, to determine whether such effects exist.

In all the three cases mentioned above, if the subsidizing country fails to take appropriate steps to implement the recommendations made, the DSB/Committee on SC could authorize the affected country to take counter measures that would affect the trade of the subsidizing country.

---

subsidies to products not previously covered. Enterprises currently benefiting from export subsidies will therefore have to prepare themselves for the withdrawal of these subsidies by their governments by the end of the transitional period, if not earlier.

It should be noted that while the SCM Agreement permits developing countries to use export subsidies during the transitional period, these subsidies can be countervailed by importing countries even during that period if they cause injury to their domestic industries. This also applies to the developing countries that are exempt from the rule prohibiting the use of export subsidies. The maintenance of export subsidies on products that are considered import sensitive by importing countries (e.g. textiles, leather and leather products, etc.), albeit permitted under the Agreements, is therefore fraught with danger. It is thus important for governments to adopt trade and foreign exchange policies that will remove the bias against their countries' exports and reduce the need for export subsidies. It is also necessary for them to examine, in consultation and in cooperation with their exporting enterprises and their associations, whether assistance, where needed, can be provided in the form of permissible subsidies and preferably those that are not actionable by importing countries.

Section 4

SAFEGUARD ACTIONS, COUNTERVAILING AND ANTI-DUMPING DUTIES (MEASURES GOVERNMENTS ARE ORDINARILY AUTHORIZED TO TAKE IF REQUESTED BY AN AFFECTED INDUSTRY)

CHAPTER 9

Safeguard measures to restrict imports in emergency situations

Summary of the main rules

*The Agreement on Safeguards authorizes importing countries to restrict imports for temporary periods if, after investigations carried out by competent authorities, it is established that imports are taking place in such increased quantities (either absolute or in relation to domestic production) as to cause **serious injury** to the domestic industry that produces like or directly competitive products. It further provides that such measures, which could take the form of an increase in tariffs over bound rates or the imposition of quantitative restrictions, should normally be applied on an MFN basis to imports from all sources.*

The investigations for the imposition of such measures can be initiated either by the government itself or on the basis of a petition from the affected industry. In practice, however, the investigations are generally initiated on the basis of petitions from the affected industry.

The Agreement lays down the criteria which investigating authorities must consider in determining whether increased imports are causing serious injury to the domestic industry. It also sets out basic procedural requirements for the conduct of investigations. One aim of the procedural requirements is to provide foreign suppliers and governments whose interests may be adversely affected by the proposed safeguard actions with an adequate opportunity to give evidence and to defend their interests.

The primary purpose of providing such temporary increased protection is to give the affected industry time to prepare itself for the increased competition that it will have to face after the restrictions are removed. The Agreement seeks to ensure that such restrictions are applied only for temporary periods by setting a maximum period of eight years for the application of a measure on a particular product. Developing countries can, however, impose them for a maximum period of 10 years.

1. General

To give industries time to adjust gradually to the increased competition resulting from reductions in tariffs and from the removal of other barriers to trade, the GATT practice has been to require that the cuts in tariffs agreed in multilateral trade negotiations should be implemented in stages over an agreed period of years. Thus tariff reductions on industrial products agreed in the Uruguay Round are to be made over five years in five equal instalments. Likewise, reductions in the agricultural sector as well as in domestic and export subsidies are to take place in stages over a period of six years. Developing countries have been given longer periods within which to implement reductions.

The GATT rules recognize that, despite the phased implementation of tariff reductions, certain industrial or agricultural sectors may face, in the short term, problems in adjusting to increased import competition. These problems may flow from their failure to rationalize production structures or to adopt the technological innovations necessary to raise productivity. To provide affected industries time to adjust to competition, Article XIX of GATT provides that where, as a result of tariff reductions, a country finds that a product is being imported "in such increased quantities and under such conditions as to cause or threaten serious injury to domestic producers", it can impose *safeguard measures* to restrict such imports for temporary periods.

GATT 1994, Article XIX:1(a)

2. Circumventing GATT rules through VERs

Largely because of the GATT requirement that safeguard measures should be applied on a non-discriminatory basis, countries entered into voluntary export restraints (VERs) or orderly marketing arrangements (OMAs). Under these arrangements, exporting countries with rising exports are required by importing countries to restrain their exports to agreed limits. Though these arrangements are called "voluntary", in reality they are not always so. As the restraints are applied only to imports from certain countries, they are also inconsistent with the rule that restrictions on imports should be employed on a non-discriminatory basis.

The use of such *grey area measures* (called so because their consistency with GATT rules is in doubt) by some developed countries, notably the United States and members of the European Union, has increased over the past three decades. The governments of these countries have also in some instances either encouraged or supported the initiatives taken by their industries to enter into voluntary export restraint arrangements with their counterparts in exporting countries. It is estimated that there are at present over 200 such bilateral or plurilateral arrangements. They cover products ranging from agricultural goods like beef; simple merchandise such as leather and rubber products, travel goods, pottery and chinaware; to sophisticated manufactures like television sets, motor cars and trucks.

3.   Agreement on Safeguards

3.1.   Commitment to abolish VERs

The main aim of the Uruguay Round negotiations in this area was to ensure that restrictive measures like VERs and other similar discriminatory measures are brought into conformity with GATT principles and rules. The Agreement on Safeguards (negotiated in the Round) does this by requiring that existing grey area measures must be phased out within a period of four years (i.e. by 1 January 1999[12]). In addition, countries are committed "not to seek, take or maintain any voluntary export restraints, orderly marketing arrangements or any other similar measures on the export or import side". They are also required not to "encourage or support the adoption or maintenance" of inter-industry arrangements that are comparable to the governmental measures described above.

3.2   Serious injury standard

The Agreement further provides that safeguard measures should be applied only after it has been determined by the investigating authorities that:

AS, Article 2

❑   A product is being imported in increased quantities (absolute or relative to domestic production); and

❑   In such conditions as to cause or threaten to cause serious injury to producers of like or directly competitive products.

AS, Article 4:1

The term "serious injury" is defined as the "significant overall impairment in the position of a domestic industry." It must be established that imports are causing such injury to the domestic industry, defined as the "producers as a whole of the like or directly competitive products" or those "whose collective output of the like or directly competitive products constitutes a major proportion of the total domestic production of those products." In other

---

12 Each member country can, however, maintain one such measure over an additional period of one year.

words, it is not permissible to take safeguard measures to restrict imports where only a few producers are finding it difficult to meet import competition.

3.3   Rules governing investigations

The Agreement requires each member country to designate authorities to be responsible for carrying out investigations and to publish the procedures it proposes to follow, so that these are known to the public.

The request for the initiation of such investigations can be made by the government itself or by an industry whose collective output constitutes a major portion of the total domestic production of the imported product. However, in practice, investigations are generally triggered by an application made by producers or on their behalf by an association of producers. Such applications typically claim that increased imports are causing the producers serious injury, leading for instance to loss of profits, reduction in production and under-utilization of capacity and/or requiring cuts in the labour force.

AS, Article 3

The investigating authorities must give public notice of investigations and arrange for public hearings or other appropriate means in which "importers, exporters and other interested parties could present evidence and their views." The authorities should also examine views and comments against the requested safeguard action and on whether the application of such a measure would be in the public interest.

AS, Article 4:2

The investigating authorities can authorize a safeguard action only after an evaluation of all relevant factors of an objective and quantifiable nature establishes that there is a "causal link between increased imports of the product concerned and serious injury or threat thereof" to the industry. Safeguard actions should not be authorized if the problems the industry is encountering arise from factors other than increased imports (e.g. decline in overall demand for the product). In order to provide transparency, the investigating authorities are further required to publish their reports and conclusions.

3.4 Application of safeguard measures

AS, Preamble

The Agreement emphasizes that, in taking safeguard measures, the aim of the governments should be to promote "structural adjustment" and to "enhance rather than limit competition in international markets". To this end it provides that such safeguard measures should be applied only for temporary periods to enable the affected industry to take steps to adjust itself to the increased competition that will follow the removal of those measures. Adjustment could take the form of the adoption of improved technology or the rationalization of production structures.

AS, Article 5

Furthermore, safeguard measures should be applied only "to the extent necessary to prevent or remedy serious injury and to facilitate adjustment" and on a "non-discriminatory basis to imports from all sources". The type of safeguard action to be taken — increase in the bound rate of tariffs or imposition of quantitative restrictions on imports — is decided by the investigating authorities. Where a quantitative restriction is used, quotas may be allocated among the main supplying countries. In such cases, individual shares are allocated in consultation with the supplying countries on the basis of their shares in imports during a previous representative period. In allocating shares on this basis, the interests of new suppliers should also be adequately taken into account.

The Agreement permits, in exceptional situations, member countries to depart from the non-discriminatory rule and to apply quota restrictions only to one or more countries when imports from these countries "have increased in disproportionate percentage in relation to the total increase of imports of the product concerned in the representative period". In order to ensure that such actions are taken only in exceptional situations, the Agreement stipulates that they should be taken after consultations with, and approval by, the Committee on Safeguards. The Committee has been established under the Agreement.

3.5   Compensation for the loss of trade

AS, Article 8

A member country proposing to apply safeguard measures is expected to offer adequate trade compensation to countries whose trade interests would be adversely affected by such measures.[13] If agreement on an adequate trade compensation cannot be reached by the country proposing to apply a safeguard measure and the affected exporting member countries, the exporting members may take retaliatory action.[14] However, the right to retaliatory action cannot be exercised for the first three years that the measure is in effect, where the safeguard measure has been taken in accordance with the provisions of the Agreement and as a result of an absolute increase in imports (and not relative to domestic production).

---

13 The compensation is generally a concession, in the form of tariff reductions, from the country wishing to take safeguard actions to the countries whose trade would be restricted, on other products of export interest to them.

14 Such retaliatory action is generally the suspension of a concession or other obligation to which the country applying the safeguard measure is otherwise entitled.

3.6 Special and differential treatment to developing countries

AS, Article 9

The Agreement provides for special and differential treatment to developing countries in the application of safeguard measures. Imports from a developing country are exempt from safeguard measures if its share in the imports of the product concerned into the country taking the measure is less than 3%. This exemption does not apply if developing countries with individual shares of imports smaller than 3% collectively account for more than 9% of the imports.

3.7 Duration of safeguard measures

The other provisions of the Agreement are mainly directed towards ensuring that safeguard measures are applied for temporary periods. It is thus provided that:

❑ Safeguard measures in force on 1 January 1995, when the Agreement went into effect, must be terminated after eight years or by 1 January 2000, whichever comes later.

❑ The maximum initial period for the application of a safeguard measure is four years. This initial period may be extended up to a maximum of eight years (10 years for developing countries).

AS, Article 7

In order to assist affected industries in preparing themselves for the increased competition that will follow the ultimate lifting of safeguard measures, the Agreement requires any measure with a duration of more than one year to be progressively liberalized. There should also be mid-term reviews of measures with durations of over three years, to see whether they should be withdrawn or liberalized faster.

In addition, the Agreement prevents countries from circumventing the time limits on safeguard measures by prohibiting the reimposition of protection on the same product for a period equal to that of the original safeguard action. In no event can a measure be reapplied within an immediately following period of less than two years. However, temporary safeguards that have been imposed for six months or less may be reinstated after one year, as long as actions are not taken on the same product more than twice in a five-year period. Here again, developing countries are subject to less rigorous obligations and may reimpose actions on the same product after a period equal to half the duration of the previous measure (but not within a period of less than two years).

4.   Business implications

The new and improved rules on safeguards reinforce the GATT rules providing for security of access. Importing countries are prohibited from requesting exporting countries to ask their enterprises to restrain their exports under VERs or similar arrangements. It is important to note that by providing further that governments should not encourage their industries to conclude such arrangements with industries in other countries, the Agreement has cautioned industries against entering into similar arrangements even on an informal basis.

As has been mentioned, almost all tariffs of developed countries and a high proportion of the tariffs of developing countries have been bound against further increases, thus restricting the right of countries to raise tariffs. Under the rules of the Agreement on Safeguards, importing countries will therefore be able to take measures to restrict imports only when investigations have established that increased imports are causing *serious* injury to their domestic industries. The rules further try to protect the interests of exporting enterprises by giving them the right to defend their interests during the investigations and to produce, if necessary, evidence to establish that the imposition of restrictions would not be in the interest of the consuming public in the importing country.

It is, however, important to note that these general rules on safeguard actions do not immediately apply to textile products. The Agreement on Textiles and Clothing, negotiated in the Uruguay Round, provides that the discriminatory restrictions currently applied to textile products by some importing countries should be phased out in four stages over a period of 10 years. During this phase-out period the Agreement permits countries to take safeguard actions to restrict imports on a discriminatory basis from those exporting country or countries, where as a result of "sharp and substantial increase in imports" from these countries, "serious damage" is caused to the domestic industry.

The trade in textiles will be governed by the rules of the Agreement on Safeguards on non-discriminatory application of safeguard measures only after 1 January 2005. On that date, the Agreement on Textiles and Clothing, after having been under implementation for 10 years, will cease to exist.

It is essential to look at these rules not only from the viewpoint of exporting enterprises but also from the perspective of enterprises which as a result of a sudden surge in imports are finding it difficult to compete with foreign suppliers in their domestic markets. These enterprises have the right to petition their governments to take safeguard actions to restrict imports. Such petitions cannot be made by a single firm or a few enterprises, but by producers whose "production constitutes a major proportion of total domestic production". In practice, such petitions or applications are often made on behalf of producers by the associations to which they belong. Petitions can be submitted only when it is possible to establish that there is a *causal link* between increased imports and the alleged *serious injury* to the industry. The ability of the affected industries to take advantage of these provisions will depend on how far they are able to build up the case for such temporary protection, taking into account the Agreement's strict conditions for the imposition of safeguard measures.

CHAPTER 10

Safeguard actions for economic development purposes: special flexibility available to developing countries

---

Summary of the main rules

GATT rules provide special flexibility to developing countries to take safeguard measures to restrict imports, for temporary periods, in order to promote the development of new or infant industries. However, GATT lays down strict conditions for the invocation of these rules. Furthermore, safeguard measures can ordinarily be introduced only with WTO approval.

1. General

GATT 1994, Article XVIII: Section C; Tokyo Round Declaration: Safeguard Action for Development Purposes

The GATT rules recognize that governments of developing countries, in pursuance of their programmes and policies of economic development, may find it necessary to provide assistance to new or infant industries or for the further development of existing industries and that such assistance may take the form of safeguard actions restricting imports for temporary periods. As the imposition of these restraints could adversely affect the interests of exporting countries, the rules lay down stringent conditions for their adoption.

2. Conditions for the invocation of safeguard provisions

The government wishing to provide higher protection through the imposition of restrictions is expected to notify the WTO secretariat of the:

❑ Particular industry or industries, either existing or new, for the development of which such higher protection is necessary;

❑ The nature of the proposed restrictive measure (increase in tariffs that are bound against further increases, imposition of quantitative restrictions on imports or the introduction of a licensing system);

❑ The special difficulties that imports pose for the development of such industries; and

❑ Why measures other than import restrictions are not practicable.

The notification must be made before the measure is introduced. In exceptional cases, where delay in the introduction of the measure is expected to pose special difficulties to the industry concerned, the notification can be made immediately after the measure is imposed.

The introduction of safeguard measures or their continuation where notification is made after the measures have been introduced is ordinarily[15] possible if WTO member countries, after examining the reasons for it, approve it.

3. Business implications

In practice, the special flexibility available to developing countries under these provisions has rarely been invoked. One of the main reasons for this was that, until the conclusion of the Uruguay Round, the tariffs of nearly all developing countries were not bound against increases. This enabled them to protect developing infant industries, where necessary, by raising their tariffs.

In the Uruguay Round, as noted earlier, a large proportion of the tariffs of member countries has been bound against further increases. Enterprises in developing countries which believe that they need more protection to develop new industries or further develop existing ones will therefore have to request their governments to invoke the provisions on "safeguard actions for development purposes". WTO ap-

---

15 If the tariff on a product is bound against further increases, restrictive measures can be taken only with WTO's prior approval. Where, however, the duty is not bound, two courses are open to the developing country wishing to give higher protection. It may raise the rate of duty. As a rise in the rates of tariffs that are not bound is permissible under GATT rules, it can take such an action without invoking the provisions of GATT Article XVIII:C. Where, however, it proposes to give higher protection by imposing restrictions that are not permissible under GATT (such as the application of quantitative restrictions or a restrictive licensing system), it has to notify WTO and enter into consultations with other member countries in order to obtain approval of the proposed measure. While the Article provides that, in such cases, the developing country concerned could apply the measure even if the approval is not granted, in practice, this is not possible. The reason is that the Article also gives other member countries the right to take retaliatory actions if they consider the measure to be adverse to their trade interests.

proval of proposed measures to restrict imports (e.g. increase in bound rates of tariffs or imposition of quantitative restrictions) will have to be obtained. As the adoption of such measures will be a derogation from the basic rules, WTO will grant such approval only if member countries are satisfied that, taking into account such factors as available natural resources and existing production and consumption trends, the higher level of protection will help the industry to become internationally competitive within a reasonable period. Furthermore, in granting such approval, WTO will be expected to impose strict conditions to ensure that the restrictions are maintained only for temporary periods and that steps are taken for their gradual withdrawal during these periods.

CHAPTER 11

Response to unfair trade practices: rules on the use of countervailing and anti-dumping duties

Summary of the main rules

The GATT rules deal with two types of "unfair" trade practices which distort conditions of competition. First, the competition may be unfair if the exported goods benefit from subsidies. Second, the conditions of competition may be distorted if the exported goods are dumped in foreign markets.

In common parlance, it is usual to designate all low-cost imports as dumped imports. The Agreement on Anti-dumping Practices (ADP), however, lays down strict criteria for determining when "a product is to be considered as being dumped". In general, a product is considered to be dumped if the export price is less than the price charged for the like product in the exporting country. A product is also considered to be dumped if it is sold for less than its cost of production.

The Agreements on Anti-dumping Practices and on Subsidies and Countervailing Measures (SCM) authorize countries to levy compensatory duties on imports of products that are benefiting from unfair trade practices. However, an importing country can levy countervailing duties on subsidized imports and anti-dumping duties on dumped imports only if it is established on the basis of investigations carried out by it that such imports are causing "material injury" to a domestic industry. Investigations for the imposition of such duties should ordinarily be initiated on the basis of a petition made by or on behalf of an industry, alleging that imports are causing it injury.

The two Agreements lay down similar criteria for determining injury. The procedures for carrying out investigations of petitions for the levy of anti-dumping and countervailing duties are likewise similar.

1. General

As noted in chapter 9, the rules permit countries to take safeguard actions restricting imports for temporary periods when, as a result of a sudden and sharp increase in imports, serious injury is caused to the domestic industry of the importing country. The increased imports covered by these particular rules are not attributable to unfair trade practices by foreign suppliers.

However, the GATT rules acknowledge that the rise in imports may indeed be due to the adoption of unfair trade practices by foreign suppliers. The rules therefore lay down the basis on which governments may levy compensatory duties on imports of products benefiting from such unfair practices. They deal with two forms of unfair trade practices which distort conditions of competition. First, the competition may become unfair if the exported goods benefit from specific subsidies. Second, the conditions of competition may be distorted if the producer dumps its goods in foreign markets.

The basic provisions of GATT 1994 on the use of subsidies have been elaborated by the Agreement on SCM. As noted earlier, the basic aim of these provisions is either to prohibit or to restrain the use of subsidies that cause adverse effects to the interests of other Members. However, where the use of permitted subsidies results in material injury to a domestic industry in an importing Member, the rules permit that importing Member to take remedial measures which could take the form of countervailing duties on subsidized imports. Likewise the Agreement on Anti-dumping Practices (ADP), which elaborates the basic GATT rules on dumping, authorizes Members to levy anti-dumping duties on dumped imports.

In general, a product is considered to be dumped if the export price is less than the price charged for the like product in the exporting country. Broadly speaking, a producing enterprise is able to charge higher prices on sales in domestic markets if, as a result of high level of protection, foreign competition is absent or weak. Even if the export price is not less than the price charged in the exporting country, a product is considered to be dumped if it is sold for less than its cost of production.

The rules of the Agreements on SCM and ADP do not *per se* condemn dumping or subsidization. They recognize that the lower prices of imported goods arising from dumping or subsidization could benefit industrial users and consumers in the importing countries. The two Agreements therefore lay down an important principle: that compensatory duties in the form of countervailing duties on subsidized imports and anti-dumping duties on dumped imports cannot be levied solely on the ground that product has benefited from subsidy or that it is being dumped. They can be levied only if it is established after an investigation, which must normally be initiated on the request of a domestic industry, that dumped or subsidized imports are causing "material injury" to that industry.

Similar principles apply when governments take safeguard measures to restrict imports in order to assist a domestic industry that is being injured by a sudden and sharp increase in imports. The standard of "injury" to the industry that must be established to justify safeguard actions is, however, much higher than that required for the levy of countervailing or anti-dumping duties. In the case of safeguard actions, injury to the industry must be "serious"; in the case of countervailing and anti-dumping duties, a lower standard of proof of material injury is adequate. The difference in standards is attributable to the fact that, in the first instance, the industry's problems do not arise from unfair competition, while in the second, these are due to the unfair trade practices of foreign producers.

This chapter discusses the following subjects:

❑ The concept of dumping as embodied in GATT law;

❑ The rules and procedures that countries must follow in levying anti-dumping and counter-vailing duties.

The rules that the Agreements on SCM and ADP lay down for the levy of these compensatory duties are similar. Furthermore, at the national level, the authorities responsible for investigating petitions for the levy of countervailing and of anti-dumping duties are the same in most cases.

2.   Concept of dumping as embodied in GATT law

In common parlance, it is usual to designate all low-cost imports as dumped imports. The Agreement on Anti-dumping Practices, however, lays down strict criteria for determining when an imported product should be treated as being dumped. In particular it states that "a product is to be considered as being dumped", if its export price is less than the price at which a like product is sold for consumption in the exporting country. In other words, if on the basis of a comparison of the export price and the home consumption price in the exporting country it is found that the latter price is higher, the product could be treated as being dumped.

ADP, Article 2:1

The Agreement, however, provides that the determination of dumping on the above basis may not be appropriate:

❑   Where sales in the domestic market of the exporting country are not in the ordinary course of trade (e.g. sales below the cost of production); and

❑   Where the volume of sales in domestic markets is low.

In these cases, the Agreement permits dumping to be determined by comparing the export price with:

❑   A comparable price charged for the like product when exported to a third country; or

❑   A constructed value, calculated on the basis of the production costs of the imported product, plus general, selling and administrative costs, and profits.

However, in order to ensure to the maximum extent possible that dumping is being determined on the basis of a comparison of the export price with the price for home consumption in the exporting country, the Agreement lays down the so-called *5% representative test*. The investigating authorities must use for price-comparison purposes prices charged to third country markets or use constructed values calculated on the basis of the cost of production if the value of sales in the domestic market of the exporting country constitutes 5% or more of the sales of the products to the importing country.

3. Rules and procedures for levying countervailing and anti-dumping duties

3.1 Main criteria for the levy of duties

3.1.1 Injury to the domestic industry

The basic rule which the Agreements on ADP and SCM lay down is that anti-dumping and countervailing duties should be levied only where it has been established on the basis of investigations that:

❑ There has been a significant increase in dumped or subsidized imports, either in absolute terms or relative to production or consumption; or

ADP, Article 3
SCM, Article 15

❑ The prices of such imports have undercut those of the like domestic product, have depressed the price of the like product or have prevented that price from increasing; and

❑ As a result, injury is caused to the domestic industry or there is a threat of injury to the domestic industry of the importing country.

3.1.2 Causal link between dumped, subsidized imports and injury to the domestic industry

The two Agreements specify that, in determining whether dumped imports are causing injury to the domestic industry, "relevant economic factors having a bearing on the state of the industry" should be taken into account (see box 20 for a listing of these factors). Furthermore, for anti-dumping or countervailing duties to be levied, it must be clearly established that there is a causal link between dumped or subsidized imports and the injury to the industry. Where the problems which the industry is encoun-

---

Box 20

FACTORS TO BE TAKEN INTO ACCOUNT IN DETERMINING
MATERIAL INJURY TO DOMESTIC INDUSTRY
(ADP, Article 3; SCM, Article 15)

The Agreements on SCM and ADP provide that the determination of whether subsidized or dumped imports are causing injury to a domestic industry should be made on the basis of all "relevant economic factors having a bearing on the state of the industry". Such factors include:

- Actual or potential decline in output, sales, market share, profits, productivity, return on investments, or utilization of capacity;
- Effects on domestic prices;
- Actual or potential effects on cash flow, inventories, employment, wages, growth, ability to raise capital or investments.

In the case of anti-dumping investigations, one of the other factors to be taken into account is the *magnitude of the margin of dumping*. Likewise in investigations for the levy of countervailing duties on imports of *agricultural products*, an additional factor to be taken into account is whether there has been an increased burden on government support programmes.

The two Agreements clarify that the above list of economic factors is illustrative and not exhaustive, and that "one or several of these factors necessarily give decisive guidance".

The Agreements further stipulate that the investigating authorities must also examine whether any factors other than subsidized or dumped imports are causing injury to domestic industry. Countervailing or anti-dumping duties should not be levied if the main factors responsible for the difficulties of the industry are factors other than subsidized or dumped imports. Such factors could include:

- Contraction in demand or changes in the patterns of consumption;
- Trade restrictive practices of, and competition between, foreign and domestic producers;
- Developments in technology and export performance; and
- Productivity of the domestic industry.

---

tering are caused by such factors as "contractions in demand or changes in the pattern of consumption" and cannot be directly attributed to dumped or subsidized imports, anti-dumping or countervailing duties should not be levied. Furthermore, such duties should not be levied where increased imports are adversely affecting only a few producers. They can be levied solely when it has been established that the imports are posing problems to the producers "whose collective output of the product constitutes a major proportion of the total domestic production" of the industry.

3.1.3 Cumulation of imports

Normally when imports from several countries are subject to investigations, the assessment of whether such imports are causing injury to the domestic industry has to be made separately for each country. The Agreements, however, allow the investigating authorities in certain situations to assess the combined effects of all imports under investigation in determining injury. Such cumulation of imports is allowed only if:

ADP, Article 3.3
SCM, Article 15.3

❑   The dumping margin or the amount of subsidization of each individual country exceeds *de minimis* level;

❑   The volume of imports from each country is not negligible; and

❑   Such cumulative assessment is appropriate in the light of conditions of competition between imported products and the conditions of competition between the imported products and like domestic products.

3.1.4 Standing of petitioners

It is important to note that the two Agreements stipulate that, save in exceptional situations,[16]

---

16 The government of an importing country can initiate action for the levy of anti-dumping and countervailing duties only in exceptional circumstances.

anti-dumping or countervailing investigations should be initiated only on the basis of a complaint made "by or on behalf" of the domestic industry.

Further, in order to ensure that applications for the levy of such duties are made only when a substantial number of producers are affected, the Agreements lay down two complementary criteria:

ADP, Article 5.4
SCM, Article 11.4

❑   First, the producers supporting the application must account for over 50% of the production of the producers who express an opinion either in support of, or against, the petition.[17]

❑   Second, the producers supporting the application should account for at least 25% of the industry's total production.

The investigating authorities are under an obligation to ascertain whether petitioners have such *standing* before initiating an investigation.

3.2   Procedural rules

3.2.1   Information to be provided in the application

The Agreements further stipulate the type of information (see box 21) that the petitioning industry must provide in its application in order to substantiate its claim that dumped or subsidized imports are causing it injury.

A large number of applications that are unsubstantiated or do not meet the criteria described above are in practice rejected by investigating

---

17 A section of the producers may not wish to express an opinion either for or against the petition. The share of such producers is to be excluded in arriving at the percentage.

Box 21

INFORMATION TO BE PROVIDED IN APPLICATIONS FOR THE LEVY OF ANTI-DUMPING OR COUNTERVAILING DUTIES

The application for the levy of anti-dumping and countervailing duties should contain the following information:

- The volume of the domestic production of the producers making the application;

- Description of the alleged dumped or subsidized product;

- The names of the exporting countries, each known exporter or foreign producer, and a list of the importers of the product;

- Information on dumping/subsidization:

  - In applications for anti-dumping action, such information should include prices at which the product is sold in the domestic market of the exporting country and information on export prices.

  - In applications for countervailing duties, such information should include evidence of the existence, amount and nature of the subsidy.

  - Information regarding injury and causality.

  - Information on the volume of dumped or subsidized imports.

  - Information on the adverse effects of such imports:

    ❏ On domestic prices, and

    ❏ On the domestic industry.

ADP, Article 5.5
SCM, Article 11.5

ADP, Article 12.1
SCM, Article 22.2

authorities. As the mere submission of such applications often creates uncertainty in trade, the Agreements require the investigating authorities to avoid *publicizing* the submission of applications. However, after the decision is taken to initiate investigations, authorities are obliged to give public notice of the initiation of investigation giving, *inter alia,* the names of the exporting country or countries, the basis on which dumping or subsidization is alleged and a summary of the allegations on which the claim for injury is based.

3.2.2 Notification to governments

In addition, the investigating authorities are required to notify the governments of exporting Members of the receipt of a properly documented complaint and before initiating anti-dumping or countervailing investigations. As soon as an investigation is initiated, the authorities must *make available the full text of the written application* to the *governments of the exporting Members*. Furthermore, the SCM Agreement imposes an obligation on the investigating country to enter into consultations with the government of the exporting country after the petition is accepted but before the investigations begin. Such consultations provide the government of the investigating country an opportunity to ascertain whether, taking into account the information presented in the application on the alleged injurious effects of subsidies on the industry, the exporting country is prepared to modify its subsidy practices so as to reach mutually acceptable solutions.

ADP, 6.1.3
SCM, 12.1.3

SCM, Article 13

3.2.3 Right to give evidence

The rules of the two Agreements further aim at ensuring that, once investigations have begun, exporters and importers of the alleged dumped or subsidized products, the governments of the exporting countries, and other interested parties (e.g. trade or business associations of which exporters or producers are members) have adequate opportunity to tender oral and written evidence to rebut the claim made by the petitioners and to defend their interests. Towards this end, the Agreements specifically provide that:

ADP, Article 6.1
SCM, Article 12.1

❑   The full text of the application should be made available to all known exporters alleged to be dumping or benefiting from subsidies and to the governments of the exporting countries concerned;

❑   The evidence presented by one party should be promptly made available to the other parties participating in the investigations; and

❑   Parties have a right to see all information (excluding confidential information) used by the investigating authorities during the investigations to help them in preparing their presentations.

In addition, the two Agreements provide that in anti-dumping and countervailing investigations industrial users and organizations of consumers of the products under investigation shall be given an opportunity to express their views on whether the case meets the statutory criteria for the levy of such duties (i.e. dumping or subsidization, injury and causality). This provision can be used to safeguard the essential interests of users and consumers when the authorities consider that the industry has petitioned for anti-dumping or countervailing actions mainly for protectionist reasons and that the levy of such duties could lead to an unjustified rise in prices.

ADP, Article 6.12
SCM, Article 12.10

3.2.4   Provision of information by exporters and the best information rule

While giving exporting enterprises the right to defend their interests during the investigations, the Agreements also oblige them to cooperate with investigating authorities and to provide the latter with any information they may request on production costs and other matters. In practice, investigating authorities require such information to be given on the basis of a questionnaire and within a period of

ADP, Article 6.1.1
SCM, Article 12.1.1

not less than 30 days of the request for information. Where enterprises are not able to reply within that period, the Agreements call on investigating authorities to consider requests for extension with sympathy and to assist the enterprises, if requested, in providing the information in the format required. Where, however, producing enterprises refuse to cooperate or do not provide the information demanded within a reasonable period of time, the investigating authorities can take decisions on the basis of the best information available.

3.2.5 On-the-spot investigations

Investigating authorities often find it necessary to undertake on-the-spot investigations to verify the information provided by exporters or producing companies in response to the questionnaire or to collect additional information. The Agreements stipulate that such investigations can be carried out only with the agreement of the exporters or producers concerned and if the government of the exporting country does not object to the investigations. Sufficient advance notice of the intended visit should be given. The notice should indicate the type of the information needed so that the exporters/producers can prepare themselves to provide that information.

ADP, Article 6.7 and Annex I
SCM, Article 12.6 and Annex VI

A refusal to permit an on-the-spot investigation could result in use by the authorities of the best information available.

3.3   Methodological rules

The methods used by the investigating authorities to calculate the per unit subsidy received by a product or the margin of dumping can greatly influence the level of countervailing or anti-dumping duties to be paid. The two Agreements therefore provide certain guidelines for the investigating authorities to follow in making these calculations.

3.3.1 SCM Agreement

SCM, Article 14

The SCM Agreement provides that the national legislation or implementing regulations of member countries should specify the methods to be used by the investigating authorities in determining per unit subsidy. In addition, to ensure transparency, it imposes an obligation on the investigating authorities to explain in their decision how the per unit subsidization was arrived at by using the method specified in the legislation.

3.3.2 ADP Agreement

3.3.2.1 Price comparison: general principles

ADP, Article 2.4

As noted earlier, a product is considered dumped only if the foreign producer's *export price* is lower than the price charged for *home consumption* in the country of export. The margin of dumping is therefore determined primarily by comparing these two prices. The ADP Agreement sets out guidelines to ensure a fair comparison between the home consumption price and the export price. In particular, it states that such comparison should be made "at the same level of trade, normally at the ex-factory level, and in respect of sales made at as nearly as possible the same time." Due allowance should also be made for "differences in conditions and terms of sale, taxation, levels of trade, quantities, physical characteristics" and other factors affecting price comparability.

In making a price comparison, the question often arises of what benchmark to use in determining the price for home consumption when the producer is selling in the home market at prices below average production costs or at a loss. A producer who over a long period has been selling at a loss in its domestic market the product it is alleged to be dumping in foreign markets can do so only by making use of its sales profits from other products (i.e. cross-product subsidization). A number of countries have in the past excluded such domestic sales in determining domestic consumption prices. In order to ensure uniformity in the practices adopted by investigating authorities for that purpose, the Agreement provides that sales in the home market below fully allocated production costs (including administrative and selling costs) may be disregarded only when:

ADP, Article 2.1.1 and foot-notes 3, 4, 5

❑   Such sales are made over an extended period (normally one year);

❑   The average selling price in the home market is less than the weighted average unit cost; or

❑   The volume of sales below unit cost is more than 20% of the total; and

❑   The costs are not recovered over a reasonable period.

3.3.2.2   Averaging prices

ADP, Article 2.4.2

To arrive at the margin of dumping by comparing the exporter's domestic and export prices, investigating authorities often use a system of averaging, particularly when a large number of small transactions are involved. In order to ensure that, in such cases, prices are compared on an *apple-to-apple* basis, the Agreement now requires that comparison should normally be based on:

❑   Either the weighted average of home consumption prices with the weighted average of the prices of all export transactions;

❑   Or the home market prices and export prices on a transaction-to-transaction basis.

The Agreement permits an exception to this general rule when export prices differ significantly among purchasers, regions or periods. In such instances, a weighted average home consumption price may be compared with the price of an individual export transaction.

3.3.2.3   Currency conversion

ADP, Article 2.4.1

Comparing the home consumption price with the export price normally involves the conversion of the latter into the exporting country's currency. Because of fluctuations, the rate used for currency conversion could greatly influence the margin of dumping. In order to ensure consistency in the methods used by investigating authorities, the ADP Agreement provides that the exchange rate prevalent *on the date of sale* should be used for conversion purposes. However, if the transaction is based on an exchange rate stated in a forward contract, that rate should be used.

3.3.2.4   Constructed value

ADP, Articles 2.2, 2.3

The Agreement on ADP recognizes, as noted earlier, that where the volume of domestic sales is "low" the consumption price in the exporting country may not provide a proper basis for price comparison. In such cases, the Agreement permits the investigating authorities to use, for price comparison purposes, a *constructed value* instead of the domestic consumption price. The constructed value is calculated on the basis of cost to the exporting industry of

producing the product. Box 22 describes the guidelines which the Agreement on ADP lays down for
calculating constructed values.

Box 22

GUIDELINES FOR CALCULATING CONSTRUCTED VALUES
(ADP, Articles 2.2 and 2.3)

When investigating authorities decide, for price comparison purposes, to replace
the consumption price in the exporting country, with a *constructed value* calculated on the basis of the production costs of the exporting industry, the ADP
Agreement lays down principles for arriving at such a value. In particular, it states
that the costs should "normally be calculated on the basis of records kept by the
exporter or producer under investigation, provided that such records are in
accordance with the generally accepted accounting principles of the exporting
country". The Agreement further provides that the amounts for administrative,
sales and general costs and profits should be based on "actual data pertaining
to production and sales in the ordinary course of trade of the like product by the
exporter or producer under investigation." However, when it is not possible to
determine such amounts on the above basis, the Agreement provides that they
can be determined on the basis of:

• Actual data from other exporters or producers of products in the same general
  category;

• The weighted average of the costs and profits of other exporters of the same
  product; and

• Any other reasonable method, as long as the amount does not exceed that
  of the exporters or producers of the same general category of product.

3.4   *De minimis* rule

Very often during the course of preliminary
investigations, the authorities are satisfied that it will
not be possible for the petitioners to establish injury
as the margin of dumping is small or import penetra-
tion is negligible. The ADP Agreement provides that
the application should be immediately rejected and
the investigation terminated if:

| ADP, Article 5.8 | ❏ | The margin of dumping is *de minimis*, i.e. less than 2%, expressed as a percentage of the export price; or |

❏ The volume of imports from a particular country is less than 3% of all imports of like products into the importing country. However, this rule does not apply when countries with individual shares of less than 3% collectively account for more than 7% of imports of the product under investigation; or

❏ The injury is negligible.

SCM, Article 11.9   Likewise, the SCM Agreement requires the authorities to terminate investigations in the situations described below.

❏ In the case of a product originating from a developed country, where:

– The amount of subsidy is *de minimis,* i.e. less than 1%; or

– The volume of subsidized imports or the injury is negligible.

SCM, Article 27.10   ❏ In the case of a product originating from a developing country, when:

– The level of subsidies granted does not exceed 2% of the value calculated on a per unit basis;

– The subsidized imports are less than 4% of total imports of the importing country. However, the rule does not apply when developing countries with individual shares of less than 4% collectively account for more than 9% of total imports.

3.5   Lesser duty rule

ADP, Article 9.1
SCM, Article 12.2

In this context, it is also important to note that both the ADP and SCM Agreements emphasize that, after completion of the investigations, the governments should carefully consider whether additional duties should be levied even if "all requirements regarding their imposition are met". They further encourage the use of the lesser duty rule. Under this approach even after it is established that dumped or subsidized imports are causing injury to the domestic industry, the decision on whether *the amount of duty should be the full margin of dumping or the full amount of subsidy or less* should be made by the appropriate governmental authorities and, if a lesser duty is adequate to remove the injury to the domestic industry, the lesser duty should be levied. This principle is followed by some countries which, after the investigations are completed, try to determine the *injury margin* and levy duty on the basis of that margin if it is lower than the dumping margin or the amount of subsidy.

3.6   Provisional measures

ADP, Article 7
SCM, Article 17

The two Agreements further authorize provisional measures — in the form of cash deposits or bonds — to be taken when the investigating authorities judge that such measures are "necessary to prevent injury being caused during the investigation." However, the Agreements stipulate that such provisional measures should be taken only after the investigating authorities have made a preliminary affirmative determination of dumping or subsidization and *consequent injury to the domestic industry*. If a definitive decision is made to levy duty and the duty is higher than the cash deposit or bond, the difference is not collected from the importer. The importer, however, has a right to claim for reimbursement of the difference when the definitive duty is lower than the cash deposit.

3.7 Price undertakings

Exporters can avoid anti-dumping or counter-vailing duties by undertaking to increase their export prices. However, to prevent exporters from being required to give such price undertakings even when their exports are not causing injury to the domestic industry of the importing country, the Agreements permit such price undertakings only after the investigating authorities have made *preliminary affirmative determination* of injury to the domestic industry and of dumping or subsidization. They further stipulate that the decision to offer a price undertaking should be left to the exporter and that "no exporter shall be forced to enter into such undertakings." It is also possible that the authorities of the importing countries may consider the acceptance of undertakings impractical; this would be the case when the "number of actual or potential exporters is too great".

ADP, Article 8
SCM, Article 18

3.8 Disclosure prior to final determination

The two Agreements stipulate that the investigations should be completed within a period of one year, and in no case more than 18 months after its initiation. Before making the final determination, the investigating authorities are required to "disclose" to the interested parties (e.g. exporters or producers under investigation, their governments, and importers) *the essential facts* on which the decision to apply the duty is made.

ADP, Article 6.9
SCM, Article 12.8

3.9 Determination of the amounts of subsidy and dumping margins

ADP, Articles 6.10, 9.2
SCM, Article 19.3

It is important to note that the Agreements visualize that as far as possible the amounts of countervailing and anti-dumping duties should be determined separately for each exporter or producer. The amounts of duties payable could therefore vary according to the element of subsidy in the price or dumping margin determined for each exporter. However, the investigating authorities may determine duties on the basis of *statistically valid* samples (or the largest volume of exports from the country in question) when the number of exporters or producers is so large as to make the calculation of individual subsidy elements or dumping margins impracticable. In making such a selection, the investigating authorities are urged to consult the exporters or producers concerned and to make the selection preferably with their consent. In addition, any exporter or producer not included in the sample has a right to request that the dumping margin should be fixed separately for it.

3.10 Sunset clause

ADP, Article 11
SCM, Article 21

The Agreements further require that the continued imposition of anti-dumping and countervailing measures (duties and price undertakings) should be kept under constant review. Such reviews should be conducted by the authorities on their own initiative or upon request by any interested party. If as a result of such a review the authorities conclude that the measures are no longer warranted, these measures should be terminated. In addition, the Agreements have a *sunset clause*, under which anti-dumping and countervailing measures automatically expire five years after their imposition, unless a review of the cases determines that, in the absence of such measures, dumping and injury will continue or recur. Reviews for this purpose must be initiated before the sunset date and should normally be concluded within one year.

4. Business implications

For business persons, knowledge of the complex rules on the levy of anti-dumping and countervailing duties is essential in their capacities as exporters and producers whose interests may be adversely affected by the unfair price practices of producers in other countries.

In recent years, there has been a steady increase in the number of petitions for anti-dumping and countervailing actions by both developed and developing countries (see box 23). Enterprises in many developing countries are finding that as their exports of manufactured products rise, there are increasing pressures from industries in the importing countries for the levy of such duties, on the grounds that the goods are being dumped or subsidized. Such duties may be levied on any imported product.

In the circumstances, it is becoming essential for enterprises to be familiar with the rules applicable in this area. An understanding of the rules could, for instance, enable an exporting enterprise to take precautionary steps to avoid anti-dumping actions in foreign markets where there are increasing pressures from industrial and other groups for such actions. While it may continue to charge export prices that are lower than its domestic prices in markets where it faces no threat, it should avoid doing so in markets where anti-dumping actions are possible. In such markets, anti-dumping duties can be avoided if the exporter does not allow the difference between its domestic price and export price to fall below a rea-

---

Box 23

ANTI-DUMPING ACTIONS

During the period 1 July to 30 June 1993 the total member of anti-dumping investigations initiated rose to 245 from 237 in the corresponding period a year earlier. The figures by country/area are as follows:

Country/area	Number of investigations initiated
United States	68
Australia	61
Canada	37
European Union	33
Mexico	24
Korea, Rep. of	7
Austria	4
New Zealand	4
India	3

The total number of anti-dumping measures in force stood at 662 on 30 June 1993. Most of these measures were accounted for by the United States (279), the European Union (185), Canada (81) and Australia (64).

Source: *GATT Activities 1993.*

---

sonable margin. As noted, if the margin is *de minimis* or less, investigating authorities are required to reject applications for the levy of duties. Investigating authorities also take into account the share of an exporting country in total imports of a product. It would be in the interest of the exporting enterprise not to allow its exports to rise to a market where it is apprehensive of a petition for anti-dumping action and, where possible, to diversify its trade to other markets.

When investigations begin, the Agreements give exporting enterprises (and the trade or business associations to which they belong) the right to defend their interests. The ADP Agreement obliges them to provide information on the cost of production and other matters on the basis of a questionnaire sent by the investigating authorities. It is essential for exporters to cooperate with these authorities and to give them the required information, the reason being that in anti-dumping cases the duty payable is fixed separately for each exporting enterprise on the basis of the margin between the price charged by it in its domestic market and its export price.

The Agreements also oblige the investigating authorities to notify the governments of the exporting countries of their decision to begin investigations. The governments have a right to tender evidence against the petition and to defend the interests of their exporters. As the legal and other costs of participating in investigations are substantial and are often beyond the resources of small and medium-sized enterprises, it is often necessary for them to rely on their governments to defend their interests.

The Agreements also seek to protect the interests of enterprises which find that they are being injured or hurt as a result of the unfair pricing practices of foreign suppliers. The affected enterprises have the right to petition their national investigating authorities for the levy of anti-dumping duties if the imports are being dumped and for the levy of countervailing duties if the imports are being subsidized. However, the Agreements lay down strict conditions for invoking that right. In particular, an application for the levy of duties can be made only if it has *standing*, i.e. the support of producers accounting for at least 25% of the total domestic production of the product alleged to be dumped or subsidized. In addition, the application must provide information establishing a causal link between increased dumped and subsidized imports and injury to the producers in the form of loss of production, domestic sales or loss of jobs.

Complaints of dumping or subsidized imports are on the increase in most developing countries implementing liberalization measures. While many of these complaints are due to the inability of domestic industries, long accustomed to heavy levels of protection, to adjust to the changed competitive situation resulting from the removal of tariffs and other barriers, some complaints about unfair price practices of foreign suppliers are undoubtedly genuine. A better understanding of the Agreements will enable the affected producing enterprises to make appropriate use of their right to petition the authorities for the levy of anti-dumping or countervailing duties in such cases. The stringent conditions the Agreements lay down will ensure that such duties are levied only when the dumped or subsidized imports are established to be causing injury to the industry concerned.

Section 5

TRADE-RELATED INVESTMENT MEASURES

Chapter 12

Trade-related investment measures (TRIMs)

Summary of the main rules

Governments often impose conditions on foreign investors to encourage investment in accordance with certain national priorities. Conditions that can affect trade are known as **trade-related investment measures** or TRIMs.

The Agreement on TRIMs, which was negotiated in the Uruguay Round, requires countries to phase out TRIMs that have been identified as being inconsistent with GATT rules. The phasing-out period for developed countries is two years from 1 January 1995, for developing countries five years, and for transitional economies seven years.

1.   General

When the Uruguay Round of negotiations was being launched, the United States proposed that there was a need to bring under discipline *investment measures that distort trade*. It also suggested that the negotiations should cover policy issues affecting the flow of foreign direct investment. In particular it suggested that it would be necessary to consider the feasibility of applying to foreign direct investment the GATT principles of *national treatment* (which would give foreign companies the same right as domestic companies to invest in, and to establish, local operations) and *MFN treatment* (which would prevent countries from discriminating amongst sources of investment).

While these proposals received some support from other developed countries, they were not looked on with favour by developing countries. Apart from holding that GATT's mandate did not permit it to negotiate on investment issues, these countries maintained that, if any such negotiations were to be held, they would have to include the problems posed to trade by transnational corporations resorting to transfer pricing, restrictive business methods and other practices. This reluctance of developing countries to allow discussions in GATT on investment issues ultimately resulted in negotiations taking place on a narrowly defined concept of trade-related investment measures.

2.   What are TRIMs?

The measures adopted by governments to attract and regulate foreign investment include fiscal incentives, tax rebates and the provision of land and other services on preferential terms. In addition, governments impose conditions to encourage or compel the use of investment according to certain national priorities. Local content requirements, which require the investor to undertake to utilize a certain amount of local inputs in production, are an example of such conditions. Export performance requirements are another example; they compel the investor to undertake to export a certain proportion of its output. Such conditions, which can have adverse effects on trade, are known as *trade-related investment measures* or TRIMs. An illustrative list of TRIMs is presented in box 24.

Trade-related investment measures have been used mainly, if not exclusively, by developing countries to promote development objectives. For instance, the growth of domestic ancillary industries has been sought by the imposition of local content requirements and export expansion through export performance requirements. In many cases, TRIMs are designed to deal with the restrictive business practices of transnational corporations and their anti-competition behaviour.

A recent survey shows that TRIMs tend to be concentrated in specific industries — automotive, chemical and petrochemical, and computer/informatics. Local content requirements are more predominant than export performance requirements in the automotive industry and are less so in the computer/informatics industry. In the chemical and petrochemical industries both local content and export performance requirements are prominent.[18]

---

18 Patrick Low and Arvind Subramanian, "TRIMs in the Uruguay Round: An Unfinished Business" (paper presented at the World Bank Conference on the Uruguay Round and Developing Economies, 26-27 January 1995).

Box 24

AN ILLUSTRATIVE LIST OF TRIMs

Local content requirements (LCRs). Impose the use of a certain amount of local inputs in production.

Trade-balancing requirements. Oblige imports to be equivalent to a certain proportion of exports.

Foreign exchange balancing requirements. Stipulate that the foreign exchange made available for imports should be a certain proportion of the value of foreign exchange brought in by the firm from exports and other sources.

Exchange restrictions. Restrict access to foreign exchange and hence restrict imports.

Domestic sales requirements. Require a company to sell a certain proportion of its output locally, which amounts to a restriction on exportation.

Manufacturing requirements. Require certain products to be manufactured locally.

Export performance requirements (EPRs). Stipulate that a certain proportion of production should be exported.

Product mandating requirements. Oblige an investor to supply certain markets with a designated product or products manufactured from a specified facility or operation.

Manufacturing limitations. Prevent companies from manufacturing certain products or product lines in the host country.

Technology transfer requirements. Require specified technologies to be transferred on non-commercial terms and/or specific levels and types of research and development (R & D) to be conducted locally.

Licensing requirements. Oblige the investor to license technologies similar or unrelated to those it uses in the home country to host country firms.

Remittance restrictions. Restrict the right of a foreign investor to repatriate returns from an investment.

Local equity requirements. Specify that a certain percentage of a firm's equity should be held by local investors.

---

3. Agreement on Trade-Related Investment Measures (TRIMs)

The TRIMs Agreement, which was negotiated in the Uruguay Round, prohibits countries from using five TRIMs from the list in box 24. These are considered inconsistent with GATT rules on *national treatment* and the rules against the use of *quantitative restrictions*.

Agreement on Trade-Related Investment Measures (TRIMs), Article 2

TRIMs prohibited on the grounds that they extend more favourable treatment to domestic products in comparison to imports and thus infringe the national treatment principle include those that require:

❑ Purchase or use by an enterprise of products of domestic origin or from any domestic source (local content requirements); or

❑ That an enterprise's purchase or use of imported products should be limited to an amount related to the volume or value of the local products it exports (trade-balancing requirements).

TRIMs, Article 2, Annex

TRIMs considered inconsistent with the provisions of Article XI of GATT against the use of quantitative restrictions on imports and exports include those that:

❑ Restrict imports to an amount related to the quantity or value of the product exported (i.e. trade-balancing requirements constituting restrictions on imports).

❑ Restrict access to foreign exchange to an amount of foreign exchange attributable to the enterprise (i.e. exchange restrictions resulting in restrictions on imports).

❑   Specify exports in terms of the volume or value of local production (i.e. domestic sales requirements involving restrictions on exports).

The Agreement provides transitional periods for the elimination of prohibited TRIMs. For developed countries, the period is two years, for developing countries five years, and for transitional economies seven years.

4.   Business implications

For the business person, it is important to note that the Agreement is limited in scope. It identifies only five TRIMs that are inconsistent with GATT and gives countries transitional periods within which to remove them. It does not prevent countries from using at least some of the other TRIMs listed in box 24. For instance, countries are not prevented from imposing export performance requirements as a condition for investment. They are not prohibited from insisting that a certain percentage of equity should be held by local investors or that a foreign investor must bring in the most up-to-date technology or must conduct a specific level or type of R & D locally.

A number of developing countries today impose local content requirements. The abolition of these requirements may have an impact on ancillary industries that are benefiting from the protection they provide. However, most of these countries are reviewing the need for the continued maintenance of such measures in the light of the open trade policies they are now pursuing and the steps they are taking to attract foreign investment. For instance, Argentina, Brazil, India and Mexico had taken decisions to abolish local content requirements even before the conclusion of the Uruguay Round. The Agreement therefore only reinforces the trend towards the removal of TRIMs that are considered inconsistent with GATT.

The Agreement's limited coverage of TRIMs has led countries to provide that its operation should be reviewed within a period of five years of its coming into force (i.e. before 1 January 2000) and that the review should consider the desirability of complementing the Agreement with *provisions on investment and competition policy.* This indicates that proposals for negotiations on the development of multilateral rules on foreign direct investment may be revived in the future. If such negotiations take place, there will be pressures from developing countries for coverage of the problems posed to international trade by the restrictive business practices and other anti-competition behaviour of transnational corporations.[19]

---

19 Competition policy is difficult to define in precise terms because it potentially encompasses a wide range of government policies. Thus, control of protectionist abuse of technical standards or the grant of subsidies could be described as competition policies. In addition, there is competition policy *per se* which is a body of economy-wide laws and regulations governing private producer behaviour and the market structure within which interactions between producers take place. Such laws typically deal with restrictive business operations such as price fixing, output restrictions or restrictive practices involving the transfer of technologies.

Section 6

IMPROVEMENTS IN MARKET ACCESS AND NEW RULES APPLICABLE TO THE TRADE IN TEXTILES AND IN AGRICULTURAL PRODUCTS

CHAPTER 13

Market access negotiations in the industrial and agricultural sectors (Agreements on Textiles and Clothing and on Agriculture)

Summary of results

The preceding sections noted the main features of the strengthened legal system that has emerged from the Uruguay Round and how business persons can use their knowledge of the system to promote and develop their trade. The Round has also significantly improved market access, opening up additional and new opportunities for enterprises to sell abroad.

The previous rounds of GATT negotiations, particularly the Tokyo Round, had considerably reduced the tariffs applied by developed countries to industrial products. However, they made very little progress in the removal of quantitative restrictions and other non-tariff measures on imports. For instance, in the industrial sector, the developed countries' discriminatory quantitative restrictions on imports of textile products and clothing continued to be applied under the legal cover provided by the Multi-Fibre

Arrangement. The previous Rounds had also failed to modify the highly protectionist agricultural policies pursued by some developed countries which had almost closed their markets to competitive imports. Furthermore, no changes were made in their policies of subsidizing exports, which distorted conditions of competition in international trade.

The market access negotiations in the Uruguay Round have greatly improved the situation. The main features of the Round's results can be summarized as follows:

- *The **tariff cuts** countries have pledged to make on industrial products are much higher than those of the Tokyo Round.*

- *By adopting the **Agreement on Textiles and Clothing**, countries have agreed to phase out the restrictions maintained under the Multi-Fibre Arrangement within a period of 10 years, i.e. by 1 January 2005.*

- *The **Agreement on Agriculture** has created a framework for gradually bringing trade in agricultural products under GATT discipline and for liberalizing trade in this sector.*

- ***Developing countries** and **economies in transition**, which participated actively in the negotiations, have reduced their tariffs on both industrial and agricultural products.*

- *Almost all tariffs of developed countries have been bound against further increases; in developing and transitional economy countries, the proportion of tariffs that have been bound has risen significantly.*

1. General

This chapter describes first the liberalization commitments made in the industrial sector and the gradual phasing out of restrictions applicable to textiles in accordance with the provisions of the *Agreement on Textiles and Clothing (ATC)*. This is followed by a description of the framework of the new rules that have been adopted for trade in agricultural products under the *Agreement on Agriculture* and of the liberalization commitments that countries have undertaken in pursuance of the provisions of the Agreement. The chapter concludes by describing the steps that the business person will have to take to derive full advantage from these liberalization measures.

2. Industrial products

2.1 Reduction in tariffs

In the Uruguay Round, developed countries agreed to cut their tariffs by an overall percentage of 40%, and the developing countries and transitional economies by 30%.

These tariff cuts are to be made in five equal stages so as to reach the final agreed rate applicable at tariff line level by 1 January 2000. Tables 1 to 3 of the annex to this chapter show, for selected developed, developing and transitional economies, the weighted average tariffs in the pre-Uruguay Round period and those that will be applicable by 1 January 2000, the date set for the full implementation of the reductions agreed in the Round.

In the Uruguay Round negotiations, developed countries and certain developing countries also agreed to eliminate all tariffs in certain sectors, the so-called zero-for-zero sectors. These include pharmaceuticals, agricultural equipment, construction equipment, medical equipment, furniture, paper, steel and toys. As a result of these and other concessions, the proportion of industrial products entering developed country markets on a duty-free basis will more than double from 22% to 44%. The weighted average level of tariffs applicable to industrial products is expected to fall from:

❑   6.3% to 3.8% in developed countries;

❑   15.3% to 12.3% in developing countries; and

❑   8.6% to 6% in the transitional economies.

2.2   Binding of tariffs

Another important aspect of the Uruguay Round negotiations was the progress made in binding tariffs. Virtually all imports into developed countries will now enter under bound rates; the proportions for developing countries and transitional economies are 73% and around 98% respectively. As has been noted in chapter 2, one of the major advantages of binding is the security of access it provides to foreign markets. Enterprises can plan the development of their trade without fear of duties being increased or access being restricted by quantitative restrictions.

2.3   Removal of quantitative restrictions

Equally important from the point of creating improved opportunities for trade are the provisions for phasing out quantitative restrictions on industrial products. The Agreement on Textiles and Clothing provides for the gradual elimination of restrictions on textiles and clothing; the Agreement on Safe-guards will remove VERs and other grey area measures.

2.3.1 Agreement on Textiles and Clothing (ATC): background to the negotiations

World trade in textiles and clothing has been subject to an increasing array of bilateral quota arrangements over the past three decades. The range of products covered by quotas expanded from cotton textiles under the Short-Term and Long-Term Arrangements of the 1960s and early 1970s to an ever-increasing list of textile products fashioned from natural and man-made fibres under five extensions of the Multi-Fibre Arrangement (MFA).

At the end of 1994, when the Arrangement was terminated, MFA had a membership of 39 countries. Eight of these were developed countries and were designated as "importers"; the remaining 31 developing country members were considered "exporters". MFA encouraged exporting and importing countries to enter into bilateral arrangements requiring exporting countries to restrain their exports of either all or certain categories of textiles and clothing. In entering such bilateral agreements, the countries were expected to adhere strictly to MFA rules:

❑   For the determination of quotas and categories;

❑   For restraint levels; and

❑   For the inclusion of such provisions as annual growth rates, carry-over of unutilized quotas from the previous year and carry-forward of part of the current year's quota for use in the following year.

When the Agreement on Textiles and Clothing became operational on 1 January 1995, several importing countries/areas (the United States, Canada, the European Union, Norway, Finland and Australia) had a total of 90 bilateral restraint agreements with exporting countries. In addition, there were 29 non-MFA agreements or unilateral measures that imposed restrictions on imports of textiles.

2.3.2 Integrating trade in textiles into GATT

From the strictly legal point of view, the maintenance of these restrictions was not consistent with GATT rules. However, MFA provided a legal cover for derogation from GATT discipline. The basic aim of the Agreement on Textiles and Clothing is to integrate the trade in textiles into GATT by requiring member countries maintaining the restrictions to phase them out over a period of 10 years. After the expiry of the 10-year period, i.e. from 1 January 2005, it will not be possible for any member country to maintain restrictions on imports of textiles, unless it can justify them under the safeguard provisions of the Agreement on Safeguards. In other words, an importing country can impose restrictions only when, after carrying out investigations, it can establish that increased imports are causing its domestic textile industry *serious injury*. Furthermore, such restrictions will have to be applied to imports from all sources, and not on a discriminatory basis to imports from one or two countries as is the case with MFA-type restrictions.

2.3.3 Methodology for integration

Agreement on Textiles and Clothing (ATC), Article I, and Annex

The methodological base for integrating the textile trade into GATT is the list of textile products contained in the annex to the Agreement. The list covers all textile products, whether or not they are subject to restrictions. The integration process is to be carried out in four stages. At each stage, products amounting to a certain minimum percentage of the volume of the country's imports in 1990 are to be included in the integration process. These percentages are:

ATC, Article 2.8

❏ 16% of the products on the list, on the date of entry into force of the Agreement (i.e. 1 January 1995);

❏ 17% at the end of the third year (i.e. 1 January 1998);

❏ 18% at the end of seven years (i.e. 1 January 2002); and

❏ 49% at the end of the tenth year (i.e. 1 January 2005).

In assimilating products into the integration process, countries are under no obligation to limit themselves to products subject to restrictions. The only constraint the Agreement places is that they include products from each of four segments, namely, tops and yarn, fabrics, made-up-textile products, and clothing.

In the case of the United States and the European Union, in 1990 (the base year to be used for integration) the percentage of imports of products not covered by restrictions was around 34% and 37% respectively. For other countries maintaining restrictions the percentage was much higher. Notionally therefore, it may be possible for these major restraining countries to meet their obligations to integrate the textile trade in the first two stages without significantly removing restrictions. That they may in practice do so is borne out by the fact that both the United States and the European Union have refrained from including any restricted textile product and clothing in the first integration measures taken on 1 January 1995. There are therefore apprehensions that serious steps to remove restrictions will be taken only when the third stage begins in 2002, and that the bulk of the restrictions will be removed on the last day of the 10-year transitional period.

The Agreement, however, tries to provide improved and enlarged access for textile products that may continue to be restricted during the transitional period. It seeks this by requiring that the *growth factors* provided for annual increases in the quotas fixed for each category of textile products under bilateral agreements should be increased at escalated rates. Thus if the annual growth rate for a rise in the quota for a textile product (say, shirts) is fixed under a bilateral agreement at 3%, it will have to be increased by:

ATC, Articles 2.13, 2.14

❑   16% per year in the first three years;

❑   25% per year in the next four years; and

❑   27% in the next three years.

This will raise the growth rate to 5.52% in the tenth year. If the size of the quota is 100 tons at the beginning of the transitional period, it will more than double to around 204 tons in the tenth year.

2.3.4   Integration of non-MFA restrictions

ATC, Article 3

The Agreement on Textiles and Clothing also requires countries applying non-MFA restrictions to phase them out in a period of 10 years. The programme for the gradual phasing out of such restrictions is to be prepared by the importing country and presented to the Textiles Monitoring Body (TMB). The Body has been established under the Agreement for the surveillance of its operation.

2.3.5 *Transitional safeguard measures*

It is interesting to note that even though the aim of the Agreement is to facilitate the removal of restrictions on textiles, it permits countries to take *safeguard actions* during the transitional period. Such transitional safeguard actions can be taken only in respect of textile products that are not integrated into GATT, and if the importing country determines that:

ATC, Article 6

❑ The product is being imported in such increased quantities as to cause serious damage or actual threat thereof to the domestic industry producing the like product, and

❑ There is a causal link between such serious damage to the domestic industry and sharp and substantial increase in imports from the exporting country or countries whose exports are to be restrained.

Such restrictions can ordinarily be imposed only after consultations and after reaching agreement with the exporting countries on the level of imports. However, the Agreement permits countries to impose restrictions even in the absence of an agreement provided the matter is referred to the Textiles Monitoring Body. The importing country is expected to abide by the TMB decision.

2.3.6 *Removal of grey area measures*

In addition to removing restrictions applicable to textile products, countries are committed, under the provisions of the Agreement on Safeguards, to eliminate VERs and other grey area measures that apply on a discriminatory basis to imports from a few selected countries, or to bring them in conformity with the Agreement's provisions. These grey area measures are applied to such products as travel goods, footwear, machine tools, electric equipment and appliances, television sets and television tubes.

3.   Agricultural products

3.1   General

This section now turns to a description of the measures that countries have agreed to take to liberalize trade in agricultural products.

It is common practice to divide agricultural products into two groups, viz. tropical products and others. Though there is no agreed definition of tropical products, beverages like tea, coffee and cocoa; cotton and hard fibres like jute and sisal; fruits like bananas, mangoes and guavas; and other products that are almost predominantly produced in developing countries are treated as tropical products. In the years following the establishment of GATT, these products were subject to both high tariffs and internal taxes in most developed countries. As these products are predominantly of export interest to developing countries, priority was given in the past rounds of GATT negotiations to the removal of barriers affecting the trade in such products. As a result, even before the Uruguay Round, a large number of these products, in both raw and processed forms, were entering developed markets either on a duty-free basis, at low rates on MFN terms, or under preferential arrangements.

Most developed countries, however, continued to apply to imports of other agricultural products — like wheat and other grains, meat and meat products and dairy products — both high levels of tariffs and non-tariff measures such as quantitative restrictions, discretionary licensing and variable levies. The governments' basic objective in providing protection to such products (which are often referred to as temperate zone products) was to guarantee domestic producers prices that were much higher than world prices, in order to assure them reasonable incomes. These policies, apart from reducing trade opportunities for competitive foreign producers, also put heavy burdens on the budgetary resources of governments. This was inevitable, as the high cost of production in excess of domestic requirements could be disposed of in international markets only through export subsidies.

Though agriculture is not as highly protected in developing countries, many of them impose high tariffs and restrict imports through quantitative restrictions. Imports of food and other essential requirements are sometimes channelled through State trading organizations.

Agreement on Agriculture (AG), Preamble

The Agreement on Agriculture that has been negotiated in the Uruguay Round establishes a programme for the gradual reform of trade in agriculture. The programme aims at establishing "a fair and equitable market-oriented agricultural trading system" by requiring countries to adopt new disciplines governing both:

❑　　The use of border measures to control imports;

❑   The use of export subsidies and other subsidies that governments grant to support the prices of agricultural products and assure a reasonable income to farmers.

3.2   Border measures

3.2.1   Tariffication

The most important aspects of the Agreement on Agriculture are the new rules. These require countries to abolish non-tariff measures (such as quantitative restrictions, discretionary licensing and variable levies) by calculating their *tariff equivalents* and adding these to the fixed tariffs. As a result, developed countries have established new higher rates of tariffs for products (mostly temperate zone) to which they previously applied non-tariff measures. The tariff equivalent of non-tariff measures was calculated on the basis of average world market prices for the product subject to non-tariff measures and its guaranteed price in the importing countries. Tariff rates resulting from such *tariffication* as well as tariffs applicable to other products have been bound against further increases.

AG, Article 4 and footnote 1

The obligation to tariffy quantitative restrictions does not apply to restrictions maintained by developing countries in balance-of-payments difficulties, under the GATT provisions permitting them to impose such restrictions. Developing countries, including those in balance-of-payments difficulties, were, however, required to bind their tariffs. In response, they often gave *ceiling bindings* at rates that were in most cases higher than their then current tariff rates.

AG, Article 4, footnote 1

3.2.2 Percentage reductions in tariffs

Countries have agreed to reduce such bound rates by fixed percentages. The developed and transitional economy countries have undertaken to reduce tariffs by an average of 37% and developing countries by 24%. Such reductions are to be made by developed countries over a period of six years and by developing countries in 10 years. The least developed countries, even though they have bound tariffs at higher ceiling rates, were not required to reduce them.

The rules further require that a tariff on a particular product must be reduced by at least 15% by developed countries and 10% by developing countries.

3.2.3 Results of the negotiations on tropical products

In view of the importance of tropical products to the export trade of developing countries, negotiations on the reduction and elimination of tariffs and other restrictions applicable to these products were given priority attention and held separately. The negotiations brought about further progress in the removal of the remaining MFN tariffs and other restrictions applicable to these products in developed countries. Developing countries also reduced their duties on these products. Most countries implemented the reductions without staging.

3.2.4 Results on temperate zone products

For temperate zone products, the rates of tariffs that now apply, after tariffication, reflect the level of protection extended by non-tariff measures earlier. As this level was high, the new rates applicable to such products in some countries generally range between 60% and 100%; for some tariff lines they are as high as 300% to 350%. One of the basic objectives of requiring countries to tariffy their non-tariff measures was to add transparency to the protection granted. The objective has not been fully achieved as, for a number of products, countries have imposed not *ad valorem* but specific duties. These are payable in some cases on the basis of either minimum values or reference prices.

For some products with a high protection level, there was a danger that the tariffication process by itself would not have a significant liberalizing effect even after implementation. The techniques of *current* and *minimum* access commitments were therefore adopted to complement the tariffication process. (See box 25 for details.)

3.3   Export subsidies and governmental support measures

Apart from high levels of protection, distortions in the international trade in agricultural products are caused by subsidy practices mainly in developed countries. While over the years GATT was able to develop rules for subsidies on industrial products, it had failed to bring under discipline subsidies granted by governments to the agricultural sector. The Agreement on Agriculture, for the first time, makes a systematic effort to lay down rules for subsidies on agricultural products.

These rules differ from those applicable to industrial products. The Agreement on SCM, which deals with industrial products, divides subsidies into three categories according to the traffic light system: red, amber and green. Red subsidies are those that are prohibited; they include *export subsidies*. The rule against the use of export subsidies on industrial

---

Box 25

AGRICULTURAL PRODUCTS: CURRENT AND MINIMUM MARKET ACCESS COMMITMENTS

(Agreement on Agriculture, Article 5.2)

Current access commitments

A number of countries had special arrangements for imports of meat and other mainly temperate zone products up to quota limits on either a duty-free or a preferential basis. In order to ensure that such imports are not affected by the application of higher rates resulting from tariffication, importing countries have given *current access commitments* by establishing tariff quotas to cover imports that were entering the market at lower duty rates. As a result of these commitments, imports up to quota levels are allowed at the lower existing rates. The higher rates ensuing from tariffication are applicable to imports over and above quota limits.

Minimum access commitments

For products for which little or no imports took place in the past because of the highly restrictive nature of the then-existing regime, countries were required to give *minimum market access opportunity commitments.* The commitments provide for the establishment of *tariff quotas* equal to 3% of domestic consumption in the base period 1986-1988 and rising to 5% by the end of 2000 for developed countries and 2004 for developing countries. Lower rates (specified in the national schedules but generally not greater than 32% of the bound tariffied rates) are applicable to imports up to the quota limits, while the higher rate resulting from tariffication will apply to imports over quota limits. As a result of these minimum access commitments, countries will have to import modest amounts of their most restricted products. Table 4 in the annex to this chapter lists the products subject to minimum access commitments. In addition to meat, the commitments cover dairy products, and specified fresh vegetables and fruits.

---

products, previously applicable only to developed countries, now covers developing countries. However, the latter countries have a transitional period of eight years to implement the rule. Amber subsidies are subsidies that are permissible but are actionable by importing countries. Green subsidies include subsidies that are both permissible and non-actionable.

In the categorization used in the Agreement on Agriculture, there are no red or prohibited subsidies. Its approach is to require governments to reduce the use of subsidies. From this perspective, the Agreement divides subsidies into two categories: green and amber. Green subsidies are those which are permitted to be used, and to which reduction commitments do not apply. Amber subsidies include subsidies to which reduction commitments apply.

3.3.1 Green subsidies

AG, Annex 2:1

All subsidies that have "no, or at most minimal, trade-distorting effects or effects on production" and do not have the "effect of providing price support to producers" are treated as green subsidies and are exempt from reduction commitments. Thus the Agreement does not unduly restrict the rights of governments to grant subsidies for the improvement of productivity and efficiency of agricultural production or to adopt suitable measures to provide support to farmers. Box 26 contains an illustrative list of subsidy practices that are exempt from reduction commitments.

3.3.2 Amber subsidies

3.3.2.1 Domestic support

AG, Article 1(a), Article 6

Amber subsidies mainly cover domestic support subsidies. The Agreement establishes a ceiling on the total domestic support (calculated as the Aggregate Measurement of Support, AMS) that governments may provide to domestic producers. In addition, it requires that AMS should be reduced by developed countries by 20% over a period of six years from the average level reached in the base period 1986-1988. Developing countries are required to reduce AMS by 13 1/3% over a period of 10 years.

Box 26

ILLUSTRATIVE LIST Of GOVERNMENT SUBSIDIES GRANTED TO PRODUCERS THAT ARE EXEMPT FROM REDUCTION COMMITMENTS

(Agreement on Agriculture, Annex 2)

The following subsidy practices are exempt from reduction commitments, if the specific conditions prescribed by the Agreement are met:

- Government expenditure on agricultural research, pest control, inspection and grading of particular products, marketing and promotion services.

- Financial participation by governments in income insurance and income safety-net programmes.

- Payments for natural disaster.

- Structural adjustment assistance provided through:

  - Producer retirement programmes designed to facilitate the retirement of persons engaged in marketable agricultural production;

  - Resource retirement programmes designed to remove land and other resources, including livestock, from agricultural production;

  - Investment aids designed to assist the financial or physical restructuring of a producer's operations.

- Payments under environmental programmes.

- Payments under regional assistance programmes.

AMS is calculated on a product-by-product basis by using the difference between the average external reference price for a product and its applied administered price multiplied by the quantity of production. To arrive at AMS, non-product-specific domestic subsidies are added to the total subsides calculated on a product-by-product basis.

The green subsidies described above are exempt from inclusion in AMS. In addition, direct payments to producers under production-limiting programmes are exempt if certain specified conditions are met. Further, where support granted to a particular product is less than 5%, expenditure on subsidization of that product is excluded. Similarly, a non-product-specific domestic subsidy is to be excluded from the calculation if it does not exceed 5% of the value of agricultural production. For developing countries, these *de minimis* percentages are 10%.

Even though AMS is calculated on a product-by-product basis, the commitments for reductions apply to the aggregate amount. This enables countries to maintain their flexibility and to shift support between products so long as they stay within the overall ceiling resulting from the commitments. The reductions to be made in domestic support to agricultural products are shown table 5 of the annex to this chapter.

3.3.3 Export and import subsidies

AG, Article 9

The Agreement further establishes a ceiling on both the value and the volume of subsidized exports of agriculture products. Developed countries are expected to reduce their export subsidy expenditure by 36% in six years, in equal instalments (from 1986-1990 levels). The volume of subsidized imports must also be cut by 21% over six years, in equal annual instalments, from the same base period. For developing countries the percentage cuts are 24% and 14% respectively, in equal annual instalments over 10 years. The Agreement also specifies that for products not subject to export subsidy reduction commitments, no such subsidies can be granted in future.

These reductions are of particular significance to world trade in heavily subsidized products such as wheat, coarse grains, meat, dairy products and sugar. The total outlay on export subsidies for agricultural products by the end of the implementation period will be reduced from $22.5 billion to $14.5 billion, of which the European Union will account for half. Table 6 of the annex to this chapter shows the outlay on export subsidies in different countries, its allocation among different products, and the level to which it has to be reduced.

Box 27 summarizes the main features of the market access commitments assumed by countries.

4. Assessment of the liberalization gains

A number of studies have been made at the macroeconomic level by international organizations and other research organizations to assess the impact which the implementation of these commitments could have on world trade and world income. All the studies agree that reductions in trade protection will lead to an increase in both world trade and income. The debate on these estimates centres on the magnitude of the gains and on the distribution of these gains among different product groups and different countries. Variations in estimates arise from differences in the methodology used, assumptions made as well as the data and information available to researchers when the various studies were being prepared.

4.1 Income gains

The WTO secretariat has estimated that by using models with static specifications (that is, ignoring the impact of income increases on the level of savings and investment) the *annual gain in world income* will be in the range of $110 billion to $315 billion in 2005. The dynamic model (which

---

Box 27

SUMMARY OF MARKET ACCESS COMMITMENTS

Industrial products

- Reduction of tariffs: 40% in developed countries, 30% in developing and transitional economy countries.

- Binding against further increases of almost all tariffs of developed countries and a high proportion of the tariffs of developing and transitional economy countries.

- Phasing out of restrictions under MFA and other restrictions applicable to textiles over a period of 10 years in accordance with the provisions of the ATC.

- A greater percentage increase in MFA quota levels during the phase-out period to provide improved access.

- Phasing out of VERs applicable to other products over a period of four years (i.e. by 1 January 1999).

Agricultural products

- Elimination of non-tariff measures through the tariffication process.

- Binding against further increases of tariffs arrived at after tariffication and other tariffs.

- Reduction of bound tariffs by 36% in developed countries and by 24% in developing countries.

- Current access and minimum access commitments in certain cases.

- Commitments to cut both the value and the volume of export subsidies by an agreed percentage.

- Commitment to reduce by an agreed percentage domestic support on the basis of an Aggregate Measurement of Support.

---

assumes that a share of income gain is saved and invested in new capital) shifts the range upwards by some 60% to between $185 billion and $510 billion.

4.2   Gains for international trade

Of more direct relevance for the purpose of this Guide are the gains which liberalization is expected to bring to world trade in goods and how these gains will be shared by the industrial and agricultural sectors and by different product groups in each of these sectors. Here again the estimates vary. Box 28 shows the WTO estimates of increase in total merchandise exports and in main product groups expected in 2005 as a result of the implementation of the results of the Uruguay Round. Total merchandise trade will be higher by anywhere between 9% to 24%, depending on the version of the computable general equilibrium (CGE) model used. In the industrial sector, higher growth rates are expected for:

❑   Textiles and clothing;

❑   Transport equipment;

❑   Fishery products; and

❑   Other manufactures (including lumber and wood products, leather and leather products, and non-electrical machinery).

In the agricultural sector, higher growth rates will be achieved in:

❑   Forestry products; and

❑   Certain agricultural products (meat and meat products, horticultural products, etc.).

These estimated growth rates are over and above the annual increase of 4% in world trade that is expected to take place even if the Uruguay Round results are not implemented.

4.3   Factors that may affect the realization of gains

It is important to note that all these assessments assume that, in order to benefit fully from liberalization, countries will have to maintain liberal

Box 28

ESTIMATED INCREASE IN MERCHANDISE EXPORTS
AS A RESULT OF THE IMPLEMENTATION OF LIBERALIZATION
OF TRADE IN GOODS: MAIN PRODUCT GROUPS
(percentage change in volume)

	VERSION OF THE CGE MODEL			
	Version 1	Version 2	Version 3	Actual value of exports in 1992 (billions of dollars)
All merchandise [a/]	8.6	9.6	23.5	2,843.0
Grains	4.1	4.4	4.6	24.2
Other agricultural products [b/]	21.1	21.0	22.1	73.8
Fishery products [b/]	13.0	12.9	13.5	26.5
Forestry products	3.7	4.1	5.6	7.7
Mining	1.6	1.8	3.1	328.4
Primary steel	8.3	8.4	25.5	76.7
Primary non-ferrous metals	3.6	3.9	14.2	52.4
Fabricated metal products	5.3	5.4	16.0	57.2
Chemicals and rubber	5.2	5.4	21.4	251.3
Transport equipment	11.7	13.6	30.1	320.2
Textiles	17.5	18.6	72.5	93.9
Clothing	69.4	87.1	191.6	105.6
Other manufactures	4.7	4.7	12.7	1,425.1

Source: GATT Secretariat, *The Results of the Uruguay Round of Multilateral Trade Negotiations, Market Access for Goods and Services: Overview of the Results* (Geneva, November 1994).

a/ Excluding intra-European Union trade, and including trade in petroleum.

b/ The marginally smaller gains under the second version of the model, relative to the first version, are the result of resources shifting into production of those product groups whose production was stimulated by the introduction of increasing returns to scale.

Version 1: assumes constant returns to scale (no economies of scale), and perfect competition.

Version 2: assumes increasing returns to scale in industrial sectors, and perfect competition.

Version 3: assumes increasing returns to scale and monopolistic competition in industrial sectors.

and open trade policies to ensure a more efficient use of domestic resources. Enterprises in countries which — because of factors such as economic downturns, currency crises or the sudden cessation of the flow of foreign investments — find it impossible to maintain the pace of liberalization or are required to take restrictive measures may not be able to take advantage of the liberalization measures to the same extent as those in countries following open market policies. The long-term interest of industries and business enterprises therefore lies in encouraging their governments to pursue liberal trade policies.

The realization of the estimated gains may also be delayed or even blocked if the commitments assumed by countries in the negotiations are implemented in form rather than in substance. There are growing apprehensions that this may happen, at least in relation to some of the liberalization commitments undertaken in the Uruguay Round. For instance, in the industrial sector, where tariffs in developed countries are low, the increase in imports is expected to occur mainly as a result of the removal of restrictions applicable to textiles and clothing and those applied to other products under VERs or other similar measures.

As regards textiles, as has been noted, it is possible for the restraining countries to plan their programmes for the integration of textiles and clothing without including any significant number of products subject to restrictions until about the third stage, i.e. the seventh year of the phase-out period. That these countries may be compelled to do so because of pressures from their domestic textile industries or for political reasons is evident from the fact that both the United States and the European Union have not included any textile or clothing products that are subject to restrictions in their integration package for the first stage that was implemented on 1 January 1995. If this trend continues and if the bulk of the restrictions are removed only during the last stage or on the date of the termination of the Agreement on Textiles and Clothing, the estimated dramatic increase in imports may prove to be illusory at least during the first half of the 10-year period.

In relation to VERs, the Agreement on Safeguards provides two options to countries maintaining restrictions. They may eliminate these restrictions in five years or bring them in conformity with the rules of the Agreement, i.e. apply them on an MFN basis to imports from all sources. The choice of the latter option, even though legally permissible, would only broaden the restrictive effects of the measures to imports from countries to which such restrictions did not apply in the past.

In the area of agriculture, taking into account the more recent information available, some researchers now point out that their earlier estimates of increase in trade in agriculture might have been optimistic. Two factors are responsible for this revised lower assessment of benefits. First, a large number of tropical products in which developing (and particularly least developed) countries had an export interest were entering the markets of developed countries duty free or at low duty rates on either an MFN or a preferential basis. Consequently, further reductions may not by themselves have a perceptible influence on the trade in these products. Second, as regards temperate zone agricultural products like cereals and meat, it now appears that in calculating tariff equivalents there has been in some cases an over-estimation of the incidence of non-tariff measures (this is often referred to as dirty tariffication). The result is that, for a number of products, the level of protection provided by the new tariff rates even after reductions are made, may be considerably higher than that existing previously.

4.4   Business implications

Despite such partial backsliding in implementation, the Uruguay Round package will result in significant growth in world trade and income. The growth rates achieved may, however, be lower than those estimated by macroeconomic studies. In practice also, at least for some products, the implementation of commitments could have a different impact on exports from different countries. Thus exporting enterprises from developing countries that enjoy preferential access in their major developed import markets may find that the preferential margin on their export products has been reduced as a result of reductions in MFN tariffs. This possible adverse impact will depend on how far the preferential access was meaningful in trade terms, taking into account such factors as the product's quality and price. Likewise in the case of textiles, where MFA restrictions apply on a discriminatory basis, the impact of the removal of restrictions could vary for different supplying countries. This is well brought out by the case study presented in box 29.

These considerations emphasize the need to supplement the macroeconomic studies with analyses at the micro-level to take into account the possible differing impact of the implementation of the Uruguay Round commitments on some products. The information required for such analytical studies is contained in the national schedules of concessions made by each country, which are available on CD-

Box 29

CASE STUDY OF THE IMPACT OF THE REMOVAL
OF MFA RESTRICTIONS ON TEXTILE PRODUCTS

In comparison to rates on other manufactured products, the tariff rates applicable to textile imports will continue to be at a high level, even after the reductions agreed during the Uruguay Round are fully implemented. The main gains for trade are therefore expected to result from the removal of the restrictions in some developed countries.

The imposition of restrictions on imports leads to a rise in the prices of imported products, as the quantities imported are less than those demanded by consumers. Import restrictions thus penalize consumers, who pay higher prices. As to whether the importer or exporter benefits from the premium resulting from the high price depends on where the licensing system is administered. If it is at the importing end, the importer is able to capture part of the difference between the normal import price and the wholesale price in the importing country. On the other hand, if the licences are issued by the exporting countries, exporters are able to appropriate part of the premium, by charging higher export prices.

Under MFA, the licences required for the administration of restrictions are issued by exporting countries. When the quota restrictions are removed, exporting enterprises will not be able to claim the premium and will have to charge lower export prices. The decline in the value per unit of exports is expected to be compensated by a rise in earnings resulting from the growth in export volume following the removal of restrictions. However, the growth of trade will in practice depend on the elasticity of demand (i.e. whether demand will increase with the fall in prices). Demand for textiles in most restraining markets is generally assumed to be elastic. But, at the enterprise level, the main issue is whether it is elastic for the particular category of textiles - say shirts and children's clothes - which the enterprise is exporting and on which restrictions have been removed. If it is not, the enterprise may not benefit from the removal of restrictions and may even lose unless it is able to diversify its production and exports into other lines for which demand is elastic.

The removal of restrictions will lead to increased competition among supplying countries in the restraining importing market. As restrictions under MFA are applied on a discriminatory basis, the impact of such competition on different supplying countries could vary. For instance, exporting firms in country A, whose exports of shirts and children's clothing are restricted, may have to develop strategies to take advantage of the removal of restrictions. On the other hand, suppliers in other countries whose exports of such textile products were not restricted will have to prepare themselves to meet increased competition from the suppliers in country A.

ROM. Appendix III indicates how such and other relevant information can be obtained by interested business enterprises.

Studies at the micro-level will have to be supplemented by subsequent research on, and analysis of, potential demand in liberalizing markets. Such analyses of demand should enable enterprises to determine the plan and strategy that they will have to adopt to take advantage of the new opportunities and, where necessary, to meet the conditions of competition as they change with the gradual implementation of the Uruguay Round commitments.

Undertaking such studies may be beyond the technical and financial resources of individual enterprises, particularly SMEs. In such instances, the initiative for carrying out the studies may have to be taken by national foreign trade research institutes or by associations of industries and chambers of commerce. In doing so, they may need financial assistance from their governments. International organizations could themselves carry out studies on selected products or assist the relevant institutions and associations in different countries in their preparation.

5.   Potential for expanding trade with developing countries

In this context, it is necessary to bear in mind an important aspect of the Uruguay Round. This is the further stimulus it has provided to the liberalization process in both developing and transitional economy countries. As has been noted, the launching of the Uruguay Round almost coincided with a change-over to more open and liberal trade policies, even in developing countries which until then had followed more restrictive trade policies. By about the same time, the transitional economies were taking initial steps towards market reform, privatization and the reorientation of economic and trade policies. Both groups of countries have consolidated in the Uruguay Round their earlier unilateral tariff reductions either by binding them at reduced rates or by giving ceiling bindings (see annex, tables 2-3). These tariffs are expected to fall further, in some cases even below the reductions agreed in the Uruguay Round. This will result from the additional liberalization measures that a number of countries are taking or propose to take in pursuance of their policies to promote export-oriented growth.

The reductions in tariffs on an MFN basis could, in certain cases, lead to a decline in the preferential margins on products that are covered by regional preferential arrangements[20] or by intraregional arrangements among developing countries[21]. The MFN rates of tariffs of most developing countries participating in such preferential systems will, however, continue to be relatively high even after reductions, with the result that the preferential margins, though narrower, may still provide meaningful trade benefits.

But more important than tariff reductions are the steps taken by developing countries to liberalize their non-tariff measures. These reduce or remove quota restrictions on, and licensing requirements for, imports, and provide for the liberal allocation of foreign exchange to the import trade. In the past,

---

20   Such as the Preferential Trade Area for Eastern and Southern African States or PTA (now known as the Common Market for Eastern and Southern Africa) and the Economic Community of West African States (ECOWAS) in Africa, the Association of South-East Asian Nations (ASEAN) in Asia, and the Asociación Latinoamericana de Integración (ALADI) in Latin America.

21   Such as the Global System of Trade Preferences (GSTP).

non-tariff restrictions blocked the development of trade in products on which preferential concessions were exchanged under regional or intraregional preferential arrangements. The liberalization of import regimes could provide a new stimulus for the expansion of this trade on both MFN and preferential terms.

Traditionally, many enterprises (particularly in some developing countries) have concentrated on markets in developed countries. The new market opportunities that have been created by liberalization measures in developing and transitional countries (taken unilaterally or under structural adjustment programmes supported by the International Monetary Fund and the World Bank) should now encourage enterprises in these countries to give equal, if not greater importance, to the development of trade among themselves.

ANNEX

Tables on various market access commitments

Table 1   Pre- and post-Uruguay Round weighted averages of tariffs applicable to industrial products[a] in individual developed countries (in millions of US dollars and percentages)

Developed country	Trade-weighted tariff averages	
	Pre-Uruguay	Post-Uruguay
Developed countries	**6.3**	**3.8**
Australia	20.1	12.2
Austria	10.5	7.1
Canada	9.0	4.8
European Union	5.7	3.6
Finland	5.5	3.8
Iceland	18.2	11.5
Japan	3.9	1.7
New Zealand	23.9	11.3
Norway	3.6	2.0
South Africa	24.5	17.2
Sweden	4.6	3.1
Switzerland	2.2	1.5
United States	5.4	3.5

Source: WTO.
a/ Excluding petroleum.

Table 2   Pre- and post-Uruguay Round weighted averages of tariffs applicable to industrial products[a/] in selected developing countries (in millions of US dollars and percentages)

Developing country	Trade-weighted tariff averages	
	Pre-Uruguay	Post-Uruguay
Argentina	38.2	30.9
Brazil	40.6	27.0
Chile	34.9	24.9
Colombia	44.3	35.1
Costa Rica	54.9	44.1
El Salvador	34.5	30.6
India	71.4	32.4
Korea, Republic of	18.0	8.3
Malaysia	10.2	9.1
Mexico	46.1	33.7
Peru	34.8	29.4
Philippines	23.9	22.2
Romania	11.7	33.9
Singapore	12.4	5.1
Sri Lanka	28.6	28.1
Thailand	37.3	28.0
Turkey	25.1	22.3
Venezuela	50.0	30.9
Zimbabwe	4.8	4.6

Source: WTO.
a/ Excluding petroleum.

Table 3   Pre- and post-Uruguay Round weighted averages of tariffs applicable to industrial products[a] in individual transitional economy
countries
(in millions of US dollars and percentages)

Transitional economy country	Trade-weighted tariff averages	
	Pre-Uruguay	Post-Uruguay
Transitional economies	8.6	6.0
Czech Republic	4.9	3.8
Hungary	9.6	6.9
Poland	16.0	9.9
Slovak Republic	4.9	3.8

Source: WTO.
a/ Excluding petroleum.

Table 4   Increases in market access under minimum access opportunity commitments: selected products (in thousands of metric tons)

Product	Increases in access opportunities between period base and end of implementation period	
	Total	Selected sub-categories
Coarse grains	1,757	Maize (1,065); barley (552)
Rice	1,076	
Wheat	807	
Dairy products	729	Milk and cream (305); milk powder (147); cheese (132); whey powder (83)
Meat	421	Bovine meat (186); pigmeat (133); poultry (94)
Vegetables	355	Potatoes (197); onions, garlic (39); cabbages (32)
Sugar	292	
Eggs	252	
Fruits	130	Citrus (64); apples, pears, peaches, plums, cherries (28); bananas (13)
Oilcakes and oilseeds	126	
Vegetable oils	110	
Cotton	61	
Coffee	21	
Chocolate	19	

Source: WTO.

Notes:

1. Selected from schedules of commitments, which contain also commitments on additional products. Figures adjusted for base period imports.

2. Countries having provided for increases in quota levels from base levels include Austria, Canada, Colombia, Costa Rica, Czech Republic, El Salvador, European Communities, Finland, Guatemala, Hungary, Japan, Republic of Korea, Mexico, Morocco, New Zealand, Nicaragua, Philippines, Poland, Romania, Slovak Republic, South Africa, Switzerland-Liechtenstein, Thailand, United States and Venezuela.

3. As products are expressed at different stages of processing in the schedules, the totals given above are only indicative.

Table 5 **Reductions in domestic support to agricultural producers (in millions of US dollars)**

Participant	Base a/	Final	Reduction
Total	**197,721**	**162,497**	**18**
European Union	92,390	76,903	17
Japan	35,472	28,378	20
United States	23,879	19,103	20
Mexico	9,669	8,387	13
Canada	4,650	3,720	20
Finland	4,186	3,349	20
Poland	4,160	3,329	20
Korea, Republic of	4,086	3,543	13
Switzerland	3,769	3,016	20
Sweden	3,429	2,743	20
Austria	2,534	2,027	20
Norway	2,247	1,797	20
Venezuela	1,305	1,131	13
Brazil	1,053	912	13
Thailand	866	745	13
Czech Republic	717	574	20
Israel	654	569	13
New Zealand	210	268	20
Hungary	613	490	20
Australia	460	368	20
Slovak Republic	435	348	20
Colombia	398	345	13
Iceland	222	177	20
Cyprus	127	110	13
Morocco	93	81	13
Tunisia	76	66	13
Costa Rica	18	16	13
South Africa	3	2	20

Source: WTO.
a/ Indicate subsidies granted in 1986 to 1988.

Table 6   Export subsidy reduction commitments by country (in millions of US dollars)

Participant	Export subsidies			Product composition of export subsidies
	Base	Final	Change	
European Union	13,274	8,496	- 36	Bovine meat (19%), wheat (17%), coarse grains (13%), butter (13%), other milk products (10%)
Austria	1,235	790	- 36	Live animals (45%), wheat (14%), bovine meat (13%), cheese (12%)
United States	929	594	- 36	Wheat (61%), skim milk powder (14%)
Poland	774	493	- 36	Meat preparations (39%), fruits and vegetables (21%)
Mexico	748	553	- 26	Sugar (76%), cereal preparations (21%)
Finland	708	453	- 36	Butter (25%), coarse grains (22%), other milk products (13%)
Sweden	572	366	- 36	Pigmeat (21%), wheat (21%), coarse grains (17%)
Canada	567	363	- 36	Wheat (47%), coarse grains (18%)
Switzerland	487	312	- 36	Other dairy products (65%)
Colombia	371	287	- 23	Rice (32%), cotton (20%), fruits and vegetables (23%)
South Africa	319	204	- 36	Fruits and vegetables (24%), cereal preparations (14%), wheat (13%), sugar (10%)
Hungary	312	200	- 36	Poultry meat (30%), pigmeat (26%), wheat (11%), fruits and vegetables (19%)
Czech Republic	164	105	- 36	Other milk products (38%), fruits and vegetables (10%)
Turkey	157	98	- 37	Fruits and vegetables (36%), wheat (23%)
New Zealand	133	0	- 100	Not available
Norway	112	72	- 36	Cheese (54%), pigmeat (19%), butter (12%)
Australia	107	69	- 36	Other milk products (32%), skim milk powder (27%), cheese (25%), butter (16%)
Brazil	96	73	- 24	Sugar (56%), fruits and vegetables (30%)
Slovak Republic	76	49	- 36	Other dairy products (19%), cereal preparations (13%), bovine meat (13%)

Table 6 (cont'd)

Participant	Export subsidies			Product composition of export subsidies
	Base	Final	Change	
Israel	56	43	- 24	Fruits and vegetables (59%), plants (22%), cotton (17%)
Indonesia	28	22	- 24	Rice (100%)
Iceland	25	16	- 36	Sheepmeat (78%), other dairy products (22%)
Cyprus	19	14	- 24	Fruits and vegetables (67%), alcohol (16%)
Uruguay	2	1	- 23	Rice (83%), butter (12%)

Source: WTO.

Notes:

1. Commitments converted to US dollars using 1990-91 average exchange rates. Reduction commitments apply to individual product categories as defined in this table.

2. Participants having submitted schedules which do not maintain export subsidies include: Algeria, Antigua and Barbuda, Argentia, Bahrain, Barbados, Belize, Bolivia, Brunei Darussalam, Cameroon, Chile, Congo, Costa Rica, Côte d'Ivoire, Cuba, Dominica, Dominican Republic, Egypt, El Salvador, Fiji, Gabon, Grenada, Gambia, Ghana, Guatemala, Guyana, Honduras, Hong Kong, India, Jamaica, Japan, Kenya, Korea, Kuwait, Macau, Malaysia, Malta, Mauritius, Morocco, Namibia, Nicaragua, Nigeria, Pakistan, Paraguay, Peru, Philippines, Saint Kitts and Nevis, Saint Lucia, Saint Vincent and the Grenadines, Senegal, Singapore, Sri Lanka, Suriname, Swaziland, Thailand, Trinidad and Tobago, Tunisia, Zambia and Zimbabwe. Least developed countries are exempt from export subsidy reduction commitments.

PART THREE

INTERNATIONAL RULES
GOVERNING TRADE IN SERVICES

CHAPTER 14

General Agreement on Trade in Services (GATS)

Summary of the main rules

*Trade in services is growing and currently ac-
counts for over 20% of all international trade. The
General Agreement on Trade in Services (GATS),
which has been negotiated in the Uruguay Round,
applies the basic rules on trade in goods to trade in
services. However, the rules have been suitably
modified to take into account the differences between
goods and services and the four modes in which
international trade in services takes place.*

The GATS consists of:

• *A framework of rules; and*

• *Liberalization commitments specific to the service sectors and sub-sectors listed in each country's schedule.*

*The framework of rules requires countries to
apply MFN treatment by not discriminating between
service products and service providers of different
countries. However, it may be possible for a country
to maintain for a transitional period of 10 years*

measures that are not consistent with the MFN principle. The national treatment principle, as embodied in the framework of rules, visualizes that countries should not treat foreign services and service providers less favourably than their own service products and service providers. While the framework does not impose a binding obligation, it requires countries to indicate in their schedule of concessions the sectors in which and the conditions subject to which such national treatment is to be extended.

Among the other important provisions of the framework of rules are those which:

* *Require member countries to ensure transparency in the regulations applicable to service industries and activities;*

* *Aim at ensuring the increasing participation of developing countries in trade in services.*

1. General

The term "services" covers a wide range of economic activities. The WTO secretariat has divided these divergent activities into the following 12 sectors:

❑   Business (including professional and computer) services;

❑   Communication services:

❑   Construction and engineering services;

❑   Distribution services;

❑   Educational services;

❑   Environmental services;

❑   Financial (insurance and banking) services;

❑   Health services;

❑   Tourism and travel services;

❑   Recreational, cultural and sporting services;

❑   Transport services;

❑   Other services not included elsewhere.

These 12 sectors have been further divided into 155 sub-sectors (see Appendix IV for a listing).

I. FOUR MODES IN WHICH THE SERVICE TRADE TAKES PLACE

2. Difference between goods and services

How do services differ from goods? One of the main characteristics of services is that they are intangible and invisible; goods by contrast are tangible and visible. Furthermore, services, unlike goods, cannot be stored.[22] These differences between services and goods were vividly highlighted by *The Economist* when it asserted that "anything sold in trade that could not be dropped on your foot" is a service.[23]

3. Four modes of international service transactions

The different characteristics of goods and services also influence the modes in which international transactions take place. While international trade in goods involves the physical movement of goods from one country to another, only a few service transactions entail cross-border movements. Examples of cross-border transactions are services that can be transmitted by telecommunications (e.g. transfer of money through banks) or services embodied in goods (e.g. a consultant's technical report or software on a diskette).

In the bulk of service transactions, however, *their time and place of consumption* cannot be separated and proximity between the service supplier and the consumer is required. Such proximity can be established through a *commercial presence* in the importing country (for instance by setting up a branch or subsidiary company) or the movement of *natural persons* for temporary periods (e.g. lawyers or architects moving to another country to provide their services). The nature of a few service transactions requires consumers to move to the country

---

22 The above description is not without limitations. Some services are visible (for example, a consultant's report on diskette). Some services are stored (for example, the telephone answering system).

23 As quoted in: *Liberalizing International Transactions in Services, A Handbook* (United Nations publication, Sales No. E.94.II.A.11), page 1.

where the services are available (e.g. tourists visiting countries of tourist interest or students going to another country for higher education).

Thus, unlike international transactions in goods which require a physical transit across a country's borders, services are supplied internationally according to one or a combination of four modes of supply, namely:

❑   Cross-border movement of service products;

❑   Movement of consumers to the country of importation;

❑   The establishment of a commercial presence in the   country where the service is to be provided; and

❑   Temporary movement of natural persons to another country, in order to provide the service there.

The total value of services traded through the last two modes is probably much greater than that of the trade in services taking place through the first two modes. However, the lack of statistics makes any concrete estimate difficult to make.

4.   How protection is granted in the service sectors

Another major difference between goods and services lies in the way protection is granted by governments to domestic industries. Industries producing goods are generally protected by the imposition of tariffs or other border measures such as quantitative restrictions. As noted in Part I, the GATT rules require countries to give such protection through tariffs and discourage them from using quantitative restrictions or other similar restrictive measures. Because of the intangible nature of services and as many service transactions do not involve cross-border movements, protection to service industries cannot be granted through measures applicable at the border. Service industries are protected mainly by national domestic regulations on foreign direct investment and the participation of foreign service suppliers in domestic industries. Such regulations may, for instance, prohibit foreign service suppliers (e.g. bank or insurance companies) from investing in or establishing a branch that is necessary for the supply of services. Regulations may be applied on a discriminatory basis to natural persons providing services, thus treating them less favourably than domestic producers (non-application of the national treatment principle). They may also provide for dissimilar treatment of service suppliers from different countries (non-application of the MFN principle).

5.   The growing importance of international trade in services

Exports of services currently account for about $1 trillion or 20% of world exports. Although the share of developing countries in total exports of services is relatively small, as annex I reveals, a few of them are already among the world's 25 leading exporters. The export trade in services is rising in importance not only in the newly industrializing countries (NICs) but also in some low-income and least developed countries.

A large number of developing countries are currently heavily dependent on imports of services. The liberal import of services is steadily on the increase. The productivity of industries is today closely linked with the ready availability, at reasonable costs, of financial, computer and information services. Enterprises looking for markets in foreign countries have also to spend far more than they did in the past on market research and development, advertising and after-sales support.

The rapid technological progress that is taking place in communications is making it possible for suppliers, heretofore confined to domestic markets, to operate internationally. Banks and insurance companies can operate far more quickly and efficiently because of the development of fax, electronic mail and other facilities. Architects can provide their architectural designs and supervise work from thousands of miles away with the aid of up-to-date information technology. Likewise, consulting engineers can transmit computer-aided designs to customers in distant countries. International trade in services is therefore expected to expand rapidly and, according to some, may overtake trade in goods within the next 10 years.

II. GENERAL AGREEMENT ON TRADE IN SERVICES (GATS)

Prior to the Uruguay Round, trade in services was not subject to any discipline at the international level. The GATS, which was negotiated in the Round, takes a first major step towards bringing the trade gradually under international discipline.

6. Objectives

GATS, Preamble

The objectives of the GATS are similar to those of GATT. It aims at "promoting the economic growth of all trading partners and the development of developing countries" through the expansion of trade in services. It seeks to achieve this by applying to the service trade the rules of GATT, with the modifications necessary to take into account its special features.

7. Structure of GATS

The GATS consists of a framework which sets out:

☐ The general concepts, principles and rules that apply to measures affecting trade in services. The annexes, which establish principles and rules for specific sectors, complement the text.

☐ Specific commitments liberalizing trade within the service sectors and sub-sectors listed in the national schedules of member countries.

8. Framework text of GATS

8.1 Scope and main obligation

The GATS applies to government measures affecting services provided on a commercial basis. It thus covers both private-sector enterprises and companies owned (or controlled) by governments if they supply services on a commercial basis. Services obtained by government departments and agencies for their own use are excluded from the purview of the Agreement. The provisions of the Agreement on Government Procurement described in Part Four cover such transactions.

GATS, Article I:3

The term "services" covers any service in any service sector,[24] including their production, distribution, marketing, sales and delivery according to the four modes described in section I of this chapter.

GATS, Part II

The obligations which the framework imposes can be broadly divided into two categories. These are:

❑ General obligations, which apply to all service sectors;

❑ Conditional obligations applicable to sectors covered by commitments specified in the national schedules.

8.1.1 General obligations

Among the important general obligations imposed by the framework text are those relating to:

GATS, Article II

❑ The extension of MFN treatment;

GATS, Article III

❑ Transparency of regulations;

GATS, Article VII

❑ Mutual recognition of the qualifications required for the supply of services;

GATS, Articles VIII and IX

❑ Rules governing monopolies and exclusive service suppliers and other business practices restraining competition;

GATS, Article IV

❑ Measures to be taken to liberalize trade, including those securing the greater participation of developing countries.

---

24 According to the Annex on Air Transport, traffic and related rights are excluded from GATS coverage.

8.1.1.1   MFN treatment

GATS, Article II

The framework text imposes an obligation to apply MFN treatment:

☐   To service products; and

☐   To suppliers of services.

GATS, Article II, Annex on Article II Exemptions

The Agreement, however, provides that it may be possible for a country to maintain for a transitional period of 10 years measures that are not consistent with the rule by incorporating them in a list of exemptions. Box 30 explains the reasons that have prompted some 60 countries to list exemptions. These exemptions are temporary and the need for maintaining them is to be reviewed periodically after five years; they are to be abolished after 10 years.

Box 30

EXCEPTIONS TO THE MFN RULE

One objective of countries in making exceptions to the MFN principle is to maintain the preferential treatment they extend to some countries in the service sector under regional cooperation or other arrangements. Thus the Nordic countries have excluded from the MFN obligation measures promoting Nordic cooperation. These measures include guarantees and loans to Nordic investment projects and financial assistance to companies of Nordic origin for the utilization of environmental technology. The European Union has, by making an exception to the MFN rule, ensured that the benefits of special arrangements which its member States have with certain countries* would not be automatically extended to nationals of other countries. The arrangements provide for the grant of temporary work permits to these countries' nationals on the basis of contracts between a company in an EU State and service providers in these countries in service sectors such as construction, hotels and catering.

Some countries with liberal import regimes have made exceptions to the MFN rule in such sectors as financial and maritime services. Their aim is to maintain their bargaining leverage when negotiating for liberalization with countries that have more restrictive regimes.

* In Central, Eastern and South-Eastern Europe (including the Russian Federation, Ukraine and Georgia) and in the Mediterranean basin.

From then on, the MFN rule will, in principle, apply unconditionally to trade in services, as it does to trade in goods.

8.1.1.2 Transparency: establishment of enquiry and contact points

GATS, Article III:4

Foreign suppliers often find it difficult to do business with firms in outside countries because of the rules and regulations applicable there. The lack of transparency of such rules poses even more serious problems in the service sectors where domestic regulations are the main means used to protect domestic producers from foreign competition. The Agreement therefore requires each member country to establish one or more *enquiry points* from which other member countries can obtain information on laws and regulations affecting trade in the service sectors of interest to their industries.

GATS, Article IV

In addition, in order to assist *service suppliers* in developing countries, the Agreement calls on developed country members to establish *contact points*. To obtain information from enquiry points, service enterprises will have to channel their requests through their national governments; requests for information from contact points can be made direct. The contact points are to be geared to providing information at the business level. In particular, the Agreement requires contact points to provide on request to service suppliers in developing countries information on:

❑   The availability of service technology;

❑   Commercial and technical aspects of the supply of services;

❑   Registering, recognizing and obtaining professional qualifications.

These enquiry and contact points are expected to be established within a period of two years from the entry into force of the Agreement, i.e. before 1 January 1997.

8.1.1.3 Mutual recognition of qualifications required for the supply of services

Companies or persons providing services have to obtain certificates, licences or other authorization entitling them to do business. Foreign suppliers often find it difficult to obtain such authorization because of differing regulatory requirements for educational qualifications and working experience. To overcome such difficulties, the Agreement urges its member countries to enter into bilateral or plurilateral arrangements for the mutual recognition of the qualifications required for obtaining authorization. It further provides that such mutual recognition systems should be open for accession by other member countries, if they can demonstrate that their domestic standards and requirements are comparable with those of the systems concerned.

8.1.1.4 Rules governing monopolies, exclusive service suppliers and other business practices restraining competition

Service industries often exercise monopoly powers in the domestic market; exclusive rights to supply services are sometimes given by governments to a small number of suppliers. In all such cases, members are under obligation to ensure that such suppliers do not abuse their monopoly or exclusive rights or act in a manner inconsistent with their general and specific obligations under the Agreement.

GATS, Article IX

The Agreement further recognizes that service suppliers could adopt practices that may distort competition and thereby restrain trade. Whenever a problem of this nature occurs, the affected member country has a right to request the member where the service supplier is situated for consultations with a view to eliminating such practices.

GATS, Article XIX

8.1.1.5 Liberalization commitments

The Agreement visualizes a continuous process of negotiations in WTO for the liberalization of trade in specified sectors. In addition, the Agreement itself provides that beginning "not later than five years from the date of entry into force of the WTO Agreement" (i.e. before 1 January 2000) a new round of negotiations should be held.

GATS, Article XVI

Market access commitments

In trade in goods, the liberalization commitments assumed by countries take the form of tariff bindings and the removal of measures (e.g. quantitative restrictions) applied at the border. Protection to domestic service industries is granted basically through domestic regulations and not through border measures. The Agreement therefore visualizes that commitments to liberalize *market access* should primarily take the form of modifications to domestic regulations for the purpose of providing increased market access both to service products and to providers of services in the four modes in which the service trade takes place. Such commitments could relate to:

❑   Maximum foreign ownership limitations: for instance, a maximum percentage limit on foreign shareholding or the total value of individual or aggregate foreign investment.

☐   Restrictions on the establishment of some kind of local representation.

☐   Limitations on the total number of service operations or on the total quantity of service output.

☐   Limitations on the total number of service personnel that may be employed in a particular service sector.

☐   Restrictions on the ability of service suppliers to choose the business form (e.g. company, partnership) in which they want to operate.

☐   Limitations on the overall number of service suppliers allowed to operate in the market, because of a quota system or a monopoly situation.

GATS, Articles XVII, XVIII

National treatment commitments

Differences in the way protection is granted to manufacturing industries and service industries also limit the extent to which the national treatment principle, as embodied in GATT, can be applied to trade in services. The national treatment rule prohibits member countries from imposing internal taxes on, or applying domestic regulations to, an imported product, which in the first case are higher and in the second case more rigorous than those applicable to a similar domestic product, after the import has entered the country on payment of customs duties and other charges payable at the border. The rule is intended to ensure that, in practice, the domestically produced product does not obtain protection higher than that resulting from the levy of tariffs. Since countries do not impose tariffs on imports of services, the application of the national treatment principle, by requiring countries to apply their national regulations on the same basis to domestic and foreign suppliers, would have resulted in the sudden loss by domestic service industries of their entire protection. In the event, it was agreed that the national treatment principle should be extended by countries through negotiations during which they would indicate the sectors or sub-sectors and the conditions and qualifications under which they would be prepared to extend such treatment.

GATS, Article IV

8.1.1.6 Increasing the participation of developing countries in trade in services

The Agreement further recognizes that there is *asymmetry* in the development of service industries in developed and developing countries and that this situation will have to be taken into account in the negotiations for the liberalization of trade in the service sector. To assist developing countries in the development of their service industries, it provides for a three-pronged approach.

First, it calls on countries to give priority to the liberalization of access in the modes of supply and service sectors of export interest to developing countries.

Second, it recognizes that in order to promote the growth of their service industries, developing countries may have to maintain higher levels of protection, both overall and in individual sectors. It therefore provides that these countries should have the *flexibility* to open fewer sectors to import competition and to liberalize fewer types of transaction.

Third, it provides that, while making commitments for liberalization, developing countries could impose conditions requiring foreign suppliers wishing to invest in the service industry and to establish a subsidiary (or other types of commercial presence) in their territory:

❑   To set up joint ventures;

❑   To provide the local company access to their technology and/or access to their information and distribution channels.

GATS, Article XX

8.1.1.7   Schedules of commitments

The commitments assumed by countries are listed in each country's schedule of commitments. The extent and conditions to which and under which the basic principles of GATS — market access, national treatment and MFN treatment — apply to individual service sectors in any country can be assessed only by referring to that country's schedule, the character of the existing regulatory regime and the nature of the limitations, if any, to which the commitments are subject.

The schedules are complex as they cover 12 sectors and 155 sub-sectors. For each sub-sector, the commitments are further listed according to the four modes in which the service trade takes place.

A detailed explanation of the nature and content of the commitments and their beneficial impact on trade is given later. At this point, it is appropriate to note the remaining important provisions of the framework text and of the annexes, which complement the text.

8.1.2 Conditional obligations and other provisions

As noted earlier, the Agreement imposes, in addition to the general obligations described above,[25] certain conditional obligations that aim at ensuring fuller implementation of the commitments assumed by countries. In relation to *sectors where specific commitments are undertaken,* these include the following obligations:

GATS, Article VI:2 ❑ To ensure that all domestic regulations of general application affecting trade in services are administered in a reasonable and objective way;

GATS, Article VI: 3 ❑ To issue to foreign suppliers the authorization required for the provision of services within a reasonable period;

GATS, Articles XI, XII ❑ Not to apply restrictions on international transfers and payments, except when the country is in serious balance-of-payments difficulties.

8.1.3 Other provisions

Box 31 summarizes the remaining provisions.

8.1.4 Annexes to the Agreement

When the Uruguay Round negotiations were being concluded, it was visualized that it might not be possible to complete the negotiations on trade liberalization in a number of sectors. It was therefore decided to complement the framework text with annexes, which lay down additional rules on *sectoral*

---

25 The obligations which the rules on monopolies (GATS, Article VIII) and on increasing the participation of developing countries (GATS, Article IV) lay down can be considered conditional obligations even though they are listed under Part II of GATS *(General Obligations and Disciplines).*

Box 31

OTHER PROVISIONS IN THE GATS FRAMEWORK TEXT

The remaining provisions in the framework text can be broadly divided into two groups. In the first group are the areas for which the text provides that negotiations should take place. In the second group are provisions granting exceptions to the general rules.

A. Provisions on further negotiations

The framework text provides that member countries should undertake further negotiations to develop rules governing the use of *subsidies* and the application of *safeguard measures* to trade in services.

B. Provisions providing for exceptions

Economic integration. The Agreement permits countries to enter into arrangements for liberalizing trade among a limited number of countries, provided substantial service sectors are covered and the other conditions prescribed are met.

Balance-of-payments restrictions. Member countries are permitted to impose restrictions on transfer of payments, even in sectors in which they have undertaken specific commitments, when they are in balance-of-payments difficulties.

Labour market integration. The Agreement does not prevent a member country from entering into an arrangement with another country for full integration of their labour markets by exempting each other's citizens from work permit requirements.

General and security exceptions. As with trade in goods, the Agreement does not prevent countries from taking measures which they consider necessary for the protection *inter alia* of public morals; human, animal and plant life; or their essential security interests.

---

specifications and provide guidelines for the continuation of negotiations for further liberalization. These annexes,[26] which constitute an integral part of GATS, cover:

---

[26] While the first four annexes deal primarily with sectoral specifications, the last two provide guidelines for further negotiations.

❑   Financial services;

❑   Movement of natural persons;

❑   Telecommunications;

❑   Basic telecommunications;

❑   Maritime transport;

❑   Air transport.

The negotiations held after the the Uruguay Round on the further liberalization of the trade in financial services and the movement of natural persons were completed by the end of July 1995. Negotiations on basic telecommunications are expected to be completed before the end of June 1996.

Annex II to this chapter summarizes the main contents of these annexes to GATS.

III. NATURE AND CONTENT OF THE LIBERALIZATION COMMITMENTS

GATS, Articles XIX, XX

9.   Liberalization commitments

This section of the Guide describes the liberalization commitments made by countries in their national schedules. Broadly speaking, by including a service sector or a sub-sector in its national schedule, the country indicates that it will apply to trade in the sector market access and national treatment obligations. It is, however, open to a country to indicate the *limitations* under which it will grant market access or national treatment for *each of the four modes* in which international trade in services takes place. Such restrictions could be:

❑   Horizontal, covering the entire range of services; or

❑   Specific to the sector or activity in question.

Box 32 presents an example of a schedule of horizontal and specific commitments. Where no limitations are indicated against any mode of supply (i.e. the term "nonc" in the schedule), the country enters into a binding commitment not to take any new measures to restrict entry into the market or the operation of the service. Where limitations have been indicated against a particular mode of supply (such as when incorporation of a company is made a condition for carrying out a service activity), the country is obliged not to impose any other limitations that would further restrict the entry of foreign suppliers. Where, however, the term "unbound" appears under either horizontal or specific commitments, the country indicates that at least at that stage it maintains its freedom to modify its regulations and possibly to change the conditions of entry for foreign suppliers.

9.1   Horizontal commitments

Almost all limitations under horizontal commitments apply to services for which a commercial presence in the importing country is necessary, and to the movement of natural persons.

Broadly speaking, developed countries have not specified many horizontal limitations on the establishment of a commercial presence by foreign suppliers. The creation of a subsidiary company or a branch by a foreign supplier to carry out a service activity or to make an investment in the domestic service industry will therefore continue to be permitted under their existing legislations. These, as a rule, provide for the grant of authorization on liberal terms.

		Box 32 **FORMAT AND EXAMPLE OF A SCHEDULE OF HORIZONTAL AND SPECIFIC COMMITMENTS**	
Commitments	**Mode of supply**	**Conditions and limitations on market access**	**Conditions and qualifications on national treatment**
Horizontal commitments (i.e. across all sectors)	Cross-border supply	None	None, other than tax measures that result in difference in treatment of R & D* services.
	Consumption abroad	None	Unbound for subsidies, tax incentives, and tax credits.
	Commercial presence (FDI**)	Maximum foreign equity stake is 49%	Unbound for subsidies. Under Law x, approval is required for equity stakes over 25% and for new investment exceeding y million.
	Temporary entry of natural persons	Unbound except for the following: intra-corporate transfers of executives and senior managers; specialist personnel for stays of up to one year; specialist personnel subject to economic needs test for stays longer than one year; service sellers (sales people) for stays of up to three months.	Unbound, except for categories of natural persons referred to in the market access column.
Specific commitment: Architectural services	Cross-border supply	Commercial presence required	Unbound
	Consumption abroad	None	None
	Commercial presence (FDI)	25% of senior management should be nationals	Unbound
	Temporary entry of natural persons	Unbound, except as indicated under horizontal commitments	Unbound, except as indicated under horizontal commitments.

* R & D: Research and development   ** Foreign direct investment

However, in the majority of the Uruguay Round schedules, horizontal commitments relating to *the movement of natural persons* were largely limited to:

❑   Intra-company transfers covering "essential personnel", i.e. managers and technical staff linked with commercial presence in the host country; and

❑   Business visitors who are short-term visitors not gainfully employed in the host country.

One of the key demands of developing countries was that member countries should assume firm and legally binding commitments to permit independent professionals to work abroad without being required to establish a company or other form of commercial presence. In the Uruguay Round negotiations these demands were met in only a very few instances. As a result of further negotiations held after the conclusion of the Round, six members have improved their commitments. The European Union and its member States have guaranteed to varying degrees opportunities for foreign professionals without commercial presence to perform temporary assignments in 14 member States (excluding Portugal). The additional commitments of Switzerland and Norway are similar in nature but limited in scope. Canada has added a number of professions to its Uruguay Round commitments on the entry and temporary stay of foreign, contract-based professionals. Australia has introduced some flexibility to its existing offer on business visitors. India has improved some of its earlier commitments.

A number of developing countries have prescribed conditions which require foreign suppliers to establish joint ventures with domestic service industries. These conditions further limit in some cases the share in equity which foreign suppliers can hold. Some of these countries have taken advantage of the provisions in the Agreement for *increasing participation of developing countries* and have specified that approval of proposals to establish a *commercial presence* will be granted on the basis of such factors as *economic need* and the readiness of the foreign supplier to bring in the most up-to-date technology (see box 33 for details).

Box 33

NATURE OF LIMITATIONS IMPOSED BY DEVELOPING COUNTRIES IN THEIR HORIZONTAL COMMITMENTS PERMITTING THE ESTABLISHMENT OF COMMERCIAL PRESENCE

A number of developing countries have taken advantage of the provisions for increasing the participation of developing countries and have specified that permission to establish a commercial presence will be granted on the basis of economic need criteria to strengthen domestic service capacities. The conditions imposed for the attainment of this objective include the following:

- The establishment of commercial presence will be allowed on the basis of a joint venture;

- The foreign supplier will be permitted to have less than a majority share in the equity of such a joint venture;

- A specific number of board members must be nationals of the country;

- The foreign service supplier should use appropriate and advanced technology and managerial experience;

- It should train and pass on the benefit of technology to local employees;

- It should employ, wherever possible, domestic sub-contractors;

- It must furnish accurate and prompt reports on its operations, including technological, accounting, economic and administrative data.

9.2   Sectoral commitments

Commitments undertaken by countries in their sectoral schedules complement their horizontal commitments. While developed countries have included in their schedules all service sectors, developing countries have exercised a certain degree of flexibility and have covered a limited number of sectors, taking into account such factors as the stage of their development.

The type of limitation specified in the sectoral schedules relates to the characteristics of the service activity and the modes in which service transactions primarily take place. The paragraphs that follow explain the nature and content of the commitments undertaken and the limitations imposed in four sectors. These have been drawn, for the purpose of this Guide, from among the sectors in which developing countries are considered to have a potential for developing export trade or for benefiting from import liberalization:

❑   Construction and related engineering services;

❑   Health-related and social services;

❑   Management consultancy services;

❑   Financial services.

9.2.1   Construction and related engineering services

This sector covers:

❑   General construction work for buildings;

❑   General construction work for civil engineering;

❑   Installation and assembly work; and

❑   Building completion and other work.

The national schedules of 48 countries carry commitments in this sector.

Trade in the sector does not take place through cross-border movements or through the movement of consumers to places abroad. However, suppliers of construction engineering services are required to establish an office in the country where the services are to be provided. The competitiveness of most construction engineering companies in developing countries in regard to work in outside countries is greatly dependent on how far the latter countries permit technicians like masons and plumbers and other workers to stay for temporary periods.

As regards the right to establish a commercial presence in order to engage in construction engineering activities, all developed countries and a large number of developing countries have indicated in their schedules that they impose no limitations. In other words, they will apply to foreign companies the rules applicable to domestic suppliers in regard to the establishment of companies for the conduct of such activities. A few developing countries have, however, indicated that foreign suppliers wishing to engage in the construction business must establish a joint venture with domestic companies providing such services.[27]

As regards the movement of *natural persons*, all countries have specified that this mode of providing service is unbound. In other words, the countries have not undertaken any commitment to allow per-

---

[27] The countries which require foreign suppliers to establish joint ventures or some other type of operation involving domestic suppliers include India, Malaysia, Morocco, Pakistan, Thailand and Turkey.

sons below managerial level to enter the country to work on the basis of temporary contracts in the construction industry.

9.2.2 Health-related and social services

Only a limited number of countries have made commitments in this sector. This is partly due to the fact that, in many countries, such services are provided not by the private sector but by government or public hospitals. The sector covers the following:

- ❑   Hospital services,
- ❑   Other human health services,
- ❑   Social services.

As regards the right of foreigners to establish hospitals, both the European Union and the United States have indicated that such requests will be subject to *need-based quantitative limits* taking into account such factors as the number of beds in relation to the population of each region. Some developing countries have specified that the establishment of hospitals with foreign participation will be possible only on the basis of joint ventures with local participation.

Most countries have, however, specified that the movement of natural persons to provide such services is unbound. This means that they will continue to apply their existing regulations, which do not generally recognize as equivalent degrees and other professional qualifications obtained in other countries and thus do not permit foreigners holding such qualifications to work in hospitals as doctors, nurses or midwives, or to provide other health or social services.

9.2.3   Management consultancy services

Management consultancy services cover a wide range of activities such as general, financial, production, marketing and human resource consultancy services.

It is possible to provide such services across borders through communications facilities. However, for more effective servicing, commercial presence in the country where the service is to be provided is essential. Of the 45 countries that have included management consultancy services in their schedules, a large majority have bound the supply of such services without limiting supply on a cross-border basis or requiring the establishment of commercial presence. A few developing countries have, however, not bound the supply of service on a cross-border basis and have indicated that the establishment of a branch or office will be possible only on the basis of joint ventures with local consultancy firms. None of these countries have agreed to bind the supply of such services through the movement of natural persons. This means that the existing regulations which prohibit foreign suppliers from providing such services unless they have established a commercial presence in the country will continue to apply.

9.2.4   Financial services

Financial services cover a wide range of insurance, reinsurance and other insurance-related services as well as a host of banking and other financial services.

Negotiations in this sector for the further improvement of the commitments assumed in the Uruguay Round were held after the termination of the Round and were completed in July 1995. The new commitments assumed include:

❑   Improvements in the number of licences available for the establishment of foreign financial institutions;

❑   Guaranteed levels of foreign equity participation of branches, subsidiaries or affiliates of banks and insurance companies;

❑   Removal or liberalization of nationality or residence requirements for members of boards of financial institutions; and

❑   The participation of foreign-owned banks in cheque-clearing and settlement systems.

One of the features of the agreements reached is the non-participation of the United States in the arrangement covering financial services. The United States considered that the advantages which its banking and insurance industry would obtain in other countries were not commensurate with the benefits which industries in these countries would acquire in the United States as a result of the open and liberal policies it had been pursuing in this sector and the commitments offered by it. It therefore decided to withdraw its offers.

The arrangement reached on financial services is being implemented by all WTO member countries, with the exception of the United States, for an initial period ending 1 November 1997. Further negotiations are expected to take place (during the 60 days following that date) which may meet some of the concerns of the United States and facilitate its participation in the arrangement.

IV. BUSINESS IMPLICATIONS

10. Assessment of benefits

With the assumption of the commitments described above, countries have taken the first preliminary steps towards liberalizing international trade in services. Unlike trade in goods, it is however not possible to quantify the potential trade effects of liberalization in the service sector for two reasons. First, there is no equivalent of customs duties in the service sector. As protection is granted through domestic regulations which discriminate against foreign suppliers, the effect of such measures or their removal cannot easily be quantified. Second, at least at present, the comprehensive data needed to estimate the trade effects of liberalizing particular services under different modes of supply or even in aggregate terms do not exist. Preliminary steps have only recently been taken to collect such data on a systematic basis.

The practical difficulties of quantifying trade gains should not, however, lead one to ignore the fact that the liberalization commitments which countries have undertaken and the discipline which GATS imposes do provide service industries with new opportunities for trade. They can take advantage of these opportunities both as importers and as exporters.

10.1 Importance of service imports

The commitments which some developing countries have taken in the financial sector will lead to the establishment of more foreign banks, insurance companies and securities firms in these countries. As noted earlier, the efficiency and competitiveness of manufacturing industries as well as of agricultural producers depend greatly on the availability of services (banking, insurance and other services) and the existence of a telecommunications system and information infrastructure. In most developing countries, the growth of the service industries has, however, lagged behind that of the manufacturing sector. Furthermore, because of the high level of protection extended to the service sector, its level of efficiency is low. The development of an efficient and thriving service sector is, therefore, a high priority for many countries.

10.1.1 New opportunities for collaboration with foreign suppliers

In the circumstances, the commitments assumed by governments provide service industries in developing countries a new opportunity to collaborate with foreign service industries and to benefit from their technology. In negotiating collaborative arrangements, the industry can use as bargaining leverage the limitations imposed by their governments in their schedules of commitments. These, *inter alia,* specify that approval will be granted only if foreign service suppliers agree to bring in the most up-to-date technologies and to train local employees in their use.

10.1.2 Benefits of contact points

One of the major handicaps which service industries in developing countries suffer when entering into collaborative arrangements is their lack of knowledge of the commercial and technical aspects of the services and technologies they want to obtain. The GATS therefore provides for the establishment by developed countries of contact points from which such information can be obtained by interested service industries in developing countries. As noted earlier, these contact points are to be set up before the end of 1996.

10.2 New export opportunities

On the export side, developing countries are generally considered to have a comparative advantage in service sectors that are either labour intensive or require highly skilled technical personnel. The sectors or sub-sectors in which it may be possible for these countries to develop trade, taking into account the above two factors, are listed below:

❑   Business services, including management consultancy services, computer services, professional services, R & D services, rental services;

❑   Communications;

❑   Construction and engineering;

❑   Distribution;

❑   Educational services;

❑   Environmental services;

❑   Financial (insurance and banking) services;

❑   Health services;

❑   Tourism and travel services;

❑   Recreational, cultural and sporting services;

❑   Transport services.

10.2.1 The link of commitments with domestic legislation

The description on pages 278-282 of commitments in several sectors provides a broad idea of the nature and content of the commitments that countries have assumed in regard to services. However, the commitments relate only to certain aspects of domestic regulations. In order to assess their beneficial impact, it is necessary to examine them against the full background of the domestic regulations and rules applicable to the service sector in the countries giving the commitments. In some cases, the commitment may simply reaffirm or bind an existing practice, for instance, of giving approval to the establishment of a branch or a subsidiary company. In other cases, it may amount to accepting a new obligation.

For service suppliers interested in developing trade, the information contained in the schedules will therefore be of practical value only if they have all the relevant information on the domestic legislation, rules, regulations and practices forming the backdrop to such commitments. To assist service and other industries in obtaining such information, the GATS requires member countries to establish enquiry points. These should provide information on the laws and regulations applicable to the service sector.

10.2.2 Increased opportunities for natural persons to provide services

In some sectors, the competitive advantage of a number of developing countries, particularly NICs, arises from the existence of a vast pool of technically qualified people. Many skill-intensive services are provided through the temporary movement of natural persons to the countries where the service is provided. The horizontal commitments which countries have assumed in recently concluded negotiations on the movement of natural persons will now provide new opportunities for technically and professionally qualified persons to provide such services, without having to establish an office or other form of commercial presence.

10.2.3 Importance of adopting a juridical personality

It is important to note that in their horizontal and sectoral commitments a number of countries have indicated the conditions they currently apply when permitting their companies to employ for temporary periods the services of foreign technicians and specialists. While these commitments open up only limited opportunities, knowledge of the conditions imposed should enable foreign companies to take full advantage of them. The commitments often indicate that approval will be granted if the local company enters into a contract with a legally constituted foreign business enterprise to obtain the services of a specialist. It will therefore be desirable for persons interested in providing such services to organize themselves into a company or partnership rather than to act as individuals or loosely formed groups.

10.2.4 Opportunities for the expansion of trade among developing countries

Lastly, the commitments assumed by developing countries have opened up new opportunities for the expansion of South-South trade in services through the establishment of joint ventures and other collaborative arrangements especially on a regional basis. Apart from promoting South-South trade, regional consortia have a larger potential to compete with industrialized countries in bidding for service contracts. Such consortia can offer an impressive range of skills and experience, thus enhancing their image and underlining their competence, particularly in relation to work in their own region.

ANNEX I

Leading exporters and importers in the world trade in services, 1993

Rank	Exporters	Value ($ billion)	Share (%)	Annual change in value in 1993	Rank	Importers	Value ($ billion)	Share (%)	Annual change in value in 1993
1	United States	167.5	16.4	4	1	United States	113.4	11.5	8
2	France	100.8	9.9	-2	2	Germany	111.9	11.3	-3
3	Germany	61.8	6.1	-8	3	Japan	100.7	10.2	3
4	Italy	59.0	5.8	-8	4	France	83.3	8.4	-1
5	United Kingdom	53.5	5.2	-5	5	Italy	58.8	5.9	-16
6	Japan	53.2	5.2	7	6	United Kingdom	44.4	4.5	-5
7	Netherlands	37.0	3.6	1	7	Netherlands	35.9	3.6	-2
8	Belgium-Luxembourg	36.7	3.6	2	8	Belgium-Luxembourg	32.3	3.3	-3
9	Spain	31.7	3.1	-12	9	Canada	27.1	2.7	1
10	Austria	29.7	2.9	-1	10	Taiwan Province (China)	21.3	2.2	11
11	Hong Kong	28.9	2.8	16	11	Austria	21.1	2.1	6
12	Singapore	20.8	2.0	11	12	Spain	19.3	1.9	-13
13	Switzerland	19.7	1.9	0	13	Switzerland	16.8	1.7	-6
14	Canada	16.7	1.6	3	14	Korea, Rep. of	16.5	1.7	13
15	Korea, Rep. of	15.4	1.5	20	15	Hong Kong	16.0	1.6	9
16	Mexico	14.3	1.4	6	16	Saudi Arabia	13.9	1.4	-8

Rank	Exporters	Value ($ billion)	Share (%)	Annual change in value in 1993	Rank	Importers	Value ($ billion)	Share (%)	Annual change in value in 1993
17	Taiwan Province (China)	13.8	1.4	29	17	Norway	13.9	1.4	-6
18	Denmark	12.8	1.3	-14	18	Sweden	13.6	1.4	-30
19	Norway	12.6	1.2	-6	19	Australia	13.1	1.3	-5
20	Sweden	12.6	1.2	-21	20	Thailand	11.8	1.2	20
21	Thailand	11.2	1.1	17	21	China	11.6	1.2	26
22	China	10.9	1.1	21	22	Singapore	11.5	1.2	14
23	Australia	10.9	1.1	3	23	Mexico	11.2	1.1	-3
24	Turkey	9.4	0.9	13	24	Denmark	10.0	1.0	-7
25	Greece	8.5	0.8	-1	25	Indonesia	8.8	0.8	11
26	Egypt	7.4	0.7	1	26	Brazil	8.7	0.8	36
27	Philippines	6.9	0.7	2	27	Malaysia	8.3	0.8	8
28	Portugal	6.8	0.7	19	28	Israel	7.2	0.7	12
29	Israel	6.2	0.6	5	29	Finland	6.4	0.6	-15
30	Malaysia	5.9	0.6	7	30	Portugal	5.5	0.6	20
	Total of above	883.0	86.5	-		Total of above	874.4	88.3	-
	WORLD		100.0	1		WORLD	990.0	100.0	0

ANNEX II

Summary of the main provisions of the annexes to GATS

Annex on Movement of Natural Persons Supplying Services under the Agreement

This annex specifies that natural persons who are themselves service suppliers or employed by a service supplier shall be allowed to provide services in accordance with the *specific commitments* given by countries relating to the entry and temporary stay of such persons.

Annex on Financial Services

The annex applies to insurance- and reinsurance-related services, banking and other financial services. It emphasizes that the provisions of GATS should not prevent countries from taking measures for *prudential reasons* (e.g. for the protection of investors, depositors or policyholders or to ensure the integrity and stability of the financial system).

Annex on Telecommunications

This annex requires each member country to provide all service suppliers — foreign or domestic — access to any public telecommunications transport network and service offered within or across its borders for the supply of a service included in its schedule. It further requires countries to accord MFN and national treatment to all foreign service suppliers seeking access to, and the use of, public telecommunications transport networks and services. However, it does not require such treatment for cable or broadcast distribution of radio and television programming. Service suppliers are permitted to use their own equipment and operating protocols, provided they comply with certain technical specifications. Developing countries may impose *reasonable* conditions to strengthen their domestic telecommunications infrastructures and to increase their participation in the international trade in telecommunications services. However, such conditions must be specified in the country's GATS schedule, making them more transparent and subject to future negotiations.

Annex on Negotiations on Basic Telecommunications

Negotiations for the liberalization of basic long-distance and international telecommunications services were being held at the time of the preparation of this Guide in accordance with the guidelines in the annex and the related decision. These are expected to be completed by 30 April 1996.

Annex on Negotiations on Maritime Transport Services

In the case of maritime services (international shipping, auxiliary services, and access to and use of port facilities), negotiations will continue until June 1996, at which time WTO members will implement the results of the negotiations and other actions recommended in the final report of the negotiating group. In the meantime the GATS does not apply to the sector, nor is it necessary to list MFN exemptions. Until the date on which the results of the negotiations take effect, members may improve, modify or withdraw commitments without offering compensation.

PART FOUR

GOVERNMENT PROCUREMENT AND STATE TRADING

CHAPTER 15

Government procurement

Summary of the main rules

*The rules of GATT specifically exempt purchases made by governments and the agencies controlled by them from the **national treatment rule**. Government agencies importing their requirements are also not obliged to extend **MFN treatment** to external suppliers of such products but only to give them **fair and equitable treatment**. These provisions permit purchasing agencies to buy their requirements, if they so wish, from domestic producers, even though products of comparable quality are offered for sale by foreign suppliers at lower prices.*

The Agreement on Government Procurement that was negotiated in the Tokyo Round required its member countries to accord national and MFN treatment to government purchases. The obligation to extend such treatment applied to purchases made by the government agencies listed by each member country in the annexes to the Agreement. These annexes formed an integral part of the Agreement. The Agreement further required the listed agencies to make their purchases by inviting tenders, in which foreign suppliers should have a fair and equitable opportunity to participate.

The Tokyo Round Agreement, which applied to trade in goods, was extensively revised and broadened in the Uruguay Round to cover government purchases of services.

The new Agreement on Government Procurement is, however, plurilateral and, unlike the multilateral agreements described in the preceding chapters of this Guide, WTO member countries are not obliged to join it. The Agreement's current members are predominantly developed countries. Only two developing countries/areas — Hong Kong and the Republic of Korea — have so far acceded to it.

1.   General

In almost all countries, governments and the agencies controlled by them are significant buyers of goods and services. Such purchases often represent 10% to 15% of a country's gross national product. The international trade in government-purchased products and services is steadily on the increase and currently amounts to several billion dollars.

2.   Historical background to the evolution of rules

The international rules governing this trade are evolving. When GATT 1947 was being negotiated, almost all countries required their government departments and agencies to accord price preferences to domestic producers and to buy foreign goods only if the domestic prices were higher (by, say, 10% to 15%) than the prices of imported products. In addition, where goods were imported, purchasing agencies were often obliged to buy from suppliers in countries with which their governments had close trade relations or political ties.

The practice of giving price preferences was not consistent with the national treatment principle which, as has been noted, does not permit imported products to be treated less favourably than products of domestic origin. Likewise, obliging purchasing agencies to obtain their imports only from a limited number of designated countries was not in conformity with the principle of non-discrimination embodied in the MFN rule.

As countries were not prepared at that time to change these practices, the GATT rules specifically exclude *procurement by government agencies of goods for their own use* and not intended for com-

GATT 1994, Article III, 8(a)

GATT 1994, Article XVII, 2

mercial sale from the application of the national treatment rule. The rules also do not require countries to extend MFN treatment to sources of products imported by government agencies for their own use. They are merely asked to extend fair and equitable treatment to such suppliers.

3.   The Agreement on Government Procurement

Policies which require government purchasing agencies to buy locally, even though foreign goods are available at lower prices, increase government expenditure and add to the burden on tax payers. These considerations, among others, led GATT member countries to negotiate in the Tokyo Round an Agreement on Government Procurement. This Agreement, which applied only to goods, was extensively revised and broadened to cover purchases by governments of services during the parallel negotiations that took place during the Uruguay Round.

3.1   Aim of the Agreement

Agreement on Government Procurement (GP), Preamble

The main aim of the Agreement on Government Procurement is to require governments to apply commercial considerations when procuring goods and services for their own use by not discriminating between domestic and foreign supplies and thus to utilize tax revenues and other public funds more effectively. It is, however, a plurilateral agreement and, unlike the multilateral agreements discussed earlier, does not oblige WTO members to accede to it. Its current membership is dominated by developed countries, with only two developing countries/areas — Hong Kong and the Republic of Korea — on the roster.

3.2 Coverage of the Agreement

The obligations which the Agreement imposes apply only to purchases made by the *procurement entities* that have been listed by each member country in its annexes. These annexes are an integral part of the Agreement. The entities listed include:

GP, Article I and Appendix I

☐ Ministries, departments and other central government offices;

☐ Sub-central organizations such as municipalities, corporations and other local bodies;

☐ In the case of federal States, government departments and agencies at provincial and State level;

☐ Public utilities supplying electricity and drinking water, and running airports, ports and urban transport.

It is open to member countries to specify in the annexes the products and services to be covered by the Agreement. In regard to goods, member countries have broadly indicated that the Agreement will apply to all purchases by the listed entities. The only exceptions are purchases by departments of defence of defence requirements; purchases made by such departments of non-defence requirements are, however, covered.

While the Agreement therefore applies to almost all contracts awarded by the government agencies concerned for the procurement of goods, only a beginning has been made in relation to purchases of services. All member countries have included construction services in the Agreement's coverage. Thus this service segment, on which governments spend a high proportion of their budgetary resources, has come under the Agreement's discipline. As regards other services, the rules of the Agreement apply only to those specified in each member country's annex. Among these are:

❏   Management consultancy and related services;

❏   Market research services;

❏   Computer and related services;

❏   Accounting and auditing services;

❏   Advertising services;

❏   Building cleaning services;

❏   Publishing and printing services.

3.3 Substantive provisions

GP, Article III

The Agreement's most important obligation requires purchasing entities to extend to imported *products, services and suppliers* national and MFN treatment. The first prevents them from giving price or other preferences to domestic suppliers; the second prohibits them from discriminating among outside supplying countries.

3.4 Operational provisions

In order to ensure the implementation of these substantive obligations and to provide fair and equitable opportunities for trade to interested domestic and foreign suppliers, the Agreement lays down a number of procedural rules. In particular, it requires entities making purchases above specified *threshold limits:*

GP, Articles VII to XVI

❏   To do so only by inviting tenders;

❏   To ensure that foreign suppliers have a fair and equitable opportunity to participate in the tendering process; and

❑   To award the contract to the tenderer who has been determined to be fully capable of undertaking the contract and whose tender "is either the lowest tender or which in terms of the specific evaluation criteria set forth in the notice is determined to be most advantageous".

Box 34 explains the various methods that can be used in inviting tenders and the conditions for their use.

3.5   Greater public scrutiny of award decisions

In the area of government procurement, it is not uncommon to hear complaints that contracts involving huge amounts have been awarded to a tenderer with the right political connections. Allegations are also often heard that contracts have been awarded to domestic or foreign firms that have made clandestine payments to the persons responsible for making award decisions. The Agreement visualizes bringing such malpractices under control by providing for greater public scrutiny of decisions to award contracts. It therefore requires purchasing entities to publish:

GP, Article XVIII

❑   A post-award notice stating the nature and quantity of the product or services covered by the contract;

❑   The name and address of the winning tenderer;

❑   The value of the winning award; and

❑   The highest or lowest offer that was taken into account in the award of the contract.

Box 34

RULES ON GOVERNMENT TENDERING PROCEDURES

The Agreement requires that, in order to provide fair and equal commercial opportunities to domestic and foreign suppliers and at the same time ensure efficient and expedient procurement, government purchasing entities should make their purchases by inviting tenders. These entities have an option to use one of the following three methods:

- Open tenders, under which all interested suppliers may submit a tender;

- Selective tendering procedures, under which only suppliers who have been identified as having the necessary qualifications are invited to tender; and

- Limited tendering procedures, under which in certain special circumstances purchases are made through direct negotiations with identified suppliers.

For tenders under selective procedures, enterprises generally maintain a list of *qualified* suppliers. The Agreement stipulates that in qualifying suppliers, the purchasing entities:

- Should not discriminate between foreign and domestic suppliers;

- Should impose only such conditions in regard to technical qualifications, financial guarantees, and establishing the commercial capability of suppliers as are necessary to ensure the firm's competence to fulfil the contract; and

- Should allow suppliers to apply at any time for qualification.

The Agreement provides that limited tendering systems should be used only in special situations such as:

- When no tenders are received in response to an open and selective tender;

- When the tenders submitted have been collusive;

- When additional deliveries of replacement parts are required from a supplier whose tender has been accepted.

Further, in order to ensure adequate transparency in the invitations to tender, the Agreement requires member countries to notify WTO of the list of publications in which invitations to tender are publicized.

In addition, if an unsuccessful bidder requests it, the purchasing entity is required to give the bidder its reasons for both the rejection and the selection.

3.6　Challenge procedures

GP, Article XX

The Agreement also calls on its member countries to establish at the national level an *independent* review body to hear *challenges* or complaints and requests for redress from domestic or foreign suppliers against a purchasing entity which in their view has not adhered to the rules of the Agreement in awarding a contract. The procedure for investigating such challenges should, *inter alia,* provide for:

❑　Interim measures to correct breaches of the Agreement's rules, including measures which may result in the suspension of the procurement process; or

❑　Payment of compensation to the challenging tenderer, which may be limited to the costs of preparing the tender or the challenge.

In addition, when the government of the country where the foreign supplier is situated is satisfied that the rules of the Agreement have not been followed by the entity in awarding the contract, it can invoke WTO dispute settlement procedures.

3.7　Special provisions for developing countries

GP, Article V

As noted earlier, only two developing countries/areas have so far acceded to the Agreement. The reasons for the reluctance of developing countries to join the Agreement can generally be attributed to the apprehension that, on becoming a member, they will have to change their existing policies. These policies currently require their purchasing agencies to buy locally whenever possible and, when they are allowed to invite tenders from foreign suppliers, to give price preferences to domestic producers. Further, in order to promote the development of SMEs, domestic rules often oblige purchasing agencies to prefer SME products to those of large firms.

However, the Agreement does provide for special and differential treatment. This permits developing countries to negotiate for accession without being obliged to bring all their practices in conformity with the Agreement immediately on joining. They can stipulate, for instance, that the discipline of the Agreement should apply only to a specified number of purchasing agencies. Furthermore, they can negotiate for "exclusion from the rule of national treatment" certain products or services for which they wish to continue to extend price preferences to domestic producers by buying from them even though the prices quoted by foreign suppliers are lower.

Furthermore, to enable suppliers in developing countries that have become members of the Agreement to benefit fully from the opening of the government procurement market, each developed country is required to establish information centres from which information can be obtained on:

❏   Laws, regulations and practices relating to government procurement;

❏   Addresses of entities covered by the Agreement;

❏   Nature and volume of products or services procured, including available information on future tenders.

From the strictly legal point of view, requests for such information can be made only by members of the Agreement. In practice, however, most — if not all of these information centres may be willing to provide information to developing country members of WTO even though they may not have acceded to the Agreement itself. The Agreement further visualizes the establishment at an appropriate time in the future of an *international information centre*. As such a centre will provide information and assistance to interested suppliers in developing countries, the chances of its being set up will depend greatly on how many developing countries accede to the Agreement in the near future.

4.   Business implications

For industries and business enterprises in developing countries, government procurement provides a huge and growing market. The purchases of government agencies cover a wide range of products that are at present being exported by a number of developing countries (see box 35). With some organizational effort and assistance from governments and international agencies on how to comply with the tendering procedures of foreign purchasing agencies, it should be possible for suppliers from developing countries to compete in this important market segment. It is important to note that member countries of the Agreement on Government Procurement do not prevent suppliers from countries that are not members to tender against invitations issued by their purchasing agencies. The only country making an exception to this rule is the United States. It prohibits its purchasing agencies from buying from non-member countries (other than those that are least developed).

Suppliers from developing countries are often handicapped by their inability to obtain information on invitations to tender issued by purchasing agencies in foreign markets. They may find of some

---

Box 35

**PRODUCTS PURCHASED BY GOVERNMENT AGENCIES
THAT CAN BE SUPPLIED BY ENTERPRISES
IN DEVELOPING COUNTRIES**

Textiles and clothing
Footwear
Office machines and data-processing equipment
Office furniture
Telecommunications equipment
Pharmaceuticals
Medical equipment
Food and food products
Sanitary, heating and lighting fittings
Motor vehicles
Electrical machinery
Paper, printing and publishing products
Rubber and plastic products
Cleaning materials and equipment

---

help the list given in appendix V of the publications in which such notices are posted by member countries of the Agreement. In addition, it may be possible for them to obtain additional information on the laws and regulations applicable to such purchases from the information centres listed in appendix VI.

It will be in the interest of individual countries that are not members of the Agreement to require government purchasing agencies to adopt procedures for inviting tenders and awarding contracts that are similar to those laid down by the Agreement. For governments, this can lead to reductions in costs and budgetary expenditures. For industry and business, it will provide an assurance that contracts will be awarded on the basis of criteria that are fair and objective.

The basic aim in adopting such procedures should be to prepare the country gradually to accede to the Agreement. In the initial years, however, it may not be possible for the government to throw open its entire government procurement market to foreign competition. In that situation, the procedures should provide for the following:

☐ The decision not to open tendering to foreign participation should be taken on a case-by-case basis; and

☐ Where foreign participation is permitted, the tendering notice should clearly indicate whether domestic suppliers are to be given a price preference and, if so, the quantum of such preference.

The disclosure of information on price preferences will help foreign suppliers in deciding whether to tender or not. It will also help governmental authorities in assessing the costs and benefits of requiring purchasing agencies to give preference to domestic producers, taking into account the aims and objectives of such a policy.

CHAPTER 16

State trading

Summary of the main rules

The GATT rules impose two main obligations on member countries in regard to State trading enterprises. First, they require these enterprises to conduct their business on the basis of commercial considerations. Second, in order to ensure transparency in the products imported and exported by such enterprises, they require member countries to notify the WTO secretariat of relevant information on their activities.

1.   General

Understanding on the Interpretation of Article XVII of GATT 1994, 1

Although with the increasing trend towards privatization, countries are reducing their reliance on State trading, it still continues to play an important role in at least some countries in the import and export of certain goods, particularly food and food products and commodities traded in bulk. State trading enterprises are broadly defined as:

> Governmental and non-governmental enterprises, including marketing boards, which have been granted exclusive or special rights or privileges, including statutory or constitutional powers, in the exercise of which they influence through their purchases or sales the level or direction of imports or exports.

State trading needs to be distinguished from government procurement, which is discussed in chapter 15. Under government procurement, the domestically produced or imported product is purchased by a government agency for its own use or consumption or for the production of goods or services for sale. In the case of State trading, imports are obtained primarily for sale in the home market and domestic products are purchased for sale in the home market and for export to foreign markets.

The GATT rules on State trading basically apply to State trading enterprises engaged in the import and export of goods.

2.   Main obligations

2.1   To conduct business in accordance with commercial considerations

GATT 1994, Article XVII:1

The basic obligation the GATT imposes on State trading enterprises is to require them to "act in a manner consistent with the general principles of non-discriminatory treatment". It states that, in practice, this can be achieved by:

❑   Making "purchases or sales solely in accordance with commercial considerations, including price, quality, availability and marketability, transportation and other conditions of purchase or sale"; and

❑   By affording adequate opportunity to enterprises in other countries to "compete for participation in such purchases and sales."

2.2   Transparency

The other major obligation under the Agreement is transparency. The notification obligations that the GATT imposes for this purpose have been further strengthened by the adoption of the Understanding on the Interpretation of Article XVII of GATT 1994 (State trading) in the Uruguay Round. The Understanding requires member countries to notify the Council for Trade in Goods of:

❑   State enterprises engaged in foreign trade;

❑   The products imported or exported by them; and

❑   Other information (given in accordance with a questionnaire) so as to permit a clear appreciation of the manner in which the enterprises conduct their trade.

Understanding on
Article XVII, 5

The notifications are to be reviewed by a working party established by the Council for Trade in Goods in accordance with the provisions of the Understanding. The deliberations of the working party are expected to result in the preparation of a compendium of State trading enterprises in different countries, the products which they import and export, and their relationship with their governments. The establishment of the working party will also enable member countries to exercise a greater degree of surveillance over the activities of these enterprises with a view to ensuring that in practice they conduct their business strictly in accordance with commercial considerations.

Understanding on Article XVII, 4

It is also open to a country to make a counter-notification to the Council for Trade in Goods when it considers that a State trading enterprise in another country has not met its notification obligation with respect to its State trading activities.

PART FIVE

TRADE-RELATED ASPECTS
OF INTELLECTUAL PROPERTY RIGHTS

CHAPTER 17

Agreement on trade-related aspects of intellectual property rights (TRIPS)

Summary of the main rules

*The development of international trade can be adversely affected if the standards adopted by countries to protect intellectual property rights (IPRs) vary widely from country to country. Furthermore, the lax or ineffective enforcement of such rights can encourage trade in counterfeit and pirated goods, thereby damaging the legitimate commercial interests of manufacturers who hold or have acquired those rights. The Agreement on Trade-Related Aspects of Intellectual Property Rights (TRIPS), negotiated in the Uruguay Round, therefore lays down **minimum standards for the protection** of intellectual property rights as well as the procedures and remedies for their enforcement. It establishes a mechanism for consultations and surveillance at the international level to ensure compliance with these standards by member countries at the national level.*

The structure of the Agreement is built on the existing international conventions dealing with IPRs. Its provisions apply to the following intellectual property rights:

- *Patents;*

- *Copyright and related rights;*

- *Trademarks;*

- *Industrial designs;*

- *Layout-designs of integrated circuits;*

- *Undisclosed information; and*

- *Geographical indications.*

In order to ensure that the rights available to patent holders are not abused, it provides for compulsory licensing. Compulsory licensing for the purpose of trade is, however, prohibited.

The Agreement also lays down procedures for consultations between governments when one party has reasons to believe that the licensing practices or conditions of an enterprise from another member country constitute an abuse of the Agreement or have adverse effects on competition.

The Agreement provides a transitional period of five years (i.e. up to 1 January 2000) for developing countries to bring their IPR legislation in conformity with the provisions of the Agreement. For least developed countries the transitional period is 11 years (i.e. up to 1 January 2006).

I. INTELLECTUAL PROPERTY RIGHTS (IPRs) AND THEIR IMPLICATIONS FOR INTERNATIONAL TRADE

1.   General

The objects of intellectual property are the creations of the human mind, the human *intellect,* thus the designation "intellectual property".

They include copyright, patents and industrial designs. Copyright relates to the rights of creators of literary, scientific, and artistic works. Patents give exclusive rights to inventors; however, inventions can be patented only if they are new, non-obvious and are capable of industrial applications. Industrial designs are new or original aesthetic creations determining the appearance of industrial products. These three rights are available for limited durations.

Intellectual property also includes trademarks, service marks and appellations of origin (or geographical indications). In the case of these property rights, the aspect of intellectual creation — although existent — is less prominent. However, protection is granted to trademarks and other signs to enable manufacturers to distinguish their products or services from those of others. Trademarks help manufacturers build consumer loyalty. They also assist consumers in making informed choices on the basis of the information provided by manufacturers about the quality of the product.

2.   Implications of IPRs for trade

Any unauthorized use of intellectual property constitutes an infringement of the right of the owner. Until about two decades ago, such infringements had implications largely for domestic trade. They were further considered to pose problems mainly at the national level which — apart from affecting the interests of the owners of rights — impinged on scientific progress and cultural life.

In recent years, however, there has been increasing realization that the standards adopted by countries to protect their IPRs as well as the effectiveness with which they are enforced have implications for the development of international trade. There are many reasons for this, of which three are especially worth noting.

First, industrial production in most industrialized countries is increasingly becoming research- and technology-intensive. As a result, their export products — both traditional (such as chemicals, fertilizers and pharmaceuticals) and comparatively new (telecommunications equipment, computers, televisions, videos) — now contain more patented high-technology and creative inputs. Manufacturers are therefore keen to ensure that wherever they market their products their patent rights are adequately protected to enable them to recoup their R & D expenditure.

Second, with the removal of restrictions on foreign investment by a large number of developing countries, new opportunities are emerging for the manufacture in these countries of patented products under licence or within joint ventures. The willingness of industries in industrialized countries to enter into such arrangements and to make their technology available, however, depends on how far the IPR system of the host country provides them an assurance that their property rights to technology will be adequately protected and not usurped by local partners making use of reverse engineering.

Third, the technological improvements in products entering international trade have been matched by technological advances that have made reproduction and imitation simple and cheap. In countries where laws on IPRs are not strictly enforced, this has resulted, as box 36 shows, in increased production of counterfeit and pirated goods, not only for sale in domestic markets but also for export.

3. WIPO conventions on IPRs

Efforts to develop rules providing adequate protection to intellectual property rights at the international level have been made for over a century, mainly under the auspices of the World Intellectual Property Organization (WIPO) and its predecessor organizations. As a result, a number of conventions

---

Box 36

TRADE IN COUNTERFEIT AND PIRATED GOODS

Estimates of revenue foregone by industries as a result of counterfeiting, pirating and other infringement of intellectual property rights vary widely, but there is no doubt that the value involved is significant.

Goods are treated as counterfeit when they are offered for sale particularly under well-known trademarks which the seller has no authority to use. These are generally labour-intensive products which, because of the reputation of the brand name, can be sold at high prices. They include clothing, shoes, watches, cosmetics, leather goods, and household and sporting goods.

Pirated goods are those that infringe copyright and related rights. Book publishers, producers of records, discs, films, tapes and cassettes are often the victims of violation of copyright and related rights. Technological progress has greatly facilitated the art of copying. The computer software industry is the leading victim of the speed with which intellectual property can be illegally copied and distributed on an international scale.

---

laying down international obligations to protect the rights of owners of IPRs have been adopted. Box 37 lists these conventions and indicates their coverage and main fields of application.

4.   Background to the negotiations

Proposals that action should be taken in GATT to bring under control the trade in counterfeit and pirated goods were made by developed countries as early as the Tokyo Round of negotiations. When the Uruguay Round was being launched, these countries proposed that the negotiations should not only cover trade in counterfeit goods but also aim at developing *minimum standards of protection* for adoption by member countries. While developing countries were in general not opposed to the proposals for action on counterfeit goods, they initially resisted discussion on minimum standards. They were apprehensive that such negotiations would require them to change their policies. For development and social reasons, these policies excluded certain products from patentability or provided shorter protection periods than the 20 years for which patent protection was generally granted by developed countries for inventions relating to such products as pharmaceuticals, chemicals, fertilizers, insecticides and pesticides. They were also fearful that the adoption of minimum standards would lead to increased royalty payments for the use of patented technology under licence and thus to higher prices for the products so manufactured.

These views, however, did not prevail and pressures from developed countries ultimately resulted in the negotiations focusing to a greater extent on the establishment of substantive and uniform standards providing a higher level of protection for

Box 37

INTELLECTUAL PROPERTY RIGHTS: INSTRUMENTS, SUBJECT MATTER, FIELDS OF APPLICATION AND RELATED WIPO AND OTHER INTERNATIONAL AGREEMENTS

Types of intellectual property rights	Subject matter	Main fields of application	Major international agreements
Types of instrument			
Industrial property	Patents	New, non-obvious, industrially applicable inventions	Manufacturing	Paris Convention; Patent Cooperation Treaty; Budapest Treaty.
	Utility models	Functional designs	Manufacturing	Paris Convention
	Industrial designs	Ornamental designs	Clothing, motor cars, electronics, etc.	Hague Agreement; Paris Convention; Locarno Agreement.
	Trade-marks	Signs or symbols to distinguish the goods and services of one enterprise from those of others.	All industries	Paris Convention; Madrid Agreement (international registration); Nice Agreement; Madrid Protocol (not yet in force); Trademark Law Treaty (not yet in force).
	Geo-graphical indications	Identification of the place of origin of goods indicative of the quality or other charac-teristics associated with the area.	Agricultural and food industries, notably the sectors for wine and spirits.	Lisbon Agreement; Madrid Agreement (false indications).
Literary and artistic property	Copyrights and neigh-bouring rights	Original works of authorship and related contributions from performers, producers of sound recordings, and broadcasting organizations.	Printing, entertainment (audio, video, motion pictures) software, broadcasting	Berne Convention; Rome Convention; Geneva Convention; Brussels Convention; Universal Copyright Convention.
Sui gene-ris protec-tion	Breeders' rights	New, stable, homo-genous, distinctive varieties	Agriculture and food industry	Union for the International Protection of New Plant Varieties (UPOV)
	Integrated circuits	Original layout designs	Micro-electronics industry	Washington Treaty (not yet in force)
Trade secrets		Secret business information	All industries	

Source: Carlos Braga, "Trade-Related Aspects of Intellectual Property Issues: The Uruguay Agreement and the Economic Implications" (World Bank conference paper, 26-27 January 1995).
Note: With the exception of UPOV, all treaties identified above are administered by WIPO. The Washington Treaty, not yet in force, has also been negotiated under WIPO auspices. The Rome Convention is administered jointly by WIPO, ILO and UNESCO. The Universal Copyright Convention is administered by UNESCO.

intellectual property rights. It is important to note in this context that the attitude of both developed and developing countries evolved as the negotiations proceeded. It was thus possible to reach a consensus on the Agreement on Trade-Related Aspects of Intellectual Property Rights which, among other things, lays down minimum standards for the protection of all main categories of intellectual property rights.

II. AGREEMENT ON TRADE-RELATED ASPECTS OF INTELLECTUAL PROPERTY RIGHTS (TRIPS)

5.   Structure of the Agreement

The TRIPS Agreement builds on the main international conventions on intellectual property rights by incorporating (by reference) most of their provisions. It further provides that countries may in pursuance of these conventions guarantee higher protection than is required by the TRIPS Agreement, as long as it does not contravene its provisions.

The main provisions of the Agreement can be divided into the following five groups:

❑   Basic principles and general obligations;

❑   Minimum standards of protection, including the duration of protection and the control of anti-competition practices in contractual licences;

❑   Restrictive business practices;

❑   Enforcement of intellectual property rights (court orders, customs actions, etc.);

❑   Transitional arrangements for the implementation of the rules at the national level.

5.1 Basic principles and general obligations

Agreement on Trade-Related Aspects of Intellectual Property Rights (TRIPS), Articles 3 and 4

The Agreement reaffirms the basic principle of national treatment embodied in the various intellectual property right conventions. In particular, it states that in regard to the "availability, acquisition, scope, maintenance and enforcement" of intellectual property rights foreign nationals shall not be accorded treatment that is less favourable than that accorded by a country to its own nationals. In addition countries are required to extend MFN treatment to foreign nationals by not discriminating among them.

5.2 Minimum standards including duration of protection

The Agreement breaks new ground by defining the main elements of protection, the rights to be conferred and the minimum term of protection for each of the following IPRs:

❑ Patents;

❑ Copyright and related rights;

❑ Trademarks;

❑ Industrial designs;

❑ Layout-designs of integrated circuits;

❑ Undisclosed information, including trade secrets.

❑ Geographical indications, including appellation of origin.

The Agreement also carries a section dealing with the control of anti-competition practices in contractual licences.

5.2.1 Patents

5.2.1.1 Definition and coverage

Patents provide property rights to inventions.[28] The Agreement provides that for an invention to be registered as a patent:

❑   It must be new;

❑   It must involve an inventive step; and

❑   It must be capable of industrial application.

TRIPS, Article 27 The Agreement further stipulates that countries shall grant patents for inventions in *all fields of technology* and for both:

❑   Products, and

❑   Processes, including those used in manufacturing the products.

Furthermore, patents are to be granted without discrimination as to place of invention and whether products are imported or locally produced.

The only products or processes which countries are permitted to exclude from patentability are:

❑   Diagnostic, therapeutic and surgical methods for the treatment of humans or animals;

❑   Plants and animals other than micro-organisms;

❑   Essentially biological processes for the production of plants and animals other than non-biological and microbiological processes.

---

28 "Invention" may be defined as a novel idea which permits in practice the solution of a specific problem in a field of technology.

However, where a country excludes plant varieties from patentability, it is expected to provide protection under a *sui generis* system. The system provided by the UPOV[29] Convention on the Protection of New Varieties of Plants can be used for that purpose. (See box 38.)

5.2.1.2   Rights of patent holders

TRIPS, Article 28

Patents give patent owners exclusive property rights; these allow them to prevent others from using the inventions covered. Manufacturers wish-

---

Box 38

CONVENTION FOR THE PROTECTION
OF NEW VARIETIES OF PLANTS

The objective of the UPOV Convention is to ensure that the member States acknowledge the achievements of breeders of plant varieties, by making available to them exclusive property rights on the basis of a set of uniform and clearly defined principles. To be eligible for protection, varieties have to be:

• Distinct from existing commonly known varieties;

• Sufficiently homogenous;

• Stable; and

• New in the sense that they must not have been commercialized.

Like all intellectual property rights, the rights of plant breeders are granted for a limited period of time, at the end of which the varieties protected by them pass into public domain. Authorization from the holder of the right is not required for the use of the protected variety in research, including its use in breeding further new varieties.

Note: The convention is administered by the international Union for the Protection of New Varieties of Patents (UPOV). In 1991 a Revision of the Convention was adopted; however, it has not yet entered into force.

---

29 Union for the Protection of New Varieties of Plants.

ing to use patented inventions must obtain licences or authorizations from the patent owners, who normally will require them to pay royalties.

The Agreement clarifies these exclusive rights of patent owners. In particular, it states that where the subject of a patent is a *product*, third persons can *make, sell or import* that product only with the consent of the patent owner. Where a process is patented, third parties cannot use the process without the patent owner's consent; neither can they, without this consent, sell or import products directly obtained with the patented process.

Furthermore, the Agreement provides that in civil proceedings for infringement of the patent on a manufacturing process, an infringing product shall be presumed to have been produced by using the patented process if it is identical to that produced by the patented process. In such cases, as it is generally difficult for the patent owner to gather evidence to establish that the process has actually been used, the burden of proof shall be on the defendant, i.e. he or she will have to establish that the product has been manufactured with a process different from that covered by the patent.

5.2.1.3   Compulsory licensing

TRIPS, Article 31

What happens if a patent owner refuses to license the use of the patented invention by demanding unreasonable terms? The legislation of many countries provide that where the patented product is not available or is available at exorbitant prices, the government may on grounds of public interest authorize an interested manufacturer to use the patent, requiring him or her to pay the patent owner a royalty that it considers reasonable. However, the Agreement lays down strict conditions for such licensing to ensure that compulsory licences are issued only in exceptional situations and on an objective basis. In particular, it provides that compulsory licences may be granted only when the interested manufacturer has failed in his or her efforts to obtain the authorization *on reasonable terms and conditions.* Box 39 lists some of the other conditions which

---

Box 39

CONDITIONS PRESCRIBED IN THE TRIPS AGREEMENT FOR COMPULSORY LICENSING OF PATENTS
(TRIPS, Article 31)

As a general rule, a compulsory licence for the use of a patented technology may be granted by the government of the country where the patent is registered if the interested user (which can be the government itself or a company or private individual) has been unsuccessful in obtaining the licence from the patent holder on reasonable commercial terms. In case of national emergency, other circumstances of extreme urgency and in cases of public non-commercial use, this condition does not have to be met. However, the patent holder has to be informed about the use.

The grant of such compulsory licence shall further be subject to the following conditions:

• Such licence shall be granted for supply predominantly to the domestic market.

• It shall be terminated if and when the circumstances which led to it cease to exist.

• In the case of semi-conductor technology, the licence shall only be for *public non-commercial use* or to remedy adjudicated anti-competitive practices.

• The grant of such a licence shall be for *non-exclusive use.*

• The patent owner shall be paid adequate remuneration, taking into account the economic value of the licence.

• The patent holder shall have a right to appeal against the decision to grant compulsory licence or any decision relating to the remuneration provided.

must be fulfilled before governments can intervene and license a manufacturer to use patented technology.

5.2.1.4   Disclosure of information

Although patent owners have exclusive property rights over their inventions, they cannot withhold technical information on these inventions. The legislation of most countries require applicants for patents to disclose such information on the products or processes to be patented as will enable technically qualified persons to understand and use it for further research or for industrial application after the expiry of the terms of the patents. Such information can be obtained by any interested person from the patent office, after paying the necessary charges.

TRIPS, Article 29

These provisions for public *disclosure of information* balance two conflicting objectives of governments in giving patent rights. By giving exclusive rights, governments provide inventors an incentive for research and a reward for their inventive work. The exclusive rights also enable manufacturers to recoup, and profit from, their R & D investment. At the same time, by requiring inventors to make a public disclosure of information on their inventions governments seek to ensure that they are used for the benefit of the community at large and for further technological research and development. While such information cannot be employed for commercial purposes by others until the expiry of the patent, it is open to any university, research or business organization to use it for further research. It is even open to them to apply for a secondary patent on the basis of the earlier patented invention. The Agreement clarifies this by stating that the legislation of member countries "shall require that an applicant for a patent shall disclose the invention in a manner sufficiently clear and complete for the invention to be carried out by a person skilled in the art".

5.2.2 Copyright and related rights

The subject matter of copyright protection includes works in the literary, scientific and artistic domain, whatever the mode or form of expression. For a work to enjoy copyright protection, however, it must be an original creation. The idea in the work does not need to be new but the form, be it literary, artistic or scientific, in which it is expressed must be the original creation of the author.

5.2.2.1   Rights comprised in copyright

Owners of copyright in a protected work have a right to *exclude* others from using it without their authorization. The rights of copyright owners are therefore often described as *exclusive rights* to authorize others to use the protected work. The acts usually requiring the authorization of copyright owners are listed below:

❑   Reproduction rights: copying and reproducing the work;

❑   Performing rights: performing the work in public (e.g. play or concert);

❑   Recording rights: making a sound recording of the work (e.g. gramophone records or "phonograms" in the technical language of copyright law);

❑   Motion picture rights: making a motion picture (often called cinematographic work in technical language);

❑   Broadcasting rights: broadcasting the work by radio or television;

❑   Translation and adaptation rights: translating and adapting the work.

In addition to these exclusive rights of an *economic character*, copyright laws provide original authors *moral rights*. These rights enable authors, even after they have transferred their economic rights, to claim authorship of the work and to object to any distortion or other derogatory action in relation to the work which would be prejudicial to their reputation or honour.

5.2.2.2   Neighbouring rights

Literary and artistic works are created in order to be disseminated among the public. This cannot always be done by the authors themselves, for it often requires intermediaries who use their professional skills to give to the works appropriate forms of presentation to make them accessible to a wide public.

In addition to protecting the rights of authors of works, it is therefore also necessary to protect the rights of:

❑   Performing artists in relation to their performance;

❑   Producers of phonograms in relation to their phonograms; and

❑   Broadcasting organizations in relation to their radio and television programmes.

These rights of performing artists, record producers and broadcasters are called neighbouring rights because they have developed in parallel to copyright and the exercise of these rights is often linked with the exercise of copyright. Copyright laws frequently deal also with neighbouring rights.

5.2.2.3   Provisions of the TRIPS Agreement

The main provisions on copyright and neighbouring rights are contained in the Berne and Rome Conventions. The TRIPS Agreement complements these provisions, particularly in relation to:

❑   Computer programmes and databases;

❑   Rental rights to computer programmes, sound recordings, and films;

❑   Rights of performers and producers of phonograms; and

❑   Rights of broadcasting organizations.

Box 40 summarizes these provisions.

5.2.3   Trademarks

5.2.3.1   General

TRIPS, Article 15

A trademark is a *sign* which serves to distinguish the goods (as does the *service mark* with regard to services) of an industrial or commercial enterprise from those of other enterprises. Such a sign may consist of one or more distinctive words, letters, names, numerals, figurative elements and combination of colours. Such a sign may combine any of the above-mentioned elements. As the basic purpose of a trademark is to distinguish, the laws of most countries provide that any mark to be protected must be *distinctive*.

5.2.3.2   Purpose served by trademarks

Trademarks serve a twofold purpose. They help their owners sell and promote their products by stimulating brand loyalty. They serve consumers by

---

Box 40

COPYRIGHT PROVISIONS IN THE AGREEMENT ON TRIPS*

Computer programmes. [TRIPS, Article 10] The Agreement provides that computer programmes should be considered *literary works* and protected under national copyright laws.

Rental rights. [TRIPS, Article 11] The Agreement requires countries to provide authors of computer programmes, sound recordings and cinematographic films "the right to authorize or to prohibit the commercial rental" of their copyright works. A member country "shall be excepted from this obligation in respect of cinematographic works unless such rental has led to widespread copying of such works... materially impairing the exclusive right of reproduction conferred on ... authors".

Protection of performers, producers of phonograms (sound recordings) and broadcasting organizations.

Performers. [TRIPS, Article 14] The Agreement provides that performers shall have, "in respect of a fixation of their performance on a phonogram", the right to prevent the reproduction of such fixation. They shall also have a right to prevent "broadcasting by wireless means and the communication to the public of their live performance" without their authorization.

Producers. Phonogram producers shall have the right to authorize or prohibit the direct or indirect reproduction of their phonograms.

Broadcasting organizations. These organizations shall have the right to prohibit the following acts from being carried out without their authorization:

• Fixation;
• Reproduction of fixations;
• Rebroadcasting by wireless or communication on television of their broadcasts.

* See box 42 for provisions on periods of duration.

---

assisting them in making a choice among several possibilities and by encouraging trademark owners to maintain or improve the quality of the products sold under their trademarks.

Although in some countries and in some situations the right to the exclusive exploitation of a trademark may be obtained by its extended *use* in commerce and without registration, it is generally necessary for effective protection that a trademark is registered in a government office (usually the same office as that which grants patents). Applicants wishing to register a trademark are required to state the nature of the goods in respect of which a mark is to be registered. The rationale for this rule is that registrants of trademarks should be able to use the signs in question only for the goods so stated. However, in practice, the prevention of the use of trademarks for other goods or services is contingent on the likelihood of their prejudicing the registered marks. This is tested on the basis of the similarity of the goods or the reputation of the mark.

5.2.3.3   International rules on the use of trademarks

International rules on trademarks are contained in the Paris Convention. The Agreement on TRIPS complements these rules in the following areas:

❑   Definition of "trademark".

❑   Exclusive rights of trademark owners.

❑   Prohibition of imposition of special requirements for the use of trademarks.

❑   Licensing and assignment of trademarks.

❑   Cancellation of trademarks.

5.2.3.4   Definition of "trademark"

TRIPS, Article 15

The Agreement provides that signs or combinations of signs capable of distinguishing the goods or services of one undertaking from those of other undertakings can be registered as trademarks. These include names, letters, numbers, figurative elements or combinations of colours. A country may provide that a mark that has been in use for a period is eligible for registration.

5.2.3.5 Exclusive rights

TRIPS, Article 16

The owners of registered trademarks have exclusive rights to prevent third parties from using on *identical or similar goods* signs that are *similar to those in respect of which the trademark is registered* where such use would cause confusion. When an identical trademark is used on goods and services that are identical, "a likelihood of confusion shall be presumed."

5.2.3.6 Special requirements

TRIPS, Article 20

The Agreement obliges countries to discontinue the practice of permitting the use of foreign trademarks only if these are combined with another trademark, such as one of a national origin. It also urges countries not to impose on the use of trademarks *special requirements* that, for example, would be detrimental to their capacity "to distinguish the goods or services of one undertaking from those of other undertakings."

5.2.3.7 Licensing and assignment of trademarks

TRIPS, Article 21

The Agreement leaves member countries free to determine the "conditions on the licensing and assignment of trademarks". However, it states that the owners should not be compelled to grant licences for the use of trademarks or to assign a trademark together with the business to which the trademark belongs.

5.2.3.8   Cancellation of trademarks

The protection granted to the proprietor of a registered mark is based on the assumption that he or she will use it in commerce. The laws of most countries provide for cancellation of the mark if it is not used over a certain period. The increasing emphasis in the laws of most countries on cancellation of marks that are not being used is related to the spectacular increase in the number of marks filed for registration every year. In fact, the proliferation of marks and their increasing use in commerce has led to a real dearth of symbols or trademarks available for adoption and use by new applicants. The human ingenuity for evolving new signs, by combining letters, numbers or pictures, is after all not without limits.

TRIPS, Article 19

The TRIPS Agreement lays down certain guidelines which registration authorities are expected to follow in cancelling trademarks because of non-use. It provides that a registered trademark can be cancelled "only after an uninterrupted period of at least three years of non-use". In taking such decisions, adequate weight should be given to the circumstances beyond the control of the foreign trademark owner, such as import restrictions imposed by governments on the import of products carrying a trademark. Moreover, use, for example by licensees, should be recognized as use by the owner of the mark.

5.2.4 Industrial designs

Not all countries currently protect industrial designs, which cover the ornamental features of products including shapes, lines, motifs and colours.

Industrial designs are protected mainly in consumer articles, of which textiles, leather and leather products, and motor cars are examples.

The TRIPS Agreement imposes an obligation on its member countries to protect industrial designs that are:

TRIPS, Article 25

❑   New, or
❑   Original.

The designs thus need to be either novel or original to qualify for protection.[30] The owner of the protected design has exclusive right to its use and can prevent third parties who have not obtained his or her consent from "making, selling or importing articles bearing or embodying a design which is a copy, or substantially a copy, of the protected design".

TRIPS, Article 25

The Agreement has a special provision to take into account the short life cycle and the sheer number of new designs in the textile sector. It provides that "any cost, examination or publication" must not "unreasonably impair the opportunity to seek or obtain such protection."

5.2.5   Other intellectual property rights

The provisions in the Agreement on geographical indications, undisclosed information and layout-designs of integrated circuits are briefly noted in box 41.

---

[30] In the negotiations, some countries had proposed that property rights for industrial designs should be granted only if they were "new and original". The application of such a cumulative principle was not, however, favoured by a number of countries, which felt that the application of the principle would make it difficult to obtain protection for industrial designs.

Box 41

OTHER INTELLECTUAL PROPERTY RIGHTS

Geographical indications. [TRIPS, Articles 22 and 23] Such indications aim at informing the consumer that a good has the "quality, reputation or other characteristic" which is "essentially attributable to its geographical origin." The Agreement provides that countries should not permit registration of trademarks containing a misleading indication of the geographical origin of goods. The most common example of this is "champagne", a term associated with wine produced in a certain region of France. In principle, therefore, it is not permissible to call wine produced elsewhere (in Argentina or the United States, for example) "champagne", even though the wine may be regarded in the producing country as comparable to French champagne.

Undisclosed information. [TRIPS, Article 39] The TRIPS Agreement carries provisions which, for the first time in public international law, explicitly require undisclosed information — trade secrets or know-how — to benefit from protection. The protection applies to information that is secret, that has commercial value because it is secret, and that has been subject to reasonable steps to keep it secret. The Agreement does not demand that undisclosed information should be treated as a form of property, but it does stipulate that a person lawfully in control of such information must have the possibility of preventing it from being disclosed to, acquired by, or used by others without his or her consent in a manner contrary to honest commercial practices. Furthermore, the Agreement has provisions on undisclosed test data and other data whose submission is required by governments "as a condition of approving the marketing of pharmaceutical or of agricultural chemical products". Member governments must protect such data against unfair commercial use.

Layout-designs of integrated circuits. [TRIPS, Articles 35 to 38] Except when it provides otherwise, the Agreement requires countries to protect the layout-designs of integrated circuits in accordance with the Washington Treaty on Intellectual Property in Respect of Integrated Circuits (which was negotiated in 1989). Additional provisions stipulate, *inter alia*, that importing or selling articles incorporating a protected integrated circuit without authorization from the right holder shall be considered unlawful. However, acquisition of an article by persons who do not know that it incorporates an unlawfully reproduced layout-design does not constitute an unlawful act. "Innocent infringers" may sell or dispose of stock acquired before they became aware that the use of the layout-design is unlawful; however, they shall be liable to pay the right holder a reasonable royalty. Another provision of the Agreement prohibits compulsory licensing of the protected right except in cases of public non-commercial use or to remedy practices determined by a judicial or administrative process to be anti-competition.

5.2.6   Duration of intellectual property rights

Intellectual property rights (other than trade-marks, geographical indications and undisclosed information) are limited in duration. Currently, the minimum periods of protection vary from country to country. The Agreement establishes minimum regulatory periods for the different property rights. These are set out in box 42.

Box 42

MINIMUM PERIODS OF PROTECTION FOR INTELLECTUAL PROPERTY RIGHTS

Patents	20 years from the date of filing of the application for a patent. [TRIPS, Article 33]
Copyright	Work other than cinematographic or photographic: 50 years from the date of authorized publication or life of the author plus 50 years.
	Cinematographic work: 50 years after the work has been made available to the public or, if not made available, after the making of such work.
	Photographic work: 25 years after the making of the work.
Trademarks	7 years from initial registration and each renewal of registration; registration is renewable indefinitely. [TRIPS, Article 18]
Performers and producers of phonograms	50 years from the end of the calendar year in which the fixation (phonogram) was made or the performance took place. [TRIPS, Article 14:5]
Broadcasting	20 years from the end of the calendar year in which the broadcast took place. [TRIPS, Article 14:5]
Industrial designs	At least 10 years. [TRIPS, Article 26:3]
Layout-designs of integrated circuits	10 years from the date of registration or, where registration is not required, 10 years from the date of first exploitation. [TRIPS, Article 38:2 and 3]

IPR owners lose their rights when the duration of protection expires. From then on patents, copyright, industrial designs and other property rights can be exploited by any member of the public without having to obtain authorization from any right holder.

5.2.7 Restrictive practices

As has been noted, developing countries were apprehensive during the GATT negotiations that the strengthening of intellectual property protection could open up opportunities for monopolistic abuses by suppliers who would be in a stronger position to impose restrictive conditions on the licensing of technology. To ensure that improved and increased protection of IPRs does not adversely affect the transfer of technology on reasonable commercial terms, the Agreement provides that countries may adopt appropriate measures, including legislation, to prevent intellectual property holders from:

❑ Abusing their rights;

❑ Adopting practices that unreasonably restrain trade or adversely affect the transfer of technology.

5.3 Enforcement provisions

One feature of the TRIPS Agreement which distinguishes it from the WIPO conventions is the emphasis it lays on enforcement by its member countries of its standards and rules. Towards this end, the Agreement prescribes the institutional mechanism, procedures and remedies that countries should adopt:

❑ To enable IPR holders to obtain redress, including provisional relief, under civil law;

TRIPS, Articles 42 to 61

❑   To prevent release by customs authorities of counterfeit, pirated and other goods that infringe IPRs; and

❑   For the prosecution of counterfeiters and pirates under criminal law.

5.3.1   Civil remedies

The Agreement states that national courts shall be able "to order prompt and effective provisional measures" to preserve evidence in regard to alleged infringement of intellectual property rights, and to prevent an infringement from occurring, *inter alia,* by preventing the entry of *imported goods* into the channels of commerce in their jurisdiction. Where infringement of IPRs has been established, the courts shall have the authority to order the infringer to pay to the right holder *damages to compensate for the injury.* In addition, in order *to create an effective deterrent*, the courts are authorized to order the *destruction* of the infringing goods so that they do not enter commercial channels.

5.3.2   Prevention of release of infringing goods by Customs authorities

Member countries are further required to adopt procedures under which holders of intellectual property who have grounds for suspecting that:

❑   Counterfeit goods infringing on their trademarks, or

❑   Pirated goods infringing on their copyright

are likely to be imported could request Customs authorities not to release the goods. Countries have the option to prescribe procedures for the suspension of release from Customs of products that infringe on patents and other IPRs.

5.3.3 Criminal proceedings

The Agreement further calls on countries to see that, where there is "wilful trademark counterfeiting or copyright piracy on a commercial scale", the infringer is prosecuted under criminal law and punished with imprisonment or fines sufficient to provide a deterrent.

5.4 Transitional periods

TRIPS, Articles 65 and 66

The national legislation of a number of countries, particularly developing and least developed countries, do not at present conform to the provisions of the Agreement on TRIPS described above. For instance, in the area of patents, while the Agreement requires that as a rule patents should be given for inventions in *all fields of technology*, some countries exclude from patentability chemicals, food and food products. The duration for which patents are granted for inventions relating to fertilizers, insecticides and pharmaceuticals is also much shorter in some countries than the 20 years provided for by the Agreement. Furthermore, in regard to pharmaceuticals, some countries grant protection only to processes and not to products. In the area of copyright, many countries do not treat computer programmes as eligible for protection. A number of countries do not provide protection for industrial designs.

To enable industry and trade in these countries to prepare themselves for the changes required by the Agreement on TRIPS, member countries have been given the following transitional periods within which to bring their national legislation and regulations in conformity with the provisions of the Agreement.

❏   Developed countries: one year, i.e. up to 1 January 1996;

❑   Developing countries: five years, i.e. up to 1 January 2000.

❑   Transitional economies: five years, i.e. up to 1 January 2000, if they are facing problems in reforming their intellectual property law.

❑   Least developed countries: 11 years, i.e. up to 1 January 2006.

In addition, developing countries that at present provide patent protection to processes and not to products, for example in the food, chemical and pharmaceutical sectors, can delay up to 1 January 2005 the application of the obligation to protect *products*.

During the transitional periods, member countries are required not to take any measures that will result in a lower level of protection to IPRs than that already existing in their territories. All countries are under an obligation to apply the MFN and national treatment rules from 1 January 1996.

6.   Business implications

6.1   General

The TRIPS Agreement will, to a large extent, have a harmonizing effect on standards for the protection of intellectual property rights throughout the world. With the exception of the obligation to protect pharmaceutical products, harmonization can be expected by 2000 when the transition period for the implementation of the Agreement by developing and transitional economies comes to an end. The emphasis of the Agreement on enforcement will result in stricter application at the national level of intellectual property rights both in domestic markets and at the border.

6.2   Challenges and advantages

For the business person from developing and transitional economies, the Agreement offers both challenges and advantages. The challenges arise from two factors.

First, the Agreement requires changes in the IPR regimes of many developing countries (see box 43). It will be necessary for the business community to prepare itself for these changes.

Box 43

CHANGES REQUIRED IN IPR REGIMES
IN DEVELOPING COUNTRIES

The Agreement will require significant changes in the IPR regimes of many developing countries. Several countries will, for example, need to extend patent protection in due time to pharmaceutical and chemical *products,* which today are excluded from protection under their national laws. Moreover, modifications will be required in the large number of countries which provide terms of patent protection that are shorter than the 20 years set out in the Agreement, allow exceptions to the 20-year term, or stipulate another duration.

With respect to copyright, arguably the main implication of the Agreement is the extension of copyright protection to software as literary works. A large number of developing Members (and two developed Members) did not have any type of protection for computer software as of April 1994 and a few countries provided protection through legal instruments other than copyright law.

Another issue of particular interest for developing countries is the protection of plant varieties. The Agreement requires protection of these varieties by patents, by a *sui generis* system, or by a combination of both. Most developed countries, as they are members of the UPOV Convention, accord property rights to plant breeders. By contrast, only a few developing countries are members of UPOV and only a handful have *sui generis* protection systems (e.g. Argentina, Chile, Kenya, the Republic of Korea, Uruguay and Zimbabwe).

Source: Carlos Braga, "Trade-Related Aspects of Intellectual Property Rights: The Uruguay Round Agreement and Its Economic Implications" (World Bank conference paper, 26 - 27 January 1995).

Second, stronger protection will make it more difficult for industries in developing countries to use through reverse engineering and other means the technology developed by foreign companies and for which the latter hold patent rights. In the past, reverse engineering had been an important source of technology particularly for SMEs. With the implementation of the Agreement, companies with registered patent rights can be expected to be more vigilant about ensuring that their patented technology is not used without payment of royalty.

On the other hand, strengthened IPR rules will have a positive impact on:

❏   Transfer of technology on commercial terms to business enterprises in developing countries;

❏   Controlling the trade in counterfeit goods; and

❏   Both the export and the import trade.

These aspects are taken up in greater detail in the paragraphs that follow.

6.2.1   Transfer of technology on commercial terms

First, increased protection of IPRs will greatly facilitate attempts by companies in developing countries to enter into joint ventures and other collaboration arrangements for the transfer of technology on commercial terms. There is increasing evidence to show that *IPR protection* in host countries is an important factor in decisions of companies in developed countries to invest in developing countries. It certainly plays a major role in investment decisions in the chemical and pharmaceutical industries. Recent studies indicate that it is also a significant variable in other industries,[31] particularly those manufacturing products that are imitation prone (e.g. electronic and computer products).

Second, more effective protection of IPRs will increase the number of patents registered in developing countries. As has been noted, the rules on patents seek to maintain a balance between the need to protect the rights of patent holders and the need of industries and society as a whole to benefit from new and improved knowledge. The Agreement calls on its member countries to enforce strictly the provisions requiring patent applicants to disclose the technical information that will enable technically qualified persons to reconstruct the inventions. Access to such information will make it possible for the industrial sector, particularly in newly industrializing and other countries with a sufficient number of technically qualified persons, to utilize it for further research and to develop processes or products that differ from those patented. This stimulation of the inventive process will certainly benefit the country as a whole.[32]

Third, increased protection to IPRs will encourage foreign partners in joint ventures to undertake greater research and development work in the host developing country. At present most research work is undertaken in their own countries. Such a development will enable local partners to influence to a greater extent both the content and the priorities of research work.

---

[31] Carlos Braga, "Trade-Related Aspects of Intellectual Property Issues: The Uruguay Round Agreement and Its Economic Implications" (World Bank conference paper, 26 -27 January 1995).

[32] *The Outcome of the Uruguay Round: An Initial Assessment* (United Nations publication, Sales No. E.94.II.D.28), pp. 196 - 203.

On balance, therefore, it can be argued that, over the medium and long term, IP protection as envisaged in the Agreement will have positive effects on the growth of the inventive process in developing countries. In the short term, however, as some studies show, improved protection may force industries in certain sectors such as pharmaceuticals and chemicals to pay higher prices for acquiring patented technology.[33]

6.2.2   Impact on the trade in counterfeit goods

The emphasis of the Agreement on the enforcement of its provisions is also expected to help bring under control production of, and trade in, counterfeit and pirated goods. In the coming years the WTO consultation and dispute settlement mechanism will put increasing pressure to bear on countries with a significant output of such goods to improve the enforcement of their trademark and copyright laws. It is also in the long-term interest of domestic industries to see that these laws are enforced.

The occurrence of counterfeiting is frequently due to the fact that small enterprises are not fully aware of the legal implications of using trademarks without authorization from their owners. There is some evidence to show that pirates and counterfeiters are often able to switch to legitimate activities once the legal environment changes.[34]

Counterfeiting also adversely affects the export interests of small domestic producers who produce under licence for manufacturers in outside countries. In recent years, a number of manufacturers

---

33 *Ibid.*, pp. 45-47.
34 *Ibid*, p. 48.

marketing products under their brand names have had either the product itself or parts of it produced by SMEs in developing countries to take advantage of lower production costs. These manufacturers are more willing, as the case cited in box 44 indicates, to enter into such arrangements with countries where IPRs are effectively protected.

6.2.3 Relevance to the export and import trade

Business enterprises will have to bear in mind the provisions of the TRIPS Agreement in planning their sales strategies for foreign markets. In particular, it will be necessary for them to examine whether the processes they use in manufacturing the product or any of its inputs are subject to a patent in the target export market. Likewise, where the product offered

---

Box 44

**IMPORTANCE OF THE ENFORCEMENT OF IPRs
TO PRODUCTION UNDER LICENCE: A CAUTIONARY TALE**

A large importer of carpets in a developed country (country A) was importing carpets from small manufacturers in a least developed country (country B) which had long traditions of such artisanal work. The ornamental design and motifs were provided by the importer. In order to prevent use of the design by other producers, the importing firm had registered the industrial design as an intellectual property both in its country and in the country of production. After having spent a considerable amount on advertisement and publicity, the importing firm was able in a few years to develop a market for carpets manufactured according to its design.

This led other small manufacturers in country B to produce carpets with an identical design for export to country A. The importer in country A tried to get the IPR authorities in country B to stop production and export by these manufacturers in view of its exclusive right to the use of the protected industrial design. However, because of the lax enforcement of IPRs in country B, no action was taken. The importer therefore decided to terminate the arrangement and shift production to another country which had a reputation for enforcing its intellectual property law.

---

for sale in a foreign market bears a trademark, it will be necessary to ensure that a similar mark is not in use or registered in that market. If their trademarks are considered to be confusingly similar to other trademarks, exporting enterprises may expose themselves to legal suits for infringement of property rights.

These considerations should also be kept in mind by enterprises in placing their import orders. It will be necessary, particularly in regard to products that are widely counterfeited or pirated, for importers to satisfy those concerned that, where the foreign supplier claims that the product to be imported is produced under a licence, it has the necessary authorization to do so. Otherwise, the importer will risk facing a suit for damages from the trademark owner and the possibility of the goods being confiscated by Customs on arrival.

In sum, if trade-related IPR friction is to be avoided, it is necessary for all business enterprises engaged in foreign trade not only to familiarize themselves with the system set up by the Agreement but to be fully aware of the obligations which it imposes and the rights it creates in their favour.

National enquiry points on national mandatory standards, technical regulations and voluntary standards

WORLD TRADE ORGANIZATION
Committee on Technical Barriers to Trade

NATIONAL ENOUIRY POINTS

Note by the Secretariat

The present document contains a list of names, addresses, telex, telephone and telefax numbers of the enquiry point(s) foreseen in Articles 10.1 and 10.3 of the Agreement on Technical Barriers to Trade, and any additional infomation provided by delegations concerning its (their) operations.

ARGENTINA
Dirección General de Industria
Av. Julio A. Roca 651, 1º piso, sector 25
1322 Buenos Aires
Telephone: + (54 1) 349 36 55
Telefax: + (54 1) 349 36 44

AUSTRALIA
WTO Enquiry Point
The Director
Trade Obligations Section (GTO)
Trade Negotiations and Organisations Division
Department of Foreign Affairs and Trade
Canberra, A.C.T. 2600
Telephone: + (61 6) 261 30 37
Telefax: + (61 6) 273 15 27
Telex: 62007 or 62001

AUSTRIA
(a) For technical regulations and certification systems:
Bundesministerium für wirtschaftliche Angelegenheiten
(Federal Ministry for Economic Affairs)
Abt. I/6 (Division I/6)
Stubenring 1, A-1011 Wien
Telephone: + (43 1) 711 00/Ext. 5452
Telefax: + (43 1) 715 96 51
Telex: (047) 111780 regeb a
              (047) 111145 regeb a
              (047) 112240 regeb a

(b) For non-governmental standards:
Österreichisches Normungsinstitut (ÖN)
(Austrian Standards Institute)

P.O.B. 130
Heinestrasse 38
A-1021 Wien
Telephone: + (43 1) 21 300/ Ext. 626
Telefax: + (43 1) 21 300 650
Telex: (047) 115960 norm a
Telegrams: Austrianorm

BELGIUM
CIBELNOR
Centre d'information belge sur les normes et
les règlements techniques
(Belgian Information Centre on Standards and
Technical Regulations)
Secrétariat: Institut belge de normalisation
(IBN)
(Belgian Standards Institute)
Avenue de la Brabançonne, 29
B-1040 Bruxelles
Telephone: + (32 2) 734 92 05
Telefax: + (32 2) 733 42 64
Telex: 23877 BENOR

BRAZIL
Centro de Informação e Difusão Tecnológica -
CIDIT
Instituto Nacional de Metrologia,
Normalizaçao e Qualidade Industrial -
INMETRO
Av. N.S. das Graças 50
Xerém, 25250-020 Duque de Caxias RJ
Telephone: + (55 21) 779 14 09
Telefax: + (55 21) 779 16 31
                 + (55 21) 779 14 05
Telex: 306 72

CANADA
Standards Information Service
Standards Council of Canada
45 O'Connor Street, Suite 1200
Ottawa, Ontario K1P 6N7
Telephone: + (1 613) 238 32 22
Telefax: + (1 613) 995 45 64

CHILE
Dirección de Relaciones Económicas
Internacionales
Ministerio de Relaciones Exteriores

(Directorate-General for International
Economic Relations, Ministry of External
Relations)
Alameda Bernardo O'Higgins 1315, 2º piso
Santiago
Telephone: + (56 2) 696 00 43
Telefax: + (56 2) 696 06 39
Telex: 240836 PROCH CL
                 340120 PROCH CK

COLOMBIA
(a) Productos manufacturados:
Superintendencia de Industria y Comercio
División de Normalización y Calidad
Dirección: Carrera 13 No. 27-00, 5º piso
Santafé de Bogotá
Telephone: + (57 1) 281 30 06
Telefax: + (57 1) 281 32 50

(b) Demás productos:
Ministerio de Desarrollo
División de Normas Técnicas y Calidades
Dirección: Carrera 13 No. 28-01, 6º piso
Santafé de Bogotá
Telephone: + (57 1) 320 00 77 ext. 434
Telefax: + (57 1) 287 47 37
                 + (57 1) 287 60 25

COSTA RICA
Dirección General de Normas y Unidades de
Medida
Ministerio de Economía, Industria y Comercio
Apartado Postal 1736-2050
San Pedro de Montes de Oca
Telephone and telefax: + (506) 283 51 33

CUBA
Oficina Nacional de Normalización
Contact person: Sr. Javier Acosta Alemany
Director de Relaciones Internacionales
Calle E No. 261 entre 11 y 13
La Habana
Telephone: + (53 7) 30 00 22
                 + (53 7) 30 08 25
                 + (53 7) 30 08 35
Telefax: + (53 7) 33 80 48
Telex: + (53 7) 51 22 45

CZECH REPUBLIC
Czech Office for Standards, Metrology and
Testing
WTO Enquiry Point
Václavské námÖstí 19
113 47 Praha 1
Telephone: + (42 2) 242 24 734
Telefax: + (42 2) 242 29 254

DENMARK
Dansk Standard
(Danish Standards Association)
WTO Enquiry Point
Baunegårdsvej 73
DK-2900 Hellerup
Telephone: + (45 39) 77 01 01
Telefax: + (45 39) 77 02 02
Telex: 119 203 ds stand
Telegram: Danskstandard
Tltx: 2381-11 92 03 DS STAND

DOMINICAN REPUBLIC
(a) Agricultural products
Ministerio de Agricultura
(Secretaría de Estado de Agricultura)
Km. 6 ½ Autopista Duarte
Urbanización Los Jardines del Norte
Santo Domingo, D.N.
Telephone: + (809) 547 38 88
Telefax: + (809) 227 12 68
Contact person: Mr. Luis Toral C., Secretario
de Estado de Agricultura

(b) Industrial products
Dirección General de Normas y Sistemas
(DIGENOR)
Secretaría de Estado de Industria y Comercio
Edif. de Oficinas Gubernamentales Juan Pablo
Duarte, piso 11
Avda. México, esq. Leopoldo Navarro
Santo Domingo, D.N.
Telephone: + (809) 686 22 05
Telefax: + (809) 688 38 43
Contact person: Mr. Luis Mejía

(c) Pharmaceutical products and food
additives
Secretaría de Estado de Salud Pública y
Asistencia Social (SESPAS)

Avda. San Cristóbal, Esq. Tiradentes
Santo Domingo, D.N.
Telephone: + (898) 541 84 03
                  + (898) 541 31 21
Telefax: + (809) 547 28 43
Contact person: Mr. Victoriano García Santos,
Secretario de Estado de Salud Pública y
Asistencia Social

EGYPT
Egyptian Organization for Standardization
2 Latin America Street
Garden City
Cairo
Telex: 93296 EOS UN

EL SALVADOR
Ministerio de Economía
Dirección de Política Comercial
Normas Técnicas
Paseo General Escalón 4122
San Salvador
Telephone: + (0503) 279 41 81
Telefax: + (0503) 279 39 73

EUROPEAN COMMUNITY
The head of the EC enquiry point is Mr. G.
Lohan

WTO Enquiry Point (TBT)
DG III/A/T
4th floor, Office 31
Rond-Point R. Schuman 6
Brussels
Telephone: + (322) 296 92 71
                  + (322) 296 06 98
Telefax: + (322) 296 60 26
Telex: 21877 COMEU B
There will no longer be a separate enquiry point
for agricultural products.

FINLAND
Suomen Standardisoimisliitto SFS
(Finnish Standards Association SFS)
P.O. Box 116
FIN-00241 Helsinki
Telephone: + (358 0) 149 93 31
Telefax: + (358 0) 146 49 14

FRANCE

Centre d'information sur les normes et règlements techniques (CINORTECH)
(Information Centre on Standards and Technical Regulations)
Association française de normalisation (AFNOR)
(French Standard Association)
Tour Europe CEDEX 07
F-92049 Paris La Défense
Contact person: Mme Martine Vaquier
Telephone: + (33 1) 42 91 56 69
Telefax: + (33 1) 42 91 56 56
Telex: 611974 AFNOR F
(address care of CINORTECH)

"The Centre is fully operational. CINORTECH can provide all information on AFNOR standards and on technical regulations and certification systems."

GERMANY

Deutches Informationszentrum für Technische Regeln (DITR)
(German Information Centre for Technical Rules)
Postfach 11 07, Burggrafenstr. 4-10
D-10787 Berlin
Telephone: + (49 30) 26 01 26 00
Telefax: + (49 30) 26 28 125
The DITR is being established by DIN, the German Standards Institute, in co-operation with the Federal Government. This body is the central point to which to address all questions concerning technical rules in the Federal Republic of Germany.

The Centre provides information about all technical rules (including standards, technical regulations and certification systems) valid in the Federal Republic of Germany, irrespective of whether the technical rules have been issued by federal or local authorities or by nongovernmental bodies. At present the computer-aided DITR databank comprises information about 36,000 technical rules either in force or in the draft stage.

GREECE

ELOT Information Center
Aharnon 313

11145 Athens
Telephone: + (30 1) 20 15 025
Telefax: + (30 1) 20 25 917
Telex: (21) 9621 ELOT GR.

HONG KONG

Industry Department
36th Floor, Immigration Tower
7 Gloucester Road, Wan Chai
Hong Kong
Telephone: + (852 28) 29 48 24
  (Assistant Director-General,
  Quality Services Division)
Telefax: + (852 28) 24 13 02
Telex: 50151 INDHK HX

HUNGARY

Magyar Szabvanyugyi Hivatal
(Hungarian Standards Office)
Ulloi ut 25
1450 Budapest
Telephone: + (36 1) 11 83 011
Telefax: + (36 1) 11 85 125
Telex: 22 57 23 norm h

ICELAND

Ministry of Industry and Commerce
Mr. Sverrir Júlíusson
Arnarhvoli
150 Reykjavík

INDIA

Bureau of Indian Standards
Manak Bhavan
Bahadur Shah Zafar Marg 9
New Delhi 110 002
Telephone: + (91 11) 33 21 910
Telefax: + (91 11) 33 14 062
Telex: (031)-65870 - Answer
  Back 'BIS/IN'

INDONESIA

Dewan Standardisasi Nasional (DSN)
Sasana Widya Sarwono Lt 5
Jl. Gatot Subroto 10
Jakarta 12710
Telephone: + (62 21) 520 65 74
  + (62 21) 522 16 86
Telefax: + (62 21) 520 65 74

IRELAND
(a) For technical regulations and certification systems:
EU/WTO Division
Department of Tourism and Trade
Kildare Street
Dublin 2
Telephone: + (353 1) 662 l4 44
Telefax: + (353 1) 676 61 54
              + (353 1) 676 26 54
Telex: 93418/ 93478

(b) For standards:
National Standards Authority of Ireland
Glasnevin
Dublin 9
Telephone: + (353 1) 837 01 01
Telefax: + (353 1) 836 98 21
Telex: 45301

ISRAEL
The Standards Institution of Israel
42, Chaim Levanon St.
Tel-Aviv 69977
Telephone: + (972 3) 646 51 54
Telefax: + (972 3) 641 96 83
              (Director-General)
              + (972 3) 641 27 62
              (Inf. Center, WTO Enquiry Point)

ITALY
(a) Enquiry point for WTO notifications:
MICA DGPI
Ministero Industria, Commercio e Artigianato
Direzione Generale Produzione Industriale
Divisione XIX
Via Molise 19
I-00187 Roma
Telephone: + (39 6) 478 878 60
Telefax: + (39 6) 474 44 30
Telex: 610154

(b) Enquiry point for technical regulations:
CNR STIBNOT
Consiglio Nazionale delle Ricerche
Ufficio transferimento innovazioni brevetti,
normativa tecnica

Via Tiburtina 770
I-00159 Roma
Telephone: + (39 6) 40 758 26
Telefax: + (39 6) 40 758 15
Telex: 620623

(c) Enquiry point for standards of all sectors, except electrics and electronics:
UNI
Ente Italiano di Unificazione
Via Battistotti Sassi 11-b
I-20133 Milano
Telephone: + (39 2) 70 02 41
Telefax: + (39 2) 70 10 61 06
Telex: 312481 UNI I

(d) Enquiry point for electrics and electronic standards:
CEI
Comitato Elettronico Italiano
Viale Monza 259
I-20126 Milano
Telephone: + (39 2) 25 77 31
Telefax: + (39 2) 25 77 32 22
Telex: 312207 CEI I

JAMAICA
Jamaica Bureau of Standards
6 Winchester Road
P.O. Box 113
Kingston 10
Telephone: + (809) 926 3140 6
              + (809) 968 2063 71
Telefax: + (809) 929 47 36
Telex: 2291 STANBUR JA

This government agency has responsability for standards development and standards implementation as follows:

- laboratory testing
- product and systems certification
- technical information
- training
- energy efficiency evaluation
- metrology
- ISO 9000 certification and
- laboratory accreditation

JAPAN

(a) Standards Information Service[1]
First International Organization Division
Economic Affairs Bureau
Ministry of Foreign Affairs
2-2-1 Kasumigaseki, Chiyoda-ku
Tokyo
Telephone: + (81 3) 35 80 33 11
Telefax: + (81 3) 35 03 31 36
Telex: C. J22350
A. GAIMU A-B J22350

(b) Standards Information Service[2]
Information Service Department
Japan External Trade Organizations (JETRO)
2-2-5 Toranomon, Minato-Ku
Tokyo
Telephone: + (81 3) 35 82 62 70
Telefax: + (81 3) 35 89 41 79
Telex: C. J24378
A. JETRO A-B J24378
In relation to the services of these two bodies, a Standards Agreement Office has been established in the Ministry of Foreign Affairs (MOFA). Enquiries can be made in a WTO language.

KOREA, REPUBLIC OF

(a) For industrial products:
Industrial Cooperation Division
Industrial Advancement Administration (IAA)
2, Chungang-dong, Kwachon-city
Kyonggi-do 427-010
Telephone: + (82 2) 503 79 38
Telefax: + (82 2) 503 79 41
+ (82 2) 504 52 82
Telex: 28456 FINCEN K

(b) For agricultural products:
Technical Cooperation Division

Bureau of International Agriculture
Ministry of Agriculture, Forestry and Fisheries (MAFF)
1, Chungang-dong, Kwachon-city
Kyonggi-do 427-760
Telephone: + (82 2) 503 72 94
Telefax: + (82 2) 507 20 95
Telex: (No telex)

(c) For fishery products:
Trade Promotion Division
National Fisheries Administration
Daewoo Center Building, No. 541
5-Ga Namdaemoon-Ro, Jung-Gu
Seoul
Telephone: + (82 2) 753 68 62
Telefax: + (82 2) 753 83 31

(d) For health, sanitation and cosmetic products:
International Cooperation Division
Ministry of Health and Welfare (MOHW)
2, Chungang-dong, Kwachon-city
Kyonggi-do 427-760
Telephone: + (82 2) 503 75 24
Telefax: + (82 2) 504 64 18

LUXEMBOURG
Inspection du travail et des mines
(Inspectorate of Labour and Mines)
26, rue Zithe
Boîte postale 27
L-2010 Luxembourg
Telephone: + (352) 49 92 11
Telefax: + (352) 49 14 47
Telex: (No telex)

---

1 Standards Information Service at MOFA mainly handles enquiries in the fields of drugs, cosmetics, medical devices, foodstuffs, food additives, telecommunications facilities, motor vehicles, ships, aircraft and railway equipment (excluding enquiries concerning Japanese Industrial Standards (JIS) which are handled by JETRO).

2 Standards Information Service at JETRO mainly handles enquiries in the fields of electric equipment, gas appliances, measurement scales, foodstuffs, food additives. etc. Those enquiries concerning JIS on medical devices, motor vehicles, ships, aircraft and railway equipment are handled by JETRO.

MALAYSIA

Standard and Industrial Research Institute of
Malaysia (SIRIM)
Persiaran Dato' Menteri
Section 2
P.O. Box 7035
40911 Shah Alam
Selangor Darul Ehsan
Telephone: + (603) 559 26 01
              + (603) 559 16 30
Telefax: + (603) 550 80 95
Telex: SIRIM MA 38672

MAURITIUS

(a) Director
Mauritius Standards Bureau
Réduit
Telephone: + (230) 464 76 75
              + (230) 464 06 84 Deputy Director
              + (230) 464 07 30
              + (230) 454 19 33
              + (230) 464 81 23
              + (230) 464 11 02
Telefax: + (230) 46411 44

MEXICO

Lic. María Eugenia Bracho González
Dirección General de Normas
Avda. Puente de Tecamachalco No. 6, 3° piso
Col. Lomas de Tecamachalco
C.P. 53950
Naucalpan, Estado de México
Telephone: + (52 5) 729 94 80
Telefax: + (52 5) 729 94 84

MYANMAR

Directorate of Investment and Company
Administration (DICA)
Ministry of National Planning and Economic
Development
Merchant Street, 653-691
Yangon
Telephone: + (951) 822 07
              + (951) 720 52
              + (951) 752 29
Telefax: + (951) 821 01
Telex: 21368 INVEST BM

NETHERLANDS

(a) Enquiry point mentioned in Article 10,
paragraph 1.1:
Ministerie van Economische Zaken
Centrale Dienst voor In- en Uitvoer
Att. Mr. B. Siebring
Engelse Kamp 2
Postbus 30003
9700 RD Groningen
Telephone: + (31 50) 23 91 11
Telefax: + (31 50) 23 92 19
Telex: 53009 CDIUT NL

(b) Enquiry point mentioned in Article 10,
paragraph 1.2:
Nederlands Normalisatie Instituut (NNI)
(Netherlands Standardization Institute)
Kalfjeslaan 2
2600 GB Delft
Telephone: + (31 15) 69 02 55
Telefax: + (31 15) 69 01 30
Telex: 38144

(c) Enquiry point mentioned in Article 10,
paragraph 1.3:
Stichting Raad voor de Certificatie
(Council for Certification)
Stationsweg 13
3972 KA Driebergen
Telephone: + (31 34) 38 12 604
Telefax: + (31 34) 38 18 554

NEW ZEALAND

Standards New Zealand
Standards House, 155 The Terrace
Private Bag 2439
Wellington
Telephone: + (64 4) 498 59 90
Telefax: + (64 4) 498 59 94

NORWAY

Norges Standardiseringsforbund
(Norwegian Standards Association)
P.O. Box 7020 Homansbyen
(Hegdehaugsveien 31)
N-0306 Oslo 3
Telephone: + (47 2) 46 60 94
Telefax: + (47 2) 46 44 57
Telex: 19050 nsf n

PAKISTAN
Economic Consultant
Ministry of Commerce
Government of Pakistan
Islamabad
Telephone: + (92 51) 82 17 66
Telefax: + (92 51) 82 52 41
Telex: COMDN PAK-5859

PERU
Instituto Nacional de Defensa de la
Competencia y de Protección de la Propiedad
Intelectual (INDECOPI)
Comisión de Supervisión de Normas
Técnicas, Metrología, Control de Calidad y
Restricciones Arancelarias
Calle La Prosa 138
San Borja, Lima 41
Telephone: + (51 1) 224 78 00
Telefax: + (51 1) 224 03 48
   + (51 1) 224 03 47
Postal address: P.O. Box 145, Lima

PHILIPPINES
Bureau of Product Standards
Department of Trade and Industry
Trade and Industry Building
361 Sen. Gil J. Puyat Avenue
Makati, Metro Manila 1200
Telephone: + (63 2) 817 55 27
Telefax: + (63 2) 817 98 70
Telex: 14830 MTI PS
Telegram: Philstand Manila
Postal Address: P.O. Box 2363 MCPO

PORTUGAL
Instituto Português da Qualidade
Rua C à Avenida dos Três Vales
2825 Monte da Caparica
Telephone: + (351 1) 294 8100
   + (351 1) 294 8221
Telefax: + (351 1) 294 8223

ROMANIA
Romanian Institute for Standardization
13, Jean Louis Calderon Street
Sector 2, Bucharest
Telephone: + (401) 211 32 96
Telefax: + (401) 210 08 33
Telex: (065) 11 312 ins r

SINGAPORE
**(a) For standardization and certification
undertaken by the Singapore Institute of
Standards and Industrial Research (SISIR):**
Singapore Institute of Standards and
Industrial Research (SISIR)
1 Science Park Drive
Singapore 0511
Telephone: + (65) 778 77 77
Telefax: + (65) 776 12 80
Telex: RS 28499 SISIR

**(b) For technical regulations relating to
electrical safety of specific products:**
Public Utilities Board
111 Somerset Road, PUB Building
Singapore 0923
Telephone: + (65) 235 88 88
Telefax: + (65) 731 30 20
Telex: PUB RS 34793

**(c) For technical regulations relating to
processed foods and poisons:**
Ministry of the Environment
Environment Building
40 Scotts Road
Singapore 0922
Telephone: + (65) 732 77 33
Telefax: + (65) 731 94 56
Telex: RS 34365 ENV

**(d) For technical regulations relating to
fish, meat, fruits and vegetables:**
Primary Production Department
National Development Building
Maxwell Road
Singapore 0106
Telephone: + (65) 222 12 11
Telefax: + (65) 220 60 68
Telex: RS 28851 PPD
Cable: AGRIVET

SLOVAK REPUBLIC
Slovenský ústav technickej normalizácie
WTO Enquiry Point
Karloveská cesta 63
842 45 Bratislava
Visiting address:
Stefaničova 3, 814 39 Bratislava

Telephone: + (427) 496 847
            + (427) 498 030
Telefax: + (427) 497 886

SPAIN
(a)
Ministerio de Comercio y Turismo
Dirección General de Comercio Exterior
(Subdirección General de Control, Inspección
y Normalización del Comercio Exterior)
Paseo de la Castellana, 162, planta 6ª
28046 Madrid
Telephone: + (341) 349 37 70
            + (34 1) 349 37 64
            + (34 1) 349 37 57
Telefax: + (341) 349 37 40
            + (34 1) 349 37 77

**(b) Enquiry point with regard to Spanish
national standards:**
Asociación Española de Normalización y de
Certificación
Calle Fernández de la Hoz, 52
28010 Madrid
Telephone: + (34 1) 310 48 51
Telefax: + (34 1) 310 49 76

SRI LANKA
Director of Commerce
Department of Commerce
"Rakshana Mandiraya"
21 Vauxhall Street
Colombo 2
Telephone: + (941) 29 733
            + (941) 43 61 14
Telefax: + (941) 43 02 33
Telex: 21908 COMMERCE

SWEDEN
(a) Enquiry point with regard to Article 10.1:
Kommerskollegium
(National Board of Trade)
GATT Enquiry Point
Box 1209
S-111 82 Stockholm
Telephone: + (46 8) 791 05 00
Telefax: + (46 8) 24 67 39
Telex: 11835 komkol S

(b) Enquiry point with regard to Article 10.2:
Standardiseringskomissionen i Sverige
(Swedish Standards Institution)
SIS
Enquiry Services
Box 3295
S-103 66 Stockholm
Telephone: + (46 8) 23 04 00
Telefax: + (46 8) 11 70 35
Telex: 17453 SIS-S

SWITZERLAND
Swiss Association for Standardization
SNV
Mühlebachstrasse 54
CH-8008 Zürich
Telephone: + (41 1) 254 54 54
Telefax: + (41 1) 254 54 74
Telex: 755 931 SNV CH

THAILAND
Thai Industrial Standards Institute (TISI)
Ministry of Industry
Rama VI Street
Bangkok 10400
Telephone: + (66 2) 246 19 91
            + (66 2) 245 78 02
            + (66 2) 246 40 86
            + (66 2) 246 19 94
Telefax: + (66 2) 247 87 41
            + (66 2) 246 43 27

TUNISIA
Institut national de la normalisation et de la
propriété industrielle
(National Standardization and Industrial
Property Institute)
INNORPI
B.P. 23, 1012 Tunis le Belvédère
Rue Ibn El Jazar 10 bis, La Fayette
Tunis
Telephone: + (21 61) 78 59 22
Telex: 13 602 INORPI TN

TURKEY
(a) Enquiry point with regard to Article 10.1:
Prime Ministry
Undersecretariat for Foreign Trade

General Directorate for Standardization for
Foreign Trade
06510 Emek-Ankara
Telephone: + (90 312) 212 58 96
             + (90 312) 212 87 17
Telefax: + (90 312) 212 87 68

**(b) Enquiry point with regard to Article
10.1.2:**
Turkish Standards Institution
Telephone: + (90 312) 417 83 30
Telefax: + (90 312) 425 43 95

UNITED KINGDOM
**(a) Certification Systems and
Governmental Standards:**
WTO Enquiry Point
International Trade Policy Division
Department of Trade and Industry
Room 250, Ashdown House
123 Victoria Street, London SW1E 6RB
Telephone: + (44 1) 712 15 60 61
Telefax: + (44 1) 712 15 62 12
Telex: 88 13 148 DIHQ G

(b) Non-Governmental Standards:
BSI Information Centre
389 Chiswick High Road
London W4 4AL
Telephone: + (44 1) 819 96 71 11
Telefax: + (44 1) 819 96 70 48

UNITED STATES
Standards Code and Information Program
Office of Standards Services
National Institute of Standards and
Technology
TRF Building, Room A-163
Gaithersburg, MD 20899
Telephone: + (1 301) 975 40 40
Telefax: + (1 301) 926 15 59
Telex: TRT 197674 NIST UT
The United States' enquiry point, in the National
Institute of Standards and Technology, main-
tains a reference collection of standards,
specifications, test methods, codes and recom-
mended practices. This reference material
includes United States' government agencies
regulations, and standards of United States pri-
vate standards-developing organizations and
foreign national and international standardizing

bodies. The enquiry point responds to all
enquiries for information concerning federal,
state and private regulations, standards, and
conformity assessment procedures.

ZAMBIA
**(a) Permanent Secretary/Attention of
Director of Trade**
Ministry of Commerce, Trade and Industry
P.O. Box 31968, Lusaka
Telephone: + (260 1) 228 301/9
Telefax: + (260 1) 226 673

(b) Zoo - Sanitary (Animal/animal material)
Senior Veterinary Officer
Department of Animal Production and Health
Mulungushi House
P.O. Box 50060, Lusaka
Telephone: + (260 1) 250 274
             + (260 1) 252 608
Telefax: + (260 1) 236 283

(c) Phytosanitary Service (Plant material)
Mount Makulu Research Station
P/B 7 Chilanga
Telephone: + (260 1) 278 655
             + (260 1) 278 242
Telefax: + (260 1) 230 62 22

ZIMBABWE
**(a) Standards, technical regulations and
certification schemes:**
The Director General
Standards Association of Zimbabwe
P.O. Box 2259
Northend Close, Northridge Park
Borrowdale, Harare
Telephone: + (263 4) 882 017
             + (263 4) 882 018
             + (263 4) 882 019
Telefax: + (263 4) 882 020

(b) Agricultural products:
The Permanent Secretary
Ministry of Agriculture
1 Borrowdale Road
P/Bag 7701, Causeway, Harare
Telephone: + (263 4) 708 061
Telefax: + (263 4) 734 646

National enquiry points on national health and sanitary regulations

---

WORLD TRADE ORGANIZATION
Committee on Sanitary and Phytosanitary Measures

NATIONAL ENQUIRY POINTS

Note by the Secretariat

The present document contains a list of names, addresses, telephone and telefax numbers of the enquiry point foreseen in Paragraph 3 of Annex B of the Agreement on the Application of Sanitary and Phytosanitary Measures, and any additional information provided by delegations concerning its operation, as submitted to the Secretariat as of 19 October 1995.

ANTIGUA AND BARBUDA
Plant Protection Unit
c/o Agriculture Division
Dunbars
Friars Hill
Telephone: + (809) 462 49 69
Telefax: + (809) 462 61 04

ARGENTINA
Secretaría de Agricultura, Ganadería y Pesca
Dirección de Economía Agraria y Asuntos
Internacionales
Avda. Paseo Colón 982 3º piso - oficina 162
1063 Buenos Aires
Telephone: + (541) 349 27 57/349 27 53
Telefax: + (541) 349 27 42

AUSTRALIA
Director
Development and Evaluation Division
Australian Quarantine and Inspection Service
GPO Box 858
Canberra ACT 2601
Telephone: + (616) 272 55 84
Telefax: + (616) 272 33 99

BANGLADESH
Mr. Ghulam Rahman
Joint Secretary
Ministry of Commerce
Government of the People's Republic of
Bangladesh
Bangladesh Secretariat
Dhaka

Telephone: + (8802) 83 46 65
Telefax: + (8802) 86 57 41

BOLIVIA
Dirección Nacional de Producción y
Protección Agrícola
Avda. Camacho No. 1471, Piso 5º
La Paz
Telephone: + (5912) 37 42 68/
37 42 70 interno 126
Telefax: + (5912) 35 75 35

BOTSWANA
The Permanent Secretary
Ministry of Agriculture
Private bag 003
Gaborone
Telephone: + (267) 35 05 00/35 06 03
Telefax: + (267) 35 60 27

BRAZIL
Secretaria de Defesa Agropecuária (SDA)
Ministério da Agricultura e da Reforma
Agrária (MAARA)
Esplanada dos Ministérios
Bloco 'B', Anexo 'B', sala 406
Brasilia - DF - 70.170
Telephone: + (5561) 218 23 14/218 23 15
Telefax: + (5561) 224 39 95

CANADA
WTO/NAFTA Enquiry Point
Standards Council of Canada
1200-45 O'Connor Street
Ottawa, Ontario K1P 6N7
Telephone: + (1613) 238 32 22
Telefax: + (1613) 569 03 78

CHILE
Servicio Agrícola y Ganadero
Avenida Bulnes No. 140
Santiago
Telephone: + (562) 671 23 23
Telefax: + (562) 672 18 12

COLOMBIA
Plant and animal health:
Subgerencia de Prevención y Control
Instituto Colombiano Agropecuario

Calle 37 No. 8 - 43
Santafé de Bogotá
Telephone: + (571) 320 36 54
Telefax: + (571) 232 46 95

Other sanitary measures:
Subdirección de Salud y Ambiente
Ministerio de Salud
Carrera 13 No. 32-76
Santafé de Bogotá
Telephone: + (571) 282 95 88
Telefax: + (571) 336 01 82

COSTA RICA
Ministerio de Agricultura y Ganadería
Dirección de Protección Agropecuaria
Apartado 10094-1000
San José
Telephone: + (506) 231 19 39, 231 76 73,
231 50 55
Telefax: + (506) 231 50 04

CUBA
Plant health:
Sr. Jorge Opies Díaz
Director
Calle 110 Esquina 5ta. B y eta. F, Playa
La Habana
Telephone: + (537) 29 61 89/22 25 16
Telefax: + (537) 33 50 86

Veterinary medicine:
Dr. Emerio Serrano Ramírez
Director
Calle 12 No. 355 entre 15 y 17 Playa
La Habana
Telephone: + (537) 30 66 15/30 35 35/
37 07 77/30 34 47
Telefax: + (537) 33 50 86

CYPRUS
Permanent Secretary
Ministry of Agriculture, Natural Resources and
Environment
1412 Nicosia
Telephone: + (357) 230 22 47
Telefax: + (357) 244 51 56

CZECH REPUBLIC

MVDr. Jiří Svoboda
Director
Ministry of Agriculture
External Relations Department - 110
TÖšnov 17
117 05 Praha 1
Telephone: + (422) 248 119 44
Telefax: + (422) 248 106 52

DOMINICAN REPUBLIC

Secretaría de Estado de Agricultura
Dirección General de Ganadería
- *Departamento de Sanidad Animal*
- *Departamento de Recursos Pesqueros*
Atención: Dr. Rafael Jáquez
Servicios: Análisis Zoosanitarios
- *Departamento de Sanidad Vegetal*
Atención: Dr. Pedro Jorge
Servicios de Control Sanitario de Frutas y
Vegetales
Km. 6½ Autopista Duarte
Urbanización Los Jardines del Norte
Santo Domingo
Telephone: + (1809) 547 38 88
Telefax: + (1809) 227 12 68

División de Droguas y Farmacias
Secretaría de Estado de Salud Pública y
Asistencia Social (SESPAS)
Avda. San Cristóbal, esq. Tiradentes
Santo Domingo, D.N.
Atención: Ms. Lusitania Acosta

Productos: Medicamentos y aditivos para los
alimentos
Telephone: + (1809) 541 84 03/541 3121
Telefax: + (1809) 547 28 43

EL SALVADOR

Ministerio de Agricultura y Ganadería
Dirección de Sanidad Vegetal y Animal
(DGSVA)
Cantón El Matazano de Soyapango
San Salvador
Telephone: + (503) 227 39 24
Telefax: + (503) 227 25 94

EUROPEAN UNION

European Commission
Directorate General for Agriculture and Rural
Development
Directorate VI/B.II
84 rue de la Loi
Brussels 1049
Telephone: + (322) 296 33 14
Telefax: + (322) 296 42 86

Member State Contact Points:

AUSTRIA

Bundesministerium für wirtschaftliche
Angelegenheiten
(Federal Ministry for Economic Affairs)
Abteilung I/6 (Division I/6)
Stubenring 1
A-1011 Wien
Telephone: + (431) 711 00/ext. 5452
Telefax: + (431) 715 96 51

BELGIUM

Institut belge de normalisation (IBN)
(Belgian Standards Institute)
Avenue de la Brabançonne 29
B-1040 Bruxelles
Telephone: + (322) 734 92 05
Telefax: + (322) 733 42 64

DENMARK

Landsbrugs - og Fiskeriministeriets 2.
afdeling, 4. kontor
Slotsholmsgade 10
1216 Kobenhavn K
Telephone: + (4533) 92 33 01
Telefax: + (4533) 14 50 42

FINLAND

Finnish Standards Association
SPS
P.O. Box 116
00241 Helsinki
Telephone: + (3580) 149 93 31
Telefax: + (3580) 146 49 14

FRANCE
Monsieur le Chef de la Mission de
coordination CEE et internationale
Ministère de l'agriculture et de la pêche
Direction générale de l'alimentation
175 rue du Chevaleret
75646 Paris Cedex 13
Telephone: + (331) 49 55 8120
Telefax: + (331) 49 55 44 62

GERMANY
Bundesministerium für Ernährung,
Landwirtschaft und Forsten
Referat 716
Postfach 14 02 70
53107 Bonn
Telephone: + (49228) 529 37 97
Telefax: + (49228) 529 44 10
Attention: Mr. Peter Witt
[Tel: (49228) 529 37 97]
or Ms. Kerstin Hartmann
[Tel: (49228) 529 37 82]

GREECE
Ministry of Agriculture
Division of Agricultural Policy
Department EK - AE - EM
5 Acharnon Street
Athens 10176
Telephone: + (301) 52 91 461
Telefax: + (301) 52 48 584

IRELAND
Peter Stanley
Department of Agriculture, Food and
Forestry
Agriculture House, Kildare Street
Dublin 2
Telephone: + (3531) 678 90 11
Telefax: + (3531) 661 45 15

ITALY
Mr. Marco Castellina
Ministero della Sanità
Direzione Generale Servizi Veterinari
Piazza Marconi 25
Roma EUR

Telephone: + (396) 599 438 62/
599 439 45
Telefax: + (396) 599 432 17

LUXEMBOURG
Veterinary measures:
Adm. des Services vétérinaires
B.P. 1403
93 rue d'Anvers
1014 Luxembourg
Telephone: + (352) 478 25 39
Telefax: + (352) 407 545

Phytosanitary measures:
Adm. des Services techniques de
l'agriculture
15 route d'Esch/B.P. 1904
1019 Luxembourg
Telephone: + (352) 457 172-1
Telefax: + (352) 457 172 341

NETHERLANDS
Ministry of Economic Affairs
Central Service Imports and Exports
Section EEC/WTO Notifications
P.O. Box 30003
9700 RD Groningen
Telephone: + (3150) 523 91 11
Telefax: + (3150) 526 06 98

PORTUGAL
João Manuel Machado Gouveia
IPPA - Instituto de Protecção da Produção
Agro-Alimentar
Av. Conde de Valbom No. 98-9°
1050 Lisboa
Telephone: + (3511) 795 89 84/85
Telefax: + (3511) 795 92 11

SPAIN
Dirección General de Comercio Exterior
(Subdirección General de Control,
Inspección y Normalización del Comercio
Exterior)
Paseo de la Castellana 162 - planta 6a
28046 Madrid
Telephone: + (341) 349 37 70
Telefax: + (341) 349 37 40

SWEDEN
Kommerskollegium (National Board of Trade)
WTO-SPS Enquiry Point
Box 1209
11182 Stockholm
Telephone: + (468) 79105 00
Telefax: + (468) 24 67 39

UNITED KINGDOM
B T Bibby
Ministry of Agriculture, Fisheries and Food
Trade Policy and Tropical Foods Division,
Branch A
Room 426a
Whitehall Place (East Block)
London SW1A 2HH

GABON
Mr. Eyi Metou Martin
Inspection générale de l'agriculture
Ministère de l'agriculture, de l'élevage et du
développement rural
B.P. 189
Libreville
Telephone: + (241) 76 38 36
Telefax: + (241) 72 82 75

GHANA
The Director
Plant Protection & Regulatory Services
Ministry of Food & Agriculture
P.O. Box M.37
Accra
Telefax: + (23321) 66 82 45

GUATEMALA
Dirección Técnica de Sanidad Vegetal
Dependencia de la Dirección General de
Servicios Agrícolas - DIGESA
7a. Avenida 3-87 Zona 13
Guatemala
Telephone: + (5022) 72 04 93

Dirección Técnica de Sanidad Animal
Dependencia de la Dirección General de
Servicios Pecuarios -DIGESEPE
Bárcenas, Carretera a Amatitlan, km. 22.5
Guatemala
Telephone: + (5022) 31 20 12/31 20 18

HONDURAS
Dr. Erasmo Montalbán
Director General
Ministerio de Recursos Naturales
Servicio Nacional de Sanidad Agropecuaria
(SENASA)
Bulevar Miraflores
Tegucigalpa MDC
Telephone: + (504) 32 78 67
Telefax: + (504) 31 07 86

HONG KONG
Trade Department
Hong Kong Government
19/F, Trade Department Tower
700 Nathan Road
Hong Kong
Telephone: + (852) 2398 5398
Telefax: + (852) 2789 2491

HUNGARY
Ministry of Agriculture
Department for International and Economic
Affairs
1055 Budapest, Kossuth Lajos tér 11
Telephone: + (361) 131 35 78
Telefax: + (361) 132 67 96

ICELAND
Ministry of Agriculture
150 Reykjavik
Telephone: + (354) 552 11 60
Telefax: + (354) 560 97 50

INDIA
The Joint Secretary
Plant Protection Division
Ministry of Agriculture (Department of
Agriculture & Cooperation)
Krishi Bhavan, Rafi Marg,
New Delhi - 110001
Telephone: + (9111) 338 37 44
Telefax: + (9111) 338 82 57

INDONESIA
Centre for Agricultural Quarantine
Jalan Salemba Raya No. 16
P.O. Box 1352/Jkt 10013
Jakarta 10430

Telephone: + (6221) 315 06 41/
            390 44 11/390 43 95
Telefax: + (6221) 390 46 03

ISRAEL
Prof. A. Shimshony
Director
Veterinary Services & Animal Health
Ministry of Agriculture
P.O. Box 12
50250 Beit Dagan
Telephone: + (9723) 968 16 06/612
Telefax: + (9723) 968 16 41

JAMAICA
Chief Plant Quarantine/Produce Inspector
Ministry of Agriculture
Hope Gardens
Kingston 6
Telephone: + (1809) 927 35 14
Telefax: + (1809) 927 17 01/ 927 19 04

JAPAN
Standards Information Service
First International Organizations Division
Economic Affairs Bureau
Ministry of Foreign Affairs
2-2-1 Kasumigaseki, Chiyoda-ku
Tokyo
Telephone: + (813) 3580 3311
Telefax: + (813) 3503 3136

KENYA
Director of Medical Services
Ministry of Health
P.O. Box 30016
Nairobi
Telephone: + (2542) 72 25 21
Telefax: + (2542) 72 59 02

KOREA, REPUBLIC OF
**Animal or plant health or zoonoses
(including aquatic animals):**
Technical Cooperation Division
International Agriculture Bureau
Ministry of Agriculture, Forestry and Fisheries
(MAFF)
1, Chungang-dong
Kwachon-city, Kyunggi-do 427-760

Telephone: + (822) 503 72 94
Telefax: + (822) 507 20 95

Food safety relating to food additives, veterinary drug and pesticide residues, contaminants, methods of analysis and sampling, and codes and guidelines of hygienic practice:

Food Circulation Division
Food Affairs Bureau
Ministry of Health and Welfare (MOHW)
1, Chungang-dong, Kwachon-city
Kyunggi-do 427-760
Telephone: + (822) 504 62 06
Telefax: + (822) 504 62 07

Aquatic animal health and sanitation:
Trade Division
Fisheries Administration Bureau
National Fisheries Administration
Daewoo Center Bldg, # 541
5-Ga Namdaemoon-ro
Jung-Gu, Seoul
Telephone: + (822) 753 68 62
Telefax: + (822) 753 83 31

MALAYSIA
Mr. Ahmad Rosli Joharie
Ministry of Agriculture
Wisma Tani, Jalan Sultan Sallehuddin
50624 Kuala Lumpur
Telephone: + (603) 298 69 68
Telefax: + (603) 291 56 42

MALTA
The Permanent Secretary
Ministry of Food, Agriculture and Fisheries
Barriera Wharf
Valletta
Telephone: + (356) 22 52 36
Telefax: + (356) 23 12 94

MAURITIUS
Plant Quarantine Services
Agriculture Services
Ministry of Agriculture and Natural Resources
Réduit
Telephone: + (230) 464 48 74
Telefax: + (230) 464 87 89

MEXICO

Centro de Información de la Dirección General de Normas
SECOFI
Avenida Puente de Tecamachalco No. 6
Col. Lomas de Tecamachalco
Naucalpan, 53950 Estado de México
Telephone: + (525) 729 94 85
Telefax: + (525) 729 94 84

MOROCCO

Sanitary measures:
Ministère de l'agriculture et de la mise en valeur agricole
Direction de l'élevage
Quartier administratif
Chellah-Rabat
Telephone: + (2127) 76 50 77/76 51 47
Telefax: + (2127) 76 44 04

Phytosanitary measures:
Ministère de l'agriculture et de la mise en valeur agricole
Direction de la protection des végétaux des contrôles techniques et de la répression des fraudes
Avenue de la Victoire - B.P. 1308
Rabat
Telephone: + (2127) 77 10 78
Telefax: + (2127) 77 25 53

MYANMAR

Directorate of Investment and Company Administration (DICA)
Ministry of National Planning and Economic Development
653-691 Merchant Street
Yangon
Telephone: + (951) 822 07/720 52/752 29
Telefax: + (951) 821 01

NEW ZEALAND

MAF Regulatory Authority (Tim Knox)
ASB Bank House
101-103 The Terrace
Wellington
Telephone: + (644) 474 4100
Telefax: + (644) 474 42 40

NICARAGUA

Mr. Danilo Cortés
Dirección General de Sanidad Vegetal y Animal
Ministerio de Agricultura y Ganadería
Kilometro 8 1/2, Carretera a Masaya
Managua
Telephone: + (5052) 783 412
Telefax: + (5052) 785 864

NORWAY

Ministry of Agriculture
Att: WTO-SPS
Post Box 8007 Dep
0030 Oslo
Telephone: + (472) 234 92 69
Telefax: + (472) 234 95 56

PAKISTAN

Dr. Muhammad Shafi
First Plant Protection Advisor
Jinnah Avenue, Malir Halt
Karachi
Telephone: + (9221) 457 73 82/48 20 11
Telefax: + (9221) 457 43 73

PAPUA NEW GUINEA

Director-General
Multilateral Operations
Department of Foreign Affairs and Trade
P. O. Box 422
Waigani
Telephone: + (675) 27 13 20
Telefax: + (675) 25 44 67

PARAGUAY

For information on plant health:
Ministerio de Agricultura y Ganadería
Dirección de Defensa Vegetal
Ayolas y Benjamin Constant
Edificio Mercurio, 6º piso
Asunción
Telephone: + (59521) 44 03 07/
    44 52 01/49 37 64
Telefax: + (59521) 44 03 07

For information on animal health:
Ministerio de Agricultura y Ganadería
Subsecretaría de Estado de Ganadería
Alberdi No. 611 y General Díaz

Asunción
Telephone: + (59521) 44 94 04/
44 13 94/44 06 32
Telefax: + (59521) 44 72 50

Servicio Nacional de Salud Animal
(SENACSA)
Ruta Mcal. Estigarribia, Km 10 y 1/2
San Lorenzo
Telephone: + (59521) 50 57 27/
50 13 74/50 78 62
Telefax: + (59521) 50 78 63

PERU
Dirección General de Sanidad Ambiental
(DIGESA)
Ministerio de Salud
Director General: Mr. Jorge Villena Chávez
Calle las Amapolas 350, Lince
Lima
Telephone: + (511) 442 83 53
Telefax: + (511) 422 19 78

PHILIPPINES
Department of Agriculture
Attn: Office of the Director
Planning and Monitoring Service
3rd Floor, Department of Agriculture Bldg.
Elliptical Road, Diliman
Quezon City 1100
Telephone: + (632) 97 82 47/99 87 41
Telefax: + (632) 99 05 90

POLAND
Ministerstwo Rolnictwa i Gospodarki
Żywnościowej
Departament Integracji Europejskiej i
Koordynacji Pomocy Zagranicznej
ul. Wspólna 30
00-930 Warsaw
Telephone: + (4822) 623 20 72
Telefax: + (4822) 623 15 09

QATAR
The Ministry of Public Health
P.O Box 42
Doha
Telephone: + (974) 41 71 11
Telefax: + (974) 42 95 65

ROMANIA
National Sanitary - Veterinary Agency
Ministry of Agriculture and Food
B-dul Carol I, no. 24, sector 3
70033 Bucharest
Telephone: + (401) 615 78 75/614 40 20
Telefax: + (401) 312 49 67

SINGAPORE
Head of Food Control Department
Food Control Department
Ministry of the Environment
40 Scotts Road
#19-00 Environment Building
Singapore (0922)
Telephone: + (65) 731 98 19
Telefax: + (65) 731 97 46
Area of competence: Food safety

Director of Primary Production
Primary Production Department
5 Maxwell Road #03-00
National Development Building
Singapore (0106)
Telephone: + (65) 325 76 00
Telefax: + (65) 220 60 68
Area of competence:
(a) Food safety relating to food additives, veterinary drug and pesticide residues, contaminants, methods of analysis and sampling, and codes and guidelines of hygienic practice concerning international movements of meat and meat products (including canned meat), fish and fishery products, vegetables and fruits;

(b) Animal, health and zoonoses, the standards and guidelines and recommendations developed under the auspices of the International Office of Epizootics (OIE) especially concerning the international movements of animals and birds, and their products including bones and bone meal, hides and skins, hoofs, horns, hoof meal, horn meal, offal and any other product of animal origin; semen, fodder, litter, dung of any animals or birds; veterinary biologics for use on animals or birds; and simple and compounded feedstuffs for animal consumption;

(c) Plant health including phytosanitary certifications;

(d) Fish health including certifications for ornamental fish and fishery products;

(e) International movements and certifications of endangered species of fauna and flora under agreements of the Convention on International Trade in Endangered Species (CITES).

SLOVAK REPUBLIC
Slovak Institute for Standardization
Information Centre WTO/GATT
Marta Svábová
Bezrucova 8
P.O. Box 202
81499 Bratislava
Telephone: + (427)36 74 86/36 26 69
Telefax: + (427) 36 37 51

SLOVENIA
The Ministry of Economic Relations and
Development
Kotnikova 5, Ljubljana
Telephone: + (38661) 171 35 42
Telefax: + (38661) 171 36 11

SOUTH AFRICA
The Director: Marketing
Department of Agriculture
Private Bag X791
Pretoria 0001
Telephone: + (2712) 319 65 18
Telefax: + (2712) 326 34 54

SRI LANKA
Director
Department of Animal Productions and Health
Getambe
Peradeniya
Telephone: + (948) 884 62/63
Telefax: + (948) 881 95
Telefax: + (948) 881 95

SWITZERLAND
Association suisse de normalisation
SNV
Mühlebachstrasse 54
CH-8008 Zurich
Telephone: + (411) 254 54 54
Telefax: + (411) 254 54 74

THAILAND
Thai Industrial Standards Institute (TISI)

Ministry of Industry
Rama VI Street, Bangkok 10400
Telephone: + (662) 202 34 01
              202 35 07/202 35 10
Telefax: + (662) 247 87 41

TUNISIA
Animal health, zoonoses and plant safety:
Ministère de l'agriculture
30 rue Alain Savary
1002 Tunis
Telephone: + (2161) 78 56 33
Telefax: + (2161) 79 94 57

Food safety:
Ministère du commerce
(Direction générale de la concurrence et du
commerce intérieur)
6 rue Venezuela
1002 Tunis
Telephone: + (2161) 78 77 02
Telefax: + (2161) 78 18 47

TURKEY
Mr. Muammer Yasarbas
Tarim ve Köyisleri Bakanligi
Koruma ve Kontrol Genel Müdürlügü
Akay Cad. No. 3
Ankara
Telephone: + (90312) 418 14 68
Telefax: + (90312) 418 80 05

UGANDA
Uganda National Bureau of Standards
P.O. Box 6329
Kampala
Telephone: + (25641) 23 66 06/25 86 69

UNITED STATES
Standards Code and Information Program
National Institute of Standards and Technology
(NIST)
Bldg. 411, Room 163
Gaithersburg, MD 20899
Telephone: + (1301) 975 40 37
Telefax: + (1301) 926 15 59

URUGUAY
Ministerio de Relaciones Exteriores

Dirección General de Asuntos Económicos
Avenida 18 de Julio, 1205
Montevideo
Telephone: + (5982) 92 06 18
Telefax: + (5982) 92 13 27/92 42 90

VENEZUELA
Ministerio de Agrlcultura y Cría
Servicio Autónomo de Sanidad Agropecuaria
Parque Central, Torre Este
Caracas 1010

Telephone: + (582) 509 03 77/509 05 96
Telefax: + (582) 509 03 76

ZAMBIA
Mr. F. Siame
Permanent Secretary
Ministry of Commerce, Trade and Industry
Lusaka
Telephone: + (2601) 22 14 75
Telefax: + (2601) 22 66 73

APPENDIX III

How to obtain WTO publications and documents

Copies of the following are available from the Publications Office of the WTO Secretariat and its sales agents.

- *The Results of the Uruguay Round of Multilateral Trade Negotiations: The Legal Texts*
- National schedules on tariff and other concessions on trade in goods
- National schedules of commitments on trade in services

Some of these documents are available on CD ROM.

The address of the Publications Office is:

> Publications Office
> WTO Secretariat
> Centre William Rappard
> CH-1211 Geneva 21
> Switzerland
>
> Telephone: (022) 739 5208/739 5308
> Telefax: (022) 731 4206
> Telex: 412 324 WTO CH

WTO classification of service sectors

SECTORS AND SUB-SECTORS	CORRESPONDING CPC Section B
1. BUSINESS SERVICES	
A. Professional services	
a. Legal services	861
b. Accounting, auditing and bookkeeping services	862
c. Taxation services	863
d. Architectural services	8671
e. Engineering services	8672
f. Integrated engineering services	8673
g. Urban planning and landscape architectural services	8674
h. Medical and dental services	9312
I. Veterinary services	932
j. Services provided by midwives, nurses, physiotherapists and paramedical personnel	93191
k. Other	
B. Computer and related services	
a. Consultancy services related to the installation of computer hardware	841
b. Software implementation services	842
c. Data processing services	843
d. Database services	844
e. Other	845+849
C. Research and development services	
a. R & D services on natural sciences	851
b. R & D services on social sciences and humanities	852
c. Interdisciplinary R & D services	853

D. Real estate services
  a. Involving own or leased property   821
  b. On a fee or contract basis   822

E. Rental/leasing services without operators
  a. Relating to ships   83103
  b. Relating to aircraft   83104
  c. Relating to other transport equipment   83101+83102+
                                                               83105
  d. Relating to other machinery and equipment   83106-83109
  e. Other   832

F. Other business services
  a. Advertising services   871
  b. Market research and public opinion polling services   864
  c. Management consulting service   865
  d. Services related to management consulting   866
  e. Technical testing and analysis services   8676
  f. Services incidental to agriculture, hunting and forestry 881
  g. Services incidental to fishing   882
  h. Services incidental to mining   883+5115
  i. Services incidental to manufacturing   884+885
                                                               (except for 88442)
  j. Services incidental to energy distribution   887
  k. Placement and supply services of personnel   872
  l. Investigation and security   873
  m. Related scientific and technical consulting services   8675
  n. Maintenance and repair of equipment (not including   633+
     maritime vessels, aircraft or other transport equipment) 8861-8866
  o. Building-cleaning services   874
  p. Photographic services   875
  q. Packaging services   876
  r. Printing, publishing   88442
  s. Convention services   87909*
  t. Other   8790

2. COMMUNICATION SERVICES
  A. Postal services   7511
  B. Courier services   7512
  C. Telecommunication services
    a. Voice telephone services   7521
    b. Packet-switched data transmission services   7523**
    c. Circuit-switched data transmission services   7523**
    d. Telex services   7523**

e. Telegraph services	7522
f. Facsimile services	7521**+7529**
g. Private leased circuit services	7522**+7523**
h. Electronic mail	7523**
i. Voice mail	7523**
j. On-line information and database retrieval	7523**
k. Electronic data interchange (EDI)	7523**
l. Enhanced/value-added facsimile services including store and forward, store and retrieve	7523**
m. Code and protocol conversion	n.a.
n. On-line information and/or data processing (including transaction processing)	843**
o. Other	

D. Audiovisual services

a. Motion picture and video tape production and distribution services	9611
b. Motion picture projection service	9612
c. Radio and television services	9613
d. Radio and television transmission services	7524
e. Sound recording	n.a.
f. Other	

E. Other

3. CONSTRUCTION AND RELATED ENGINEERING SERVICES

A. General construction work for buildings	512
B. General construction work for civil engineering	513
C. Installation and assembly work	514+516
D. Building completion and finishing work	517
E. Other	511+515+518

4. DISTRIBUTION SERVICES

A. Commission agents' services	621
B. Wholesale trade services	622
C. Retailing services	631+632 6111+6113+6121
D. Franchising	8929
E. Other	

5. EDUCATIONAL SERVICES

A. Primary education services	921
B. Secondary education services	922
C. Higher education services	923

D. Adult education   924
E. Other education services   929

6. ENVIRONMENTAL SERVICES

A. Sewage services   9401
B. Refuse disposal services   9402
C. Sanitation and similar services   9403
D. Other

7. FINANCIAL SERVICES

A. All insurance and insurance-related services   812**
   a. Life, accident and health insurance services   8121
   b. Non-life insurance services   8129
   c. Reinsurance and retrocession   81299
   d. Services auxiliary to insurance (including broking and
      agency services)   8140

B. Banking and other financial services (excluding insurance)
   a. Acceptance of deposits and other repayable   81115-81119
      funds from the public
   b. Lending of all types, including consumer credit,   8113
      mortgage credit, factoring and financing of
      commercial transaction
   c. Financial leasing   8112
   d. All payment and money transmission services   81339**
   e. Guarantees and commitments   81199**
   f. Trading for own account or for account of customers,
      whether on an exchange, in an over-the-counter market
      or otherwise, the following:
      - money market instruments (cheques, bills, certificates   81339**
        of deposits, etc.)
      - foreign exchange   81333
      - derivative products including, but not limited to, futures
        and options   81339**
      - exchange rate and interest rate instruments, including
        products such as swaps, forward rate agreements, etc. 81339**
      - transferable securities   81321*
      - other negotiable instruments and financial assets,   81339**
        including bullion
   g. Participation in issues of all kinds of securities, including   8132
      underwriting and placement as agent (whether
      publicly or privately) and provision of service related
      to such issues

h. Money broking	81339**
i. Asset management, such as cash or portfolio manage-	8119+**
ment, all forms of collective investment management,	81323*
pension fund management, custodial depository and	
trust services	
j. Settlement and clearing services for financial assets,	81339**
including securities, derivative products, and other	or 81319**
negotiable instruments	
k. Advisory and other auxiliary financial services on all the	8131
activities listed in Article 1B of MTN.TNC/W/50, including	or 8133
credit reference and analysis, investment and portfolio	
research and advice, advice on acquisitions and on	
corporate restructuring and strategy	
l. Provision and transfer of financial information, and	8131
financial data processing and related software by	
providers of other financial services	

C. Other

8. HEALTH-RELATED AND SOCIAL SERVICES
(other than those listed under 1.A.h-j.)

A. Hospital services	9311
B. Other human health services	9319
	(other than 93191)
C. Social services	933
D. Other	

9. TOURISM AND TRAVEL-RELATED SERVICES

A. Hotels and restaurants (including catering)	641-643
B. Travel agencies and tour operators services	7471
C. Tourist guides services	7472
D. Other	

10. RECREATIONAL, CULTURAL AND SPORTING SERVICES
(other than audiovisual services)

A. Entertainment services (including theatre, live bands and circus services)	9619
B. News agency services	962
C. Libraries, archives, museums and other cultural services	963
D. Sporting and other recreational services	964
E. Other	

11. TRANSPORT SERVICES

A. Maritime transport services
a. Passenger transportation   7211
b. Freight transportation   7212
c. Rental of vessels with crew   7213
d. Maintenance and repair of vessels   8868**
e. Pushing and towing services   7214
f. Supporting services for maritime transport   745**

B. Internal waterways transport
a. Passenger transportation   7221
b. Freight transportation   7222
c. Rental of vessels with crew   7223
d. Maintenance and repair of vessels   8868**
e. Pushing and towing services   7224
f. Supporting services for internal waterway transport   745**

C. Air transport services
a. Passenger transportation   731
b. Freight transportation   732
c. Rental of aircraft with crew   734
d. Maintenance and repair of aircraft   8868**
e. Supporting services for air transport   746

D. Space transport   733

E. Rail transport services
a. Passenger transportation   7111
b. Freight transportation   7112
c. Pushing and towing services   7113
d. Maintenance and repair of rail transport equipment   8868**
e. Supporting services for rail transport services   743

F. Road transport services
a. Passenger transportation   7121+7122
b. Freight transportation   7123
c. Rental of commercial vehicles with operator   7124
d. Maintenance and repair of road transport equipment   6112+8867
e. Supporting services for road transport services   744

G. Pipeline transport
a. Transportation of fuels   7131
b. Transportation of other goods   7139

H. Services auxiliary to all modes of transport
a. Cargo-handling services   741
b. Storage and warehouse services   742

    c. Freight transport agency services   748
    d. Other   749

I. **Other transport services**

12.   OTHER SERVICES NOT INCLUDED ELSEWHERE   95+97+98+99

The (*) indicates that the service specified is a component of a more aggregated CPC item specified elsewhere in this classification list.

The (**) indicates that the service specified constitutes only a part of the total range of activities covered by the CPC concordance (e.g. voice mail is only a component of CPC item 7523).

Publications utilized by WTO member countries for posting notices of tender and post-award notices

AUSTRIA
Amtsblatt zur Wiener Zeitung

CANADA
Government Business Opportunities (GBO)
Open Bidding Service, ISM Publishing

EUROPEAN COMMUNITIES

Belgium
Official Journal of the European Communities

Le Bulletin des Adjudications

Other publications in the specialized press

Denmark
Official Journal of the European Communities

Germany
Official Journal of the European Communities

Spain
Official Journal of the European Communities

France
Official Journal of the European Communities

Bulletin officiel des annonces des marchés publics

Greece
Official Journal of the European Communities

Publication in the daily, financial, regional and specialized press

Ireland
Official Journal of the European Communities

Daily press: *Irish Independent, Irish Times, Irish Press, Cork Examiner*

Italy
Official Journal of the European Communities

Luxembourg
Official Journal of the European

Luxembourg
Official Journal of the European Communities
Daily press

Netherlands
Official Journal of the European Communities

Portugal
Official Journal of the European Communities

United Kingdom
Official Journal of the European Communities

FINLAND
Public Procurement in Finland and EEA: *Supplement to the Official Gazette of Finland*

Official Journal of the European Communities (as long as the cost of the publication is free of charge)

HONG KONG
Annex 1
  Hong Kong Govermnent Gazette
  Daily press
Annex 2
  Hong Kong Government Gazette
  Daily press
Annex 3
  Hospital Authority
  - *Hong Kong Govermnent Gazette*
  - Daily press
  Housing Authority
  - *Hong Kong Government Gazette*
  - Daily press

Kowloon-Canton Railway Corporation
  - to be notified
Mass Transit Railway Corporation
  - to be notified
Provisional Airport Authority
  - to be notified

ISRAEL
The Jerusalem Post

JAPAN
Annex 1
  Kanpō
Annex 2
  Kenpō
  Shihō
  or their equivalents
Annex 3
  Kanpō

REPUBLIC OF KOREA
Kwanbo (the Government's official gazette
The Seoul Shinmun

NORWAY
Official Journal of the European Communities

SWEDEN
Europeiska Gemenskapernas Tidning (*Official Journal of the European Communities*)

SWITZERLAND

Annex 1

Swiss Official Trade Gazette

Annex 2

Official publications of every Swiss Canton (26)

Annex 3

Swiss Official Trade Gazette

Official publications of every Swiss Canton (26)

UNITED STATES

The Commerce Business Daily

Additional information may be available in State journals, such as the *New York Contract Reporter*.

APPENDIX VI

Information centres on laws and regulations applicable to government procurement

---

AUSTRIA

Bundesministerium für Wirtschaftliche
Angelegenheiten
(Federal Ministry for Economic Affairs)
Sektion I (Section I)
Stubenring 1
A-1011 Wien
Telephone: 222/75 000
Telex: 111145 and 111780

BELGIUM

Administration logistique
Marchés publics
Rue de la Loi 16
B-1000 Bruxelles
Telephone: 513 8020
Telex: 62400 PRIMIN B

CANADA

Corporate Relations Branch
Department of Supply and Services
Place du Portage, Phase III
14A1, 11 Laurier Street
Hull, Quebec K1A 0S5
Telephone: (819) 997 7363
Telex: 0533703

DENMARK

The State Purchasing Department
Direktoratet for Statens Indkob
Bredgade 20
DK-1260 Kobenhavn K
Telephone: 929 100
Telex: 19491 STAPUR DK

FRANCE

Ministère de l'économie et des finances
Commission centrale des marchés
Quai Branly 41
F-75700 Paris
Telephone: 550 7111
Telex: 220200 FIDOUAN PARIS

FINLAND

Ministry of Trade and Industry
Department of Trade
Aleksanterinkatu 10
SF-00170 Helsinki 17
Telephone: 3580 1601
Telex: 124645

GERMANY

Bundesministerium für Wirtschaft
(The Federal Minister for the Economy)
Villemomblerstrasse 76
D-5300 Bonn
Telephone: 6151
Telex: 886747 A BMWI D

HONG KONG

A contact point (including information centre) has been established in the Government Supplies Department.

ISRAEL

Information centres are not formally established but Israeli authorities are ready to give assistance to enhance the functioning of the Agreement. Liaison officers have been selected by each of the entities covered by the Agreement.

JAPAN

Each purchasing entity nominates its own responsible administrative body. Requests for information should be addressed to the purchasing entity itself.

IRELAND

Secretary
Government Contracts Committee
Department of Finance
Upper Merrion Street
IRL-Dublin 2
Telephone: 767 571
Telex: 30357 GEEC EI

ITALY

The appropriate office of the authority opening the tender acts as information centre. It indicates in the notice the address to be contracted.

LUXEMBOURG

Ministère des affaires étrangères
Rue Notre Dame
Luxembourg
Telex: AFFETRA 1702

or

Ministère des travaux publics
Boulevard Roosevelt, 4
Luxembourg
Telephone: 478 475

NETHERLANDS

Ministerie van Economische Zaken
(Ministry of Economic Affairs)
Postbus 20101
Bezuidenhoutseweg 30
NL-2500 EC's-Gravenhage
Telephone: (070) 796 628, 797 520
              (Mr Imans or Mr Terwindt)
Telex: 31099 ECZA NL

NORWAY

Ministry of Industry
(Naeringsdepartementet)
Postboks 8014, Dep.
N-0030 Oslo 1
Telephone: (02) 349 090

The Norwegian Import Promotion Office for Products from Developing Countries (NORIMPOD)
P.O. Box 8147 Dep.
N-Oslo 1

SINGAPORE

i. Ministry of Finance
    (Budget Division)
    43rd Storey, Treasury Building
    8 Shenton Way
    Singapore 0106

ii. Public Works Department
    12th Storey, Ministry of National

Development Building
Maxwell Road
Singapore 0106

iii. Central Supplies Department
Depot Road
Singapore 0410

SWEDEN
The Import Promotion Office for
Products from Developing Countries
(IMPOD)
Street address: Normalmstorg 1
Postal address: IMPOD, Box 7508
S-10392 Stockholm
Telephone: (46) 8-666 0190
Telex: 13426 SWEIMP
Telefax: (46) 8-660 8823

SWITZERLAND
Bundesamt für Aussenwirtschaft
Bundeshaus Ost
CH-3003 Bern
Telephone: (31) 612 211

Office fédéral des affaires économiques
extérieures
Palais Fédéral Est

Ufficio federal dell'economia esterna
(Federal Office for External Economic
Affairs of the Federal Department of the
Economy)

UNITED KINGDOM
The purchasing bodies will indicate in the
tender documents the address to which
requests for information should be sent.

UNITED STATES
Office of the United States Trade
Representative
Executive Office of the President
Winder Building, Room 507
600 17th Street
N.W. Washington D.C. 20506
Telephone: (202) 395 4647
Telex: 440051 itt

Index

INTERNATIONAL TRADE CENTRE UNCTAD/WTO (ITC)

The International Trade Centre UNCTAD/WTO (ITC) is the focal point in the United Nations system for technical cooperation with developing countries in trade promotion. ITC was created by the General Agreement on Tariffs and Trade (GATT) in 1964 and since 1968 has been operated jointly by GATT and the UN, the latter acting through the United Nations Conference on Trade and Development (UNCTAD). As an executing agency of the United Nations Development Programme (UNDP), ITC is directly responsible for implementing UNDP-financed projects in developing countries and economies in transition related to trade promotion.

Main programme areas

ITC works with developing countries and economies in transition to set up effective trade promotion programmes for expanding their exports and improving their import operations. This covers six key areas:

▪ Product and market development: Direct export marketing support to the business community through advice on product development, product adaptation and international marketing for commodities, manufactures and services. The aim is to develop and market internationally competitive products and services to expand and diversify these countries' exports.
▪ Development of trade support services: Creation and enhancement of foreign trade support services for the business community provided by public and private institutions at the national and regional levels. The objective is to ensure that enterprises have the facilities to export and import effectively.
▪ Trade information: Establishment of sustainable national trade information services and dissemination of information on products, services, markets and functions to enterprises and trade organizations. The purpose is to lay a foundation for sound international business decisions and for appropriate trade promotion programmes.
▪ Human resource development: Strengthening of national institutional capacities for foreign trade training and organization of direct training for enterprises in importing and exporting. The goal is to achieve efficient foreign trade operations based on relevant knowledge and skills.
▪ International purchasing and supply management: Application of cost-effective import systems and practices in enterprises and public trading entities by strengthening the advisory services provided by national purchasing organizations, both public and private. The aim is to optimize foreign exchange resources expended on imports.
▪ Needs assessment and programme design for trade promotion: Conception of effective national and regional trade promotion programmes based on an analysis of supply potential and constraints, and identification

of related technical cooperation requirements. The objective is to reinforce the link between trade policy and the implementation of trade promotion activities.

In all of these services ITC gives particular attention to activities with the least developed countries (LDCs).

Trade promotion projects

ITC's technical cooperation projects are carried out in all developing areas, at the national, subregional, regional and interregional levels. They are undertaken at the request of governments of the countries concerned. Projects are administered from ITC headquarters in Geneva and are implemented by ITC specialists who work in close liaison with local officials. A project may last from a few weeks to several years, depending on the number and types of activities involved.

National projects often take the form of a broad-based integrated country project, which includes a package of services to expand the country's exports and/or improve its import operations. In some cases national projects cover only one type of activity. Subregional, regional and interregional projects may also deal with either one or a combination of ITC services, depending on the trade promotion and export development requirements of the group of countries concerned.

All of ITC's technical cooperation projects are systematically monitored and evaluated to ensure that the objectives initially agreed to between the government(s) and ITC are being achieved.

Headquarters services

In addition to specific technical cooperation projects with individual developing countries and economies in transition, or groups of these countries, ITC provides services from its headquarters in Geneva that are available to all such countries. These include publications on trade promotion, export development, international marketing, international purchasing, supply management, and foreign trade training, as well as trade information and trade statistics services of various types.

Coordination with other organizations

ITC's technical cooperation work is coordinated with a number of other organizations inside and outside the UN system. ITC maintains close liaison with UNCTAD and the World Trade Organization (WTO) for specific technical cooperation activities, in addition to its more formal links with these two organizations for its overall technical cooperation programme. ITC's export market development activities are coordinated, whenever relevant, with the work of the Food and Agriculture Organization of the UN

(FAO) and the United Nations Industrial Development Organization (UNIDO). Close contacts are maintained with UNDP, which provides financing for a portion of ITC's projects with developing countries and economies in transition, and whose Resident Representatives and Resident Coordinators serve as ITC's official representatives in their countries of assignment.

ITC also works with other UN organizations, regional development banks, intergovernmental bodies outside the UN system, nongovernmental organizations and numerous trade-related institutions. In particular it has developed a close association with import promotion offices that have been set up in various countries to promote exports from developing countries into their respective national markets. ITC is continuously broadening its contacts with foreign trade and business institutions as it extends its network of technical cooperation partners.

Sources of funding

ITC's regular budget is funded in equal parts by the United Nations and WTO. It finances general research and development on trade promotion and export development, part of which results in published studies, market information and statistical services. This budget also covers overall administration of the organization.

Financing for ITC's technical cooperation activities in developing countries and economies in transition comes from UNDP, other international organizations, and voluntary contributions from individual developed and developing countries. Voluntary contributions consist of either trust funds for projects in other countries or funds-in-trust provided for projects in the donor's own country.

Status and policymaking

ITC's legal status is that of a "joint subsidiary organ" of WTO and the United Nations, the latter acting through UNCTAD. The broad policy guidelines for ITC's technical cooperation work are determined by the governing organs of ITC's parent bodies. Recommendations on ITC's future work programme are made to these two organs by ITC's annual intergovernmental meeting, the Joint Advisory Group on the International Trade Centre UNCTAD/WTO (JAG). The JAG also reviews ITC's proposals for its medium-term plan, which provides a general framework for ITC's activities over a six-year period and forms part of the overall UN Medium-Term Plan. Representatives of member states of ITC's parent organizations attend the JAG meeting. In addition to the review by these intergovernmental meetings, ITC's policies and programmes are periodically examined in meetings attended by representatives of its parent organizations and ITC's Executive Director.

Secretariat

Mr. J. Denis Bélisle, ITC's Executive Director, is responsible for the management of ITC. Staff at ITC headquarters in Geneva, Switzerland, number approximately 210. Several hundred consultants are assigned to ITC projects in developing countries and economies in transition each year.

Liaison offices

ITC does not have any regional or national field offices. However, each government with which ITC works, in both recipient and developed countries, appoints an official ITC liaison officer within its administration.

Contact information

International Trade Centre UNCTAD/WTO (ITC) Telephone: (41-22) 730 01 11
Palais des Nations Telefax: (41-22) 733 44 39
1211 Geneva 10, Switzerland Telex: 414 119 ITC CH

COMMONWEALTH SECRETARIAT

The Commonwealth Secretariat is the principal international organisation of the Commonwealth. It was established in 1965 as a visible symbol of the spirit of cooperation which animates the Commonwealth association.

The Secretariat works towards advancing the Commonwealth's fundamental values. Its primary duties include facilities and promoting consultation and exchanges among members, preparing and circulating information on issues of concern, particularly in international and economic affairs, assisting in advancing the development of member countries, acting as a focal point for specialised Commonwealth institutions and organising and servicing intergovernmental meetings.

Of the 53 Commonwealth members, 49 are developing countries for whom economic development is indispensable for the stability of their political institutions. Assistance in this area is given by the Commonwealth Fund for Technical Co-operation (CFTC) which is the development arm of the Secretariat. It was established, to take advantage of shared experiences and similarities to promote development in the Commonwealth. Within the Commonwealth — and even beyond — the CFTC stands out as a success story of cooperation for development including South-South cooperation. The Fund is responsive in nature and provides technical assistance for economic and social development.

Within the operational framework of the CFTC, the Commonwealth Secretariat has been helping its developing member countries in implementing economic reform programmes. Its Export Market Development Department provides specialised technical assistance services to developing member countries to help them establish and strengthen appropriate export promotion structures, develop the necessary infrastructure, widen the export base, improve quality standards and enlarge market access for their products. Assistance to such member countries for understanding and benefitting from the new international trade agreements is a key component of the work undertaken by the department. Provision of support for setting up strategic alliances for promoting industrial production and exports constitutes an important part of its work programme.